Social Devaluation and Special Education

of related interest

Children with Special Needs
Assessment, Law and Practice – Caught in the Act, 4th edition
John Friel
ISBN 1 85302 460 0

Young Adults with Special Needs
Assessment, Law and Practice – Caught in the Act
John Friel
ISBN 1 85302 231 4

Social Devaluation and Special Education

The Right to Full Inclusion
and an Honest Statement

John T. Hall

Jessica Kingsley Publishers
London and Bristol, Pennsylvania

The right to John T. Hall to be identified as author of this work has been asserted by him in accordance with the Copyright, Designs and Patents Act 1988.

First published in the United Kingdom in 1997 by
Jessica Kingsley Publishers Ltd
116 Pentonville Road
London N1 9JB, England
and
1900 Frost Road, Suite 101
Bristol, PA 19007, U S A

Library of Congress Cataloging in Publication Data
A CIP catalogue record for this book is available from the Library of Congress

British Library Cataloguing in Publication Data
Hall, John T.
Social devaluation and special education:
the right to full mainstream inclusion and an honest statement
1. Special education 2. School integration 3. Mainstreaming in education
I. Title
371.9'046
ISBN 1 85302 354 X

Printed and Bound in Great Britain by
Athenaeum Press, Gateshead, Tyne and Wear

Contents

List of Figures

List of Tables

Dedication

This book is for my mother, Gwennie Minns, who has been my crutch and inspiration all my life, and without whose unfailing love, support and encouragement I would not have developed the self-belief to take on new challenges.

Acknowledgements

No book has a single author and this is especially true of a book about a human service such as special needs education. Many of the ideas and practices contained in these chapters which offer advice and practical recommendations will inevitably be the product of collaborative effort and I would like to acknowledge a personal debt of gratitude to the following individuals without whose wise advice this book would be considerably more flawed than it is. In expressing my thanks, I should say that any errors, confusions and misunderstandings the reader may still detect are entirely my own responsibility.

Most importantly, I am indebted to my wife Jenny. Without her encouragement, reassurance and patient, support I could not possibly have completed this book. She has read and reread successive drafts and painstakingly corrected errors of every conceivable kind. Without her help this would have been a much worse book than it is.

I am especially grateful to Pete Ritchie for showing me, in 1984, that much of special education was largely a disservice to children, and also for helping me to see that there was a better way. Pete has been the single most influential person in my professional life, which ended in my being made redundant in June 1995. I may forgive him one day! I am also grateful to Sam Carson for his unfailingly intelligent and perceptive comments and for helping me towards a better understanding of normalisation/SRV theory.

I am indebted to John Wright for his generous support in helping me to a better understanding of the law of special education. I thank Joe Whittaker for introducing me to that new term 'inclusion' and, through that, to the people who have done so much to help us all make better sense of children's needs. Here I include: John O'Brien, Marsha Forest, Jack Pearpoint, George Flynn, Judith Snow and Herb Lovett.

For help with advice and proofreading I am grateful to the following, each of whom made their own distinctive contribution in connection with specific chapters: Jenny Hall, Gwennie Minns, Sam Carson, Martin Yates, John Wright, John Pashley and Pete Crane.

I wish to record my thanks to Ken Rowley, Paul Burrows and Rita Fred for showing me what advocacy should be about in practice. Thanks also to Brenda Brown, Bunny Pinnington, Sian Warlow, Stella Sinclair and Wendy Pownall for their commitment to inclusive education and to the support of the children and parents of Dyfatty school.

My greatest debt of gratitude is to the children I have tried to serve during my career as psychologist and teacher. They have taught me that what I *thought* I knew was mostly professional mumbo jumbo.

And a woman who held a babe against her bosom said,
Speak to us of children.
And he said:
Your children are not your children.
They are the sons and daughters of life's longing for itself.
They come through you but not from you,
And though they are with you yet they belong not to you.
You may give them your love but not your thoughts,
For they have their own thoughts.
You may house their bodies but not their souls,
For their souls dwell in the house of tomorrow, which you
cannot visit, not even in your dreams.
You may strive to be like them, but seek not to make
them like you.
For life goes not backward nor tarries with yesterday.
You are the bows from which your children as living arrows are
sent forth.
The Archer sees the mark upon the path of the infinite, and He
bends you with His might that His arrows may go
swift and far.
Let your bending in the Archer's hand be for gladness:
For even as He loves the arrow that flies, so He loves also the
bow that is stable.

Kahlil Gibran (1926)

Disclaimer

Throughout this book I have attempted to use language which is not offensive to people who have a disability or learning difficulty. On occasion I have reproduced the offensive language current at a particular time so as not to confuse the reader by sanitising, and hence fundamentally distorting, extant social perceptions and prejudices. Also, the North American term 'mental retardation' is reproduced in connection with observations within that particular context. It is important to understand that this term does not carry quite the same heavily negative connotations in North America as it does in Britain.

I have tended to use the term 'disabled' to refer generically to children who, through having a significant impairment, would typically be placed in a segregated school, special unit or separate class. The term is used to embrace children who may have a physical or sensory impairment, a learning difficulty or a combination of such impairments. I have used the word 'disabled' in preference to the word impaired because a majority of readers will find this usage more congenial and familiar, and communication is of the essence. I accept the definitions of 'impairment' and 'disability' proposed by the Disabled People's International in 1981, which sees the former as the functional limitation within the individual caused by physical, mental or sensory impairment and the latter as the loss or limitation of opportunities to take part in the normal life of the community on an equal level with others due to physical and social barriers. Choosing to use these terms in the way that I have should not be construed as an indication that I do not subscribe to the social model of disability which makes it clear that individuals have impairments which society turns into disabilities; I do, in fact, by and large subscribe to this view. I do not, however, subscribe to the currently fashionable notion that an impairment is essentially a gift.

Use of the word 'special'

Much as I deprecate the use of the word 'special', because it seems to embody everything which is destructive about services for children with additional needs, I have, nevertheless, decided to use it, because this book is aimed primarily at an audience whose use of the term is deeply ingrained. This should not be taken as an endorsement of the term's ability to describe anything in particular, because it is inherently incapable of doing anything of the sort. It is a vague and fuzzy umbrella kind of word with all manner of hidden, and usually damaging, assumptions about the nature and character of the children it purports to describe.

I am aware that the language we use plays an important part in the creation and maintenance of destructive social stereotypes of disabled people and, where I may have used language which is not absolutely current or which has not, as yet, passed the test of acceptability to disabled people who are rightly sensitive to terminology, I can only apologise and ask for their indulgence. However...

Political correctness

'Political Correctness' (PC) changes the way we talk about people and services, without necessarily changing the assumptions we make about them, the way we relate to them or the services we provide for them. PC is now rampant and a minority of people in the disability movement are as concerned to victimise those who fail to keep pace with linguistic fashion as they are to seriously challenge unacceptable established practice in the service system. This growing trend threatens the development of strong alliances between disabled people and those professionals and others who would like to offer the hand of solidarity in their struggle. Few though there may be of the latter, it would be a great shame were they to be misidentified and pilloried as enemies simply because their use of language is a month or so out of date or because they earn a living in the service system which is, for understandable reasons, viewed as largely oppressive. It would be as wrong to assume that all who work within the system share its ideology as that none do. In its more virulent manifestations, the mania for PC is frequently rooted in a deeply puritanical nature riddled with free-floating guilt and, as such, is more a comment on the inner turmoil of the determinedly correct individual than on his or her real commitment to social justice.

Without in the least understanding the psychology of the negative dynamics of unconsciousness within human services, many activists like to make the easy assumption that those who use outdated language actually hold members of oppressed minority groups in lower esteem than those who, like themselves, observe the latest linguistic fashion. They are quick to conclude that there is equivalence between the use of 'correct' terminology and the proper valuing, and hence decent treatment, of other human beings. There may well be a correlation but, in my view, it will turn out to be a rather weak one.

A basic tenet of PC is, for example, the belief in an identity between language and thought. Hence if a teacher, doctor or social worker refers to a child as a 'Mongol' then she must view that child in ways similar to her predecessors – who colluded with a system which, more than a quarter of a century ago, saw such children as ineducable. This may, of course, be the case, but it is also possible that this particular individual does not move in the sort of linguistically enlightened circles which would have enabled her to update her language. It might equally be the case that the person who uses more appropriate language nevertheless holds to those outdated views but would rather others did not know. This is not in any way to defend outdated and offensive labels but rather to highlight the fact that we can very easily massage our own public personas so as to appear more humane and enlightened than others, simply by paying close attention to the way we use language; and this without changing anything else of importance. Hence the shrewd psychologist is able to continue his practice of sticking a disabling label on a child in readiness for a segregated education without having to utter a single offensive outdated epithet.

Sadly, getting the language right has, for many, taken precedence over sorting out their own underlying beliefs, attitudes and practices, and it is clear why this is so – it is easier for us to learn new terminology than change our behaviour. The reality is, of course, that we are continuously reinventing our lexicography for children and their needs, whilst being apparently happy to run the same tired old devaluing and segregating services. None of this is intended to minimise the importance of using appropriately respectful language, because there is never an excuse for describing or addressing others in gratuitously devaluing ways. My own strength of feeling on this issue will be evident in the following pages. Yet even to challenge the current obsession with politically correct language is guaranteed to raise the hackles and provide an opportunity for someone to play the disablist, racist, sexist, or whatever, card. It is absolutely right that we should be sensitive about social prejudice but not that we should behave stupidly because we are afraid of being unjustly labelled as 'oppressor'.

It is getting harder to engage in intelligent debate about these issues because to say anything other than that which is deemed 'ideologically sound' is, apparently, to betray one's real underlying prejudice. Hence serious debate over important issues is stifled because individuals are afraid of being dismissed as part of the oppressive system, rather than being seen as the allies they either feel they are or would like to become. An example of this is the frustration felt by some in certain voluntary sector advocacy organisations working with people who have learning difficulties. Here the dilemma is over just how much responsibility for self-advocacy it is possible or desirable to pursue. If people with learning difficulties were left to fend for themselves, then this might be construed as abandonment rather than liberation. Yet how can it be right to make decisions on behalf of other adults, and how much does a policy for so doing undermine the individual's personal growth and development? We are still a long way from a serious discussion, let alone a resolution of these important issues, and such a debate is being stifled by our fear of being misunderstood.

Introduction

SPECIAL EDUCATION IN MORAL CRISIS

This book is about the malaise afflicting the practice of special education in Britain in the 1990s. If, for you the reader, there is no evident malaise, then this may be because you are aware of the major improvements that have taken place over the past half-century which, without question, have improved the lot of children with sensory, physical or learning disabilities. To adopt such a positive view of circumstances is certainly justified, yet it fails to take account of the consequences of our growth of understanding of the needs of children set against our ability to make provisions which adequately address those needs. Put simply, our desire to provide what children need still lags some way behind our understanding of those needs.

I have described this mismatch between our understanding and our will as a moral crisis because, in the – albeit short – history of special education, this discrepancy is of fairly recent origin and has a moral dimension because of our growing shared awareness of the fact that we are perpetuating an injustice – the injustice of compulsorily segregating children on the basis of their perceived impairments. The Oxford English Dictionary (1991) describes a crisis as '*a vitally important or decisive stage in the progress of anything; a turning-point; also, a state of affairs in which a decisive change for better or worse is imminent.*' I believe we are now in such a critical stage in the evolution of special education and that, over the next few years, important decisions will be made as to what we, as a society, feel we owe to children who experience a significant difficulty in learning.

What follows is, broadly speaking, in two distinct parts. The first outlines a new perspective on special needs education, drawing upon normalisation theory and the evolving social model of disability, while the second deals with the more practical aspects of securing a socially just education for children who, historically, have been sidelined in the 'backward' or 'special school'.

Chapters 1 and 2 deal with a brief historical analysis of the evolution of special education in Britain and an outline of the current legal basis of special needs provision from the perspective of the child's rights. Chapter 3 presents the current ideological framework within which special education is practised and Chapter 4 includes an analysis of the highly confused notion of 'integration'. The second half of the book is very much more practical in that Chapter 5 begins with a discussion of how service evaluation is conducted and discusses the shortcomings of the current inspection paradigm before going on to propose a more values-based approach. Chapter 6 looks at securing an inclusive school placement for a child who would otherwise be segregated and the final two chapters (7 and 8) deal with the politics of Statementing and advocacy support.

A WARNING TO PROFESSIONALS

It is likely that you will experience certain aspects of what follows as implicitly, if not explicitly, critical of your own practice, the practice of certain colleagues or that of allied professionals in other services or agencies. I hope that what I have said is not open to the criticism that it is unfair or in any respect personal. I have tried to offer reasoned argument to support my sometimes admittedly quite trenchant criticism of service organisation and professional practice. In making such criticism, I have tried, in most cases, to make it clear that it is not the individual professional who must carry the burden of responsibility for ineffective or damaging practices but the service system and the larger society – which together dictate how things should be. This is not to say that individual professionals are not at times personally culpable, for they certainly are, but rather that it would not only be unjust but plainly ludicrous to blame professionals for running services in a way that society clearly requires them to do.

One difficulty that many special needs professionals may have with much of what follows is that it is rooted in, what is for them, an unfamiliar analysis of the nature and underlying dynamic of service development – the analysis offered by principle of normalisation – which has, as yet, made virtually no impact on the practice of special education. I would just ask that you be patient as you make your way through what follows and I hope things will eventually become clear.

SO WHAT'S WRONG WITH SPECIAL EDUCATION?

'What's wrong with special education?' The question is being asked by parents, teachers, psychologists, governors, academics, administrators and a number of the leading children's charities. The question was also asked by Her Majesty's Inspectorate (HMI) and the Audit Commission who jointly undertook a piece of research – *Getting in on the Act* – which asked the very same question and came up with some quite devastating answers (Audit Commission/HMI 1992a).

The Government responded to this unparalleled level of public concern by enacting a major revision of the 1981 Education Act, which is Section 3 of the 1993 Education Act (HMSO 1993). This introduced some major new provisions aimed at strengthening the rights of parents, the most important of which is the right to appeal to the Special Needs Tribunal (SNT) against a decision by their Local Education Authority (LEA) with which they disagree. To complement the Act, the Government also issued a Code of Practice (1994) to guide LEA practice on the identification, assessment and Statementing of children with special educational needs (SENs).

Important though the new provisions of the 1993 Act are, I do not think they will serve to quell the doubts and widespread discontent amongst parents and we shall soon witness an insistent renewal of the questioning: 'what's wrong with special education?' – which should once again reach a crescendo as we approach the millennium. So what *is* wrong with special education?

THE PROBLEMS GO DEEP

A large part of the historical problem has been that the answers to the question have generally been quite superficial and, more often than not, concerned with administrative, resourcing or even training issues. This indeed was the level of answer provided by HMI/Audit Commission researchers. The assumption implicit in this kind of response has been that the schools only need to be a little better organised and resourced, the LEA and schools more accountable, the teachers better trained and more effectively deployed and everything will be fine. If this is the kind of analysis favoured by the overwhelming majority of professionals and the government itself, then it is not one which is supported by a growing body of parents of children with SENs who have long sensed a much deeper malaise.

This book is concerned to show that the problems with special education go much deeper than is usually acknowledged and that asking the question 'what's wrong with special education?' in the way that it is currently asked is merely a symptom of the depth of current misunderstanding. The government's response to parental anger and frustration has, once again, been to repackage tired legislation (the 1993 Act) in the hope that it will remove the heat from wounds which have festered over the decade since they last attempted to placate disaffected parents (the 1981 Act). However, the sticking plaster approach will do little to solve problems which are, at root, to do with what a growing body of parents and their advocates view as fundamental human rights issues. At present neither the government nor the various professional groups involved see the problems in this light.

In the following pages I shall explore three broad themes with which I have become increasingly preoccupied during my years as a special education professional. These are:

- the integration/segregation debate
- assessment and Statementing of children with SENs
- advocacy support for children with SENs.

Segregation and dishonest Statements are at the heart of the, now widespread, parental discontent and, although integration has for long been the really big and overarching moral issue in special education, problems over the assessment and Statementing process have been of increasing concern. Both integration and Statementing require a knowledge of complex legal and administrative matters as well as a sound grasp of child development and special education practice, at a level beyond the understanding of most laymen, so organised advocacy support is now necessary if parents are to achieve what they want for their children.

INTEGRATION

The debate over whether, and to what extent, we should integrate has always been around within our education service, as it has within our society. We have private and public schools (fee-paying and state-run), grammar and comprehensive schools, and mainstream and special schools. For whatever reason, it seems, as a society we have always felt the need to sort the 'wheat' from the 'chaff'; what has never been in doubt is that we always know how to distinguish between the two. This book is concerned with what we, as a society, have decided is the 'chaff' within the education system – children with SENs; the children we choose to segregate.

On the face of it, our school system would seem to be a reflection of the sort of people we are and of the kind of society we would like to become. Thus, when we arrange things so that a child with a severe disability does not have a place in his local school and must travel to a 'special' school some miles away, that decision represents society's wish for that child. Yet it seems odd that we should have to accept this as fact, as though it had arisen as a conscious decision of citizens generally, since what we find through talking to people about children who experience segregated schooling is that many would prefer it if they were present in their local schools – if they would not be disadvantaged through being there. It has to be said, though, that there is sometimes also an issue of whether the presence of some children might act to the detriment of others, but this tends to be more of a minority concern.

WHO KNOWS WHAT GOES ON IN THE SPECIAL SCHOOL?

Whatever the individual view on the issue of schooling for disabled children, there is as much mystery and confusion over the role of special schools as there is over the needs of the children who attend them. Since most people have never been inside a special school, it is hardly surprising that ignorance about the role and function of these institutions is widespread. How different to the knowledge we have about the ordinary schools which most of the rest of us have attended, even if we have long since given up trying to understand what is taught in them and how.

Given this level of ignorance, there is, on the face of it, no obvious reason why people should not simply accept that special schools provide a good and appropriate education for their pupils and this is, no doubt, what most do believe. Yet one frequently senses a nagging doubt in some minds as to why certain children should have to be separated from their peers to receive their education, since it has been noticed that such separation has consequences for the child's life outside school. However, even if the public at large remain blissfully unaware of these issues, more and more parents of disabled children are becoming concerned about the level of social isolation experienced by their children through such enforced segregation.

INVOLUNTARY SEGREGATION IS CULTURALLY DEVIANT

That compulsory segregation requires justification is not a matter for concern solely within the education service. Most modern democratic states build in substantial safeguards to protect citizens from the worst excesses of the police and the bureaucracy and, apart from the protection of life itself, the next most important area to safeguard is the liberty and rights of the individual.

As far as liberty is concerned, there is an expectation that the individual will be able to move freely within society and participate fully in the life of the community – making use of its services and opportunities on an equal footing with all other citizens. There is also an expectation that such freedoms will only be curtailed if an individual knowingly engages in violent or otherwise anti-social behaviour or becomes dangerous to himself or others through developing a mental illness – in such circumstances there is an understanding that society has a right to protect itself against the individual for as long as he or she remains a threat. When this occurs, a common consequence is the temporary, or even permanent, loss of liberty – but this is invariably a matter to be dealt with by the courts.

It is hard to think of examples of involuntary segregation which fall outside this scenario of perceived societal threat yet, with scarcely a second thought, we continue to segregate (in many cases compulsorily) a minority of our children for the duration of their educational careers. It is high time we seriously asked ourselves why this is. An exploration of this phenomenon is a key theme throughout this book.

THE NEED FOR A DIFFERENT ANALYSIS AND LANGUAGE

Certain sections of this book draw heavily upon the work of Wolf Wolfensberger, who has elaborated the principle of normalisation (1972) to explain the process of social devaluation of certain individuals and groups within society. This body of research remains largely unknown to professional educationalists – although it has had a major impact upon the training of social services and health professionals working with adults with learning difficulties. An attempt is made to spell out the implications of the principle of normalisation for the practice of special education and, in particular, to explore its relevance to children with severe and complex needs – which is the main model for this book. Such children are likely to attend separate schools or special classes in ordinary schools.

In what follows, frequent reference is made to the 'medical model' of disability – which is overwhelmingly the value/belief system of choice for service planners, managers and professionals. Perhaps 'choice' is putting it a little strongly since it implies that these individuals sit down and read up on the relevant paradigms before making an informed decision as to which will best meet the needs of those they are to serve. The reality is, of course, that we grow up within a society and culture which, in large part, conditions our habitual ways of making sense of experience so that we 'inherit' much of what we come to believe. Those involved in services by and large accept the status quo, for to do otherwise would be uncomfortable.

The 'social models' for the conceptualisation of need and the design of services will also be examined. The medical and social models represent almost diametrically opposed views of the needs of disabled people. It will be argued that the medical model is responsible for much of the existing inappropriate practice and that the slowly evolving social model offers a better analysis of what disabled children and adults need in their lives.

The language we use to describe the placement arrangements we make for children with SENs is still much too general and vague to support special needs professionals in developing more relevant and accountable practice. In Britain, until quite recently, we have unnecessarily restricted our thinking about placement differentiation through the use of such terms as *locational, social* and *functional* integration and there is an extended discussion of this issue in Chapters 3 and 4. In 1990, we in Britain acquired a new term –

inclusion – from colleagues in North America and this has served to raise expectations of what could and should be possible. This new term comes in the form of a *prescription* of what it is right to provide for children and not merely as a *description* of current practice as has largely been the case with British integration terminology hitherto.

INCLUSION – THE FINAL GOAL OF INTEGRATION

The inclusion philosophy offers renewed hope for parents who are desperate to have their children attend their local mainstream schools, and indeed many have been reinvigorated by attending conferences and workshops on inclusive education. What they take away from these events is a confirmation of their belief that what they want for their child is nothing more than should have been provided from the outset. Also, many parents are confirmed in their belief that their children will *only* grow and learn optimally in an ordinary classroom amongst their typical neighbourhood peers.

In describing and interpreting the philosophy of inclusion I will attempt to draw out its obvious advantages whilst offering a public health warning on the dangers inherent in believing that it can be easily achieved. There are particular dangers in overselling the possibility of inclusion to parents who generally know less about the system and its workings than the professionals who earn their living running it. That there is a deep institutionalised resistance to including certain children is beyond serious doubt, and it will take more than an inclusive education workshop to convince many professionals, and their employing LEAs, that they should change their traditional beliefs and practices.

None of this should be taken to imply that where there *is* goodwill, inclusion is difficult, because it is not. It is just that professionals find it difficult when they don't want to do it, either because they think it is a bad idea or because it frightens them.

THERE IS A LITTLE PROGRESS

There are also grounds for optimism that, eventually, we, as a society, will come to a clearer understanding of what children need. Such an understanding will inevitably have to be rooted in a shared paradigm of what it is to be a child growing and learning in society, since without a more coherent set of understandings and assumptions on this we will remain as confused as we are at present. It is a central thesis of this book that, in respect of severely disabled children, we are operating on the basis of a set of implicit assumptions about needs which are at odds with those we hold about typical children. Unless we address this contradiction, we are unlikely to be able to provide what those children actually need.

One of the more promising signs of a shift in attitude is provided by a policy statement made by the Council for Disabled Children in April 1994. The Council adopted the following principles:

1. No child should be denied inclusion in mainstream education provision.

2. Mainstream provision should offer the full range of support and specialist services necessary to give all children their full entitlement to a broad and balanced education.

3. Parents of children with SENs should be able to choose a mainstream school for their child on the same basis as parents of children without such special needs, and that the present element of compulsion in placement is inequitable and against the best interests of disabled people and their families.

4. The Council for Disabled Children endorses the UN Convention on the Rights of the Child, which recognises the rights of all children to education, to be achieved progressively and on the basis of equal opportunity and to facilitate the child's active participation in the community.

In adopting these four principles on integration the Council acknowledges the need for legal reform and more advice and advocacy for children, young people and their parents.

ASSESSMENT AND STATEMENTING

The Statementing process has become the focus of much parental frustration over what they increasingly see as the failure of the education service to meet their children's needs. Since its appearance in 1983, as a supposedly important safeguard for the SEN child's right to essential special services, the Statementing process has been under a cloud. The continuing failure of LEAs throughout Britain to undertake assessments and issue Statements which meet with parental approval has resulted in the proliferation of parent support organisations and a major redrafting of the legislation. At the time of writing (summer 1995), it is too early to say whether the 1993 Act will produce what parents are demanding but I am not optimistic.

The issues around most aspects of assessment and Statementing are largely, although by no means exclusively, about resourcing. On the integration issue, however, many LEAs would not change their policy if their budget were quadrupled because, for reasons I shall

the integration issue, however, many LEAs would not change their policy if their budget were quadrupled because, for reasons I shall outline later, they wish to maintain a system of segregated schools and classes. On many other Statementing issues it really does come down to money.

That there is evidence of widespread LEA contempt for the law on special needs education is no longer in doubt following the publication of the joint Audit Commission/HMI report *Caught in the Act* (1992) and the report by the Centre for Studies on Inclusive Education (Norwich 1994) on trends in integration and Statementing. It is also clear that services are in large part *means* rather than *needs* led, and this has serious implications for the working practices of special needs professionals in each of the relevant statutory services. The pressure to make recommendations which minimise the need for additional resources is evident in the way in which needs are characterised and reports are written. However, following the House of Lords ruling in July 1995 that professionals have a duty of care (and should be aware of the risks they may run if they choose to err on the side of appeasing their employer in denying the existence of genuine needs), professionals may have to take much greater care in future.

SEN ADVOCACY SUPPORT

It is the view of a number of parents and an increasing number of disabled people who have been subjected to the system of segregated education that many professionals have chosen to betray vulnerable children. For that reason advocacy support is another key theme in this book. It is still believed in some quarters that part of the role of the special needs professional is as *advocate* on behalf of the client/pupil, but this is no longer a realistic expectation given the inevitable conflict of interest that such advocacy support could engender.

Advocacy has remained a low-key, if not overlooked, issue in special needs education – probably because it is assumed parents will be willing and able to speak up on behalf of their own children. It has also been naïvely assumed that professionals will invariably be free to choose to act in the best interests of the child, hence the proliferation of such projects in the field of adult services has not been matched by a similar development in education. Whilst we are now beginning to see the development of *Parent Partnership* schemes run by LEAs and the national Special Needs Advisory Project (SNAP) in Wales, these remain largely concerned with providing information for parents rather than standing shoulder-to-shoulder with them as advocates as they battle to achieve justice for their children. Few of these schemes have the requisite level of independence from the statutory services to completely avoid a conflict

cacy. This book will explore the potential role of an advocacy service in education.

Implicit in its three main themes, this book sets out three core premises concerning the state of special education in Britain. The first is that it is a fundamentally devaluing process for many of the children who experience it. Second, many professionals are leaned on to betray the trust placed in them by largely unwitting parents. And third, in spite of a considerable amount of analytical and research effort, special education remains a non-subject and does not warrant its own army of specialists; therefore, because there is really no such thing as 'special' education, there is no justification for running two parallel service systems.

TWO SEPARATE SYSTEMS

Our education system is said to be highly inefficient, if not broken, because it fails to produce children who are sufficiently well-educated to support the needs of the workplace and the economy, hence rendering Britain a third-rate industrial economy. This is a debate that will run and run and, interesting though it is, it will not be discussed further since our main focus will not be on whether the system is inefficient but on why it is divided.

We have two education services which run in parallel: mainstream and special. These two systems have separate funding arrangements, different career structures and also compete for resources. It is said (HMSO 1978) that approximately 20 per cent of the pupil population have SENs, so it is clear where the major focus on service development must lie: in the mainstream.

The attempted revolution (reform) of our education system during the past decade has been marked by a constant stream of legislation (notably the 1988 Act) which has profoundly changed the administrative and curricula responsibilities of schools, and probably forever changed the nature of the relationship between the school and the LEA. Mainstream schools and some special schools now have full control of their own budgets and are able to hire and fire their staff.

All of this reform did little to improve the lot of children with special needs until the 1993 Act provisions began to take effect in 1994. It is still too early to predict the eventual impact of this major piece of legislation, which has indeed put in place some welcome safeguards for children in need of assessment for a possible Statement. However, much of the optimism being expressed in some quarters is both premature and probably naïve. We are, though, just beginning to see the sort of grounds on which parents are prepared to appeal, and this will be discussed in Chapter 8.

FORGOTTEN AGAIN – GUILT BY ASSOCIATION?

One interesting aspect of this whole process of devolving power from the centre to schools is that special education has been trailing every step of the way. Not only were pupils with special needs not considered in the early development of the National Curriculum but they have been years behind in coming into the formula funding arrangements and with the devolution of their budgets. Whilst most mainstream schools have been operating autonomously for a number of years, many special schools will not receive fully devolved powers until April 1996. This is also the case with the National Curriculum, which was implemented in the mainstream much earlier than in special schools.

This lag effect at national level is mirrored in local government, where special schools are dealt with as a lower tier of the service – usually as an afterthought and, on some issues, perhaps even forgotten altogether. During my years in teaching, I lost count of the number of times I had to call the central education office to remind someone they had once again forgotten the special schools. To those in the service there is a creeping suspicion that the lower valuation placed on the children contaminates perception of the staff – guilt by association?

When any individual or societal group find themselves lagging behind or separated out, it is natural to ask 'why me?'; 'why us?'. This is another question which I shall try to answer in the chapters which follow. That children with special needs are at risk of being left behind or separated out is not in question. This is not a risk; it is a fact. Britain, like most developed capitalist economies, invests a high proportion of its gross national product in educating its children, and in all such countries there has been a reluctance to acknowledge the needs of disabled children. Until just twenty-five years ago, the children who are the main focus of this book were still considered ineducable in Britain. Likewise, this same group still remain separated out from their peers and have to attend schools which are often miles from their own home neighbourhoods. Therefore, a further question we need to ask about our education system is: 'why does it continue to treat some children as though they were of less value?'.

SPECIAL EDUCATION IS FALLING BEHIND

A further important theme in this book is the view that amongst the statutory services, education has remained aloof from the debate on perceived social deviancy and the consequences of social devaluation whilst the 'care in the community' legislative programme has created a major shift in the thinking of health and social services professionals. The understandings that have dawned, often painfully slowly, for those running the big hospital institutions have hardly touched educationalists – who seem to have no means of understanding that their own services are falling behind in their treatment of vulnerable and socially devalued children and young people.

This deficit amongst educationalists is evident in three key areas: service conceptualisation and organisation, staff training and service evaluation. These three areas are, of course, linked and subsumed within a single ideology. The difficulty for educationalists is that, unlike their counterparts in health and social services, they have no coherent philosophy, or even a defensible values framework, for running a special needs service. Many in health and social services are able to point to normalisation theory or the social model of disability as the theoretical underpinning of their programmes and services, but those in education remain largely ignorant of this body of knowledge. In examining some of these ideas in the following pages, I shall be looking closely at the big moral issue in special education: our failure to integrate. The reasons for this will be explored showing how our language and general conceptualisation of integration has lacked clarity. There is a need to rethink our essentially segregationist policy and to develop new and more prescriptive terminology to describe what children need in their lives. The recently imported term *inclusive education* comes packaged with a functional definition of what an *included* child might reasonably expect, but it is all too frequently presented with gratuitous razzmatazz and can be construed as a simple panacea requiring no serious effort. This issue will be explored in the context of the real underlying ideology for inclusion – normalisation theory, or social role valorisation (SRV) as it has come to be known, which is all too frequently barely acknowledged or even understood by its proponents.

THE GOOD NEWS – THERE IS A ROLE FOR THE SPECIAL SCHOOL

To the reader who can cope with only so much bad news, I extend my sympathy but no apology. If any professional reading this book ends up feeling devalued, then I would ask them to reflect for a moment on what life is like for the children who, month in month out, year by year, have to endure many of our ill-conceived and life-wasting 'services', cut off from the real world and subjected to sometimes bizarre and untested practices. Such may be the world of the special school.

Yet there really is some good news too. Special schools, at their best, develop clever and innovative practice which, suitably adapted, could serve children well in the mainstream. There is a role for the special school teacher and classroom assistant supporting children in mainstream schools. Teachers who have discovered how to differentiate the curriculum for children with all manner of learning difficulties and teachers who know how to communicate with, position, toilet, feed and assess children with complex needs are indispensable if children from special schools are to move into the mainstream. Because good teachers have been encouraged to engage in some unhelpful practices in some equally unhelpful settings does not detract from the fact that they are still good teachers.

So, there will be a transitional role for special schools and their staff in supporting the mainstream to become mature and competent in its attitude and abilities to meet the needs of all children. Just such a role was mooted by the Warnock report (Warnock 1978, 8.12–8.15), although only as part of a system predicated upon the idea of a continuum of provision. Such a role is particularly important for the severe learning difficulty school because of the need for multidisciplinary teamwork. Once all mainstream schools are able to cope, there should be a complete closure of all segregated schools and separate classes.

Throughout this book, the chosen model for special needs provision is that for the child who is one of the approximately two per cent of children who have, or will eventually have, a Statement of their SENs (Audit Commission/HMI 1992). Such children will probably have severe learning difficulties or physical disabilities and some, perhaps, an additional sensory impairment. Whatever the particular impairment or combination of impairments, it is important to understand that many of the arguments used are specifically about the needs and life experiences of such children and are not intended to be taken as a description of the plight of the whole 20 per cent of school children with SENs.

Finally, a word for those managers and professionals whose job it is to run special needs education services. This book will probably cause many of you some pain, frustration and, perhaps, anger. If it does, this is not my intention. I simply wish to highlight a painful and enduring injustice. There is much wrong with our system that is in urgent need of reform. If you doubt this, please contact some of the national parent organisations and local groups and they will tell you what they have told me – that they are sick to death of the treatment they and their children receive at the hands of the 'system'. As a service professional, you will, of course, have the very best interests of those you serve at the forefront of your day-to-day concerns. Since you are almost certainly not the architect of the system (or even a small fragment of it) which fails so many children, you cannot accept responsibility for the undoubted damage it does. However, we each have a personal responsibility to try and ensure that the service in which we work constantly reviews its policies and practices, and that is the point at which each of us has a duty to remind ourselves, our colleagues, our line managers and the politicians that certain practices need to change if the most vulnerable learners in our school system are to receive social justice.

Chapter 1

The Context of Special Education

In this chapter I shall be looking at the historical, organisational and administrative context of special education, leaving aside the ideological context for the next and succeeding chapters. There is clearly a relationship of interdependence between the development of any legal and organisational framework for a public service and the underlying value system or ideology of which it is an expression, but, for convenience, the latter will be dealt with separately.

In order to be able to look intelligently towards the future it is important to have some acquaintance with the past, and this is especially true if one is concerned with the development of human services. Our understanding of what people need in their lives is not invented anew with each succeeding generation, but evolves out of a perception of what people had yesterday and how that affected what they were able to do in their lives.

Special education in Britain has a relatively short history – the first school for the blind was opened in 1791 – and the impression one gains looking back over those two hundred years is that tremendous strides have since been made, not only to bring all children into the education system but also to surround them with specialist supports to ensure they are able to make the most of their school years. In fact, so great seem the advances, that one could be forgiven for concluding that these technical developments must have been accompanied by, if indeed not caused by, a moral progress, since to bring children into school and community who have hitherto been excluded is surely a sign of a compassionate and caring society. An important part of what we shall be concerned with throughout the remainder of this book, therefore, is just that question: are we now a compassionate, caring and inclusive society? In what follows, this question will be addressed through looking at what has gone before and how this has shaped what we have today.

A BRIEF HISTORY OF LEGISLATION AND SPECIAL EDUCATIONAL NEEDS SERVICE DEVELOPMENT

Some have found cause for pride in the development of special education in Britain and one such commentator (Adams 1990) observes that:

> The story of special education in the United Kingdom is surely one of which the nation has every right to be proud. If it is true (as many educationalists would claim) that the mark of a civilised society is the care and concern which it shows for those of its children whose needs are greatest, the record of the United Kingdom in the development of special educational services will stand comparison with that of any other 'western' country, and British ideas and examples in this field have commanded – and still do – attention, admiration and imitation in many other countries. (p.5)

The author of this somewhat naïve eulogy goes on to redeem himself partially by observing that, according to certain sociologists, the main drive to improve the lot of children with special needs may have been rooted in the determination of the more privileged and advantaged in society to protect their own interests 'by segregating the disadvantaged in order to ensure that they remain so' (p.6). This latter explanation deserves at least as much credence as that favoured by this particular commentator who goes on to observe that 'human motivation is seldom totally pure and unselfish, but it would surely require a peculiarly virulent form of prejudice to fail to identify within our special education system a great deal of caring concern, compassion and genuine humanitarianism' (p.6).

This particular form of special pleading really only betrays the weakness of the argument being advanced. To try to develop a case for the UK as a civilised society because we demonstrate 'caring concern, compassion and genuine humanitarianism' towards disabled children is to expose his own hidden reservations about our real societal motivation (and probably his own unconscious feelings) in providing for such children.

The question we might ask here is: 'why would we not demonstrate 'caring concern, compassion and genuine humanitarianism' towards children with disabilities and learning difficulties?' Given that we would feel all those things about children generally, why would we not feel them about children with special needs? That this commentator and many others feel the need to emphasise the point is evidence that, even here in the UK, there is still a question mark hanging over these children and that question is: 'do they really deserve our care and compassion?'

Another question provoked by Adams' statement is: why are we using this kind of language to describe our feelings towards disabled children? Why the need to speak in such a condescending tone about our 'caring concern', 'compassion' and 'genuine humanitarianism'? We shall deal with underlying societal beliefs and expectations about disabled people when we look at some of the ways in which devalued people are construed by people generally, and also by those who plan and run the service system in Chapter 3.

An alternative view of the same reality (of the special needs system) is offered by a disabled person who was educated in segregated schools (Barnes 1991):

> Institutional discrimination against disabled people is ingrained throughout the present education system. The data show that most of the educational provision for disabled children and students remains basically segregative, is dominated by traditional medically influenced attitudes, and commands a low priority within the education system as a whole. As a result, rather than equipping disabled children and young people with the appropriate skills and opportunities to live a full and active life, it largely conditions them into accepting a much devalued social role and in so doing condemns them to a lifetime of dependence and subordination. In addition, by producing dependence in this way it helps to create the negative stereotypes by which all disabled people are judged, and therefore a firm basis for the justification of institutional discrimination in society at large. (p.28)

The possibility of two such contrasting views is due, at least in part, to the fact that the first commentator is speaking (as an ex-Director of Education) from the perspective of a service provider and the second (as an ex-special school pupil) from that of a consumer of special education, and it is not unusual to find that things look very different from these two somewhat divergent perspectives.

The reality was, of course, that, in Britain, a disabled child (a child with a learning difficulty, a physical disability or a sensory disability) received pretty harsh treatment until very recent times and that any real attempt to educate such children was very slow in coming. Although the first school for the blind appeared towards the end of the 18th century, it offered training in music and manual crafts for both children and adults and the ethos was more that of a workshop than an educational establishment.

At around the same time, schools for the deaf also began to appear – although they too provided *training* rather than *education*. Certainly children with sensory impairments were the first to be deemed worthy of some form of education and one commentator (Hurt 1988) describes these early efforts on behalf of deaf and blind children in the following way:

Blindness, deafness and dumbness attracted the sympathy and attention of philanthropic individuals and the state earlier, and to a greater extent, than did other impediments to the receipt of a normal education. Blind, deaf and dumb children received special consideration in the Poor Law Amendment Act, 1834, under which parents seeking relief in respect of such children did not suffer disenfranchisement, the political-social penalty imposed on all other recipients of relief at that time. (p.92)

It was not until the 1850s that children with physical disabilities were acknowledged as worthy of consideration, and here again these early institutions were concerned with training for possible employment and not education. Children who attended them came mainly from poor homes and the goods they made for sale contributed to their maintenance.

Prior to the 1850s, children who were then known as 'mentally defective' or 'feeble-minded' (other terms used to describe children with more severe learning difficulties included 'idiot', 'imbecile' and 'lunatic') were placed in workhouses and infirmaries if they were not able to remain at home. There was enormous stigma attached to the workhouse – which housed many children who had no disability but were simply from poverty-stricken homes. Adults and children coexisted in these dreadful places, which were intended to be a refuge from the rigours of a life of poverty in the outside world.

Towards the very end of the 19th century, legislation gave schools the power, but not a duty, to make special educational provision for such children. There was great confusion over classification and children ended up in one of a number of institutions – depending upon local provision, parental preference or the attitude of the local school board. So diverse were the options that a child might have ended up in a workhouse, an 'idiot asylum', a school of some kind, or may have simply remained at home.

The Royal Commission on the blind and the deaf was constituted in 1886 with a brief to include other groups in need of exceptional methods of education. The Commission distinguished between the 'feeble-minded', 'imbeciles' and 'idiots', concluding that this latter group were fundamentally ineducable. The 'feeble-minded' were deemed to be educable in 'auxiliary' schools separate from the mainstream while 'imbeciles' were thought not to need the care of an asylum or a workhouse, although they would need to remain in an institution concentrating upon their sensory, speech and physical development. Children with physical disabilities were categorised along with those described as 'feeble-minded', under the generic title 'defective', while those with 'normal' intelligence could attend ordinary schools. Children with epilepsy could attend ordinary schools if their attacks were relatively infrequent. The rest were placed in residential special schools.

Towards the end of the 19th century the word 'special' was being used quite widely and the first 'special' class for children described as 'defective' was opened in Leicester in 1892. Further schools opened in London around the same time. Describing these early efforts to acknowledge the needs of children with sensory, physical or learning disabilities, the Warnock report (HMSO 1978) summarised the state of affairs towards the end of the 19th century:

> These first, hesitant efforts by a few school boards to cater for some handicapped children owed nothing to educational legislation. The middle of the nineteenth century had seen a stirring of social conscience over the plight of the disabled, especially of the blind, but it was primarily concerned to relieve their distress, not to educate them. (p.10)

Progress in extending educational rights to children with different impairments was slowly gathering pace as the 20th century progressed, but there remained a hierarchy of perceived rights with the greatest opportunities being accorded to those with sensory impairments, who were favoured before those with physical impairments while children with significant learning difficulties trailed along behind in what we might call the 'impairment pecking order'.

As local services continued to improve (albeit unevenly) in both scope and quality, so did societal aspirations for a more comprehensive system of state provision for children with special needs. However, resources were to put a brake upon service development and, throughout the early years of the century, there remained a hierarchy of priorities which, in 1922, A.H. Wood, then Secretary to the Board of Education, decreed to be: blind, deaf, crippled and tubercular children requiring open-air schools. 'High and low grade mentally defective children' were the lowest priority. This exercise in prioritisation was said to reflect the differential public sympathy felt for these different conditions (impairments).

As legislation began to bring about increasing differentiation of categories of handicap, so the pressure increased for more 'special' education. The young and emerging discipline of educational psychology played a part in this and the French psychologists, Binet and Simon, began to develop tests aimed at classifying children according to their 'intelligence'. Cyril Burt was the first English educational psychologist and was appointed to the London County Council in 1913. Burt set about establishing the systematic use of intelligence testing, which carried with it the assumption that ability is both fixed and innate. This system eventually came into general use as a means of sorting out those children who should attend the grammar or secondary modern schools – the now infamous, though possibly (in certain quarters) resurgent, 11+ system.

In the lead-up to the 1944 Education Act, special education was a very low priority and, in government documents preceding the Bill and the Act, children with disabilities were dealt with under the heading of *Health and Welfare*. It was assumed that reform was already taking place with the generally increased provision for a range of needs having been addressed during preceding years prior to the advent of the Second World War. However, the Act did extend the range of duties of LEAs and oblige them to make appropriate provision for eleven categories of need: blind, partially sighted, deaf, partially deaf, delicate, diabetic, educationally subnormal, epileptic, maladjusted, physically handicapped and those with speech defects. Most of the children in each of these groups would be educated outside the mainstream, although some might attend ordinary schools if appropriate provision could be made.

The 1944 Act also brought in the abolition of certification, a process by which patients had been admitted to lunatic asylums, and such children were now to be known as *educationally subnormal*. Also, children over the age of two years with a disability of mind or body would need to be assessed to ascertain whether they were incapable of receiving education in an ordinary school. It was the 1944 Act which really established the firm foundations of special education as we have come to know it and, in so doing, it also shifted the power of diagnosis and determination of need from the medical profession to the education authority.

Prior to the 1944 Act, most schools – mainstream and special – were either private or run by the church under the supervision of local boards and there was little incentive for the government to become involved and provide a blueprint for service development. The general ability testing programme of recruits for the Second World War provided a warning to government that the widespread ignorance would need to be tackled eventually, and this too influenced the Act.

The Act brought in free education for every child to 15 years of age and there was an egalitarian spirit as the country began to build again after the ravages of war. However, this new-found enthusiasm for equality of opportunity did not embrace children with disabilities and learning difficulties. The 11+ examination (naturally based upon general ability testing) system was established to separate out the academically able who would attend the grammar schools from the great majority who were characterised as 'practical' and were to attend what were called the secondary modern schools. This tidy separation of the 'academic' from the 'non-academic' still left out children with additional needs, who were to be catered for in separate provision so that they would not obstruct the education of children in the two mainstream school settings.

This increased attention to categorisation then led to the development of provision within LEAs, in line with guidance from central government. The one category of children still deemed unworthy of education *per se* were those seen to be 'so low grade as to be ineducable'. These children were transferred to the health service. The Act described these children as 'suffering from such a disability of mind of such a nature or to such an extent as to make them unsuitable for education at school' (Education Act, 1944 Section 57). These children were, for the time being, to remain the responsibility of the local Health Authority.

Other children with lesser degrees of intellectual impairment were either to be educated in ordinary schools or in separate special schools. During the decade following the end of the Second World War, there was a steady increase in provision for children in most categories of disability but, for those described as 'educationally subnormal', there remained an insufficiency. The rate at which such children were being identified was constrained by the number of places available and this remained at a level much lower than the burgeoning demand from ordinary schools to transfer such children. Throughout this post-war period many children continued to be educated in hospital schools, some of which were run by voluntary bodies. Also during this time, there was an enormous increase in the number of children placed in Educationally Subnormal (ESN) schools. I was myself confronted by a situation which was precisely the reverse of this when I worked as a local authority educational psychologist many years ago. The LEA was concerned over the falling roll of a particularly dreadful special school and directed its small team of psychologists to go out and identify children whose IQ would suit them for education in such an establishment. It seems that having created categories of 'differentness' or facilities designed to cater for such categories, there will always be pressure to shuffle children around to meet the needs of the system rather than any needs the children themselves may have.

During the immediate post-war years, the number of children classified as 'Moderately Educationally Subnormal' (ESN-M) increased enormously and the schools catering for these children developed huge waiting lists. These children were seen to have only mild learning difficulties and teachers in mainstream schools were operating a policy of 'cleansing' their classrooms of all children who might present a serious teaching or behavioural challenge.

With the increased emphasis upon categorisation, the use of IQ assessment came into greater prominence and children increasingly came to be labelled according to their scores on such tests. Around 10 per cent of all children with special needs were described as 'educationally subnormal' (ESN) with a cut-off point for ineducability around IQ 50–55. Hurt (1988) refers to observations made in the much earlier (1924) Wood Report in which LEAs were firmly reminded of the dangers inherent in misplaced kindness in trying to educate children of low IQ in ordinary schools:

> In the past, numbers of children who have been recognised by their teachers and even by School Medical Officers to be ineducable or detrimental to others, have, on sentimental grounds, been allowed to attend school. In future this practice should cease. One detrimental or low-grade child in a class can cause havoc... It is too great a price to pay... He should be reported to the local mental deficiency authority. (p.180)

The guiding principle during this period was that where a child had a disability that was serious, then the child's education should take place in a separate special school. Where the disability was less serious, then education could take place in an ordinary school. Section 57 of the 1944 Act made a distinction between children who are educable and those who are not, and this was to be the cause of much parental anguish and protest as well as appeal.

Gradually the attitude of professionals changed in response to this evident injustice, and this was probably caused by a softening of attitude on the subject amongst the general public. There was also an inconsistent pattern, nationally, of children attending special schools, so that in some areas children were receiving education who would not have been educable in other parts of the country. Such ineducable children would have been attending training centres. This situation was summarised by the Warnock report (HMSO 1978) in the following way:

> Increasing unease about the principle and practice of excluding large numbers of mentally handicapped children from school found expression in the Mental Health Act 1959. The Act replaced Section 57 of the Education Act 1944 (as amended) by less rigid provisions. Parents were allowed extra time in which to appeal to the Minister against a local education authority's decision that their child was incapable of being educated in school; and given a right to call for a review after one year, with like opportunity to appeal. Parents were to be given more detailed information about the functions of the local authority in relation to treatment, care and training, and, wherever possible, a statement of the arrangements proposed to be made for their child by the local authority in discharge of those functions. Thus co-operation between local education and health authorities was enforced by statute'. (p.28)

However, in spite of this concession to the wishes of parents for their children to be properly educated, concern continued to mount and, in April 1971, the Education (Handicapped Children) Act 1970 came into force – requiring local authorities to take responsibility for mentally handicapped children. This resulted in 24,000 children in Junior Training Centres and Special Care Units being transferred to the education service. Such children were described as 'severely educationally subnormal' (ESN-S). Administratively, this meant that, centrally, the then Department for Education and Science (DES), now the Department for Education (DFE), became responsible for the education of these pupils.

This somewhat belated decision by the then government marked something of an ethical watershed in that it confirmed the right of *all* children, irrespective of the nature or degree of their disability, to a state education. Having at last decided that it is the fundamental human right of every child to receive an education, numbers in special schools rapidly increased – such that, in 1977, the number of children in special schools in England and Wales reached nearly 177,000 (or 1.8%) of the school population (HMSO 1978).

In 1974, a group of people, later to become known as the *Warnock Committee* (their report has already been referred to above), was established to review the educational provision in England and Wales 'for children and young people handicapped by disabilities of body or mind'. The committee reported in 1978 (HMSO 1978) and their recommendations were to progressively transform the approach to special needs education. Barnes (1991, p.32) points to the fact that, amongst its 27 members the committee comprised 27 professionals only one of whom was a parent of a child with special needs.

The report, in spite of adopting a somewhat pragmatic approach, produced a body of recommendations of which the scope was unprecedented. Its most enduring achievement was to begin to do away with the categorisation and labelling approach to special needs education and to highlight the importance of systematic and detailed assessment. Its least endearing recommendation was to endorse the notion of a continuum of provision to match the perceived continuum of need, which did little to promote integration. The report was also deficient in failing to address the underlying social causes of segregation and it provided no account of the phenomenon of social devaluation which surrounds children with more severe impairments.

One positive feature of the report was its recommendation that all teachers have an awareness of special needs and that in-service training be developed to achieve this. There was also an endorsement of the notion of parent-professional partnership, which has since become something of a slogan amongst special needs professionals but which still receives only lip service from most professionals whose training, as well as the culture of their services, tells them that they really do know best.

It was not until the 1960s and 70s that serious consideration began to be given to children with learning difficulties being educated in ordinary schools and this occurred just as remedial education began to develop along with the policy of attaching special classes to ordinary schools.

The Warnock report is sometimes mistakenly credited with having been an 'integrationist's charter', yet its commitment to integration was really only half-hearted because, as has been said, it strongly endorsed the concept of a 'continuum of provision'. It was this report which identified the three different forms of integration (locational, social and functional) which still form the bedrock of many professionals' understanding today, and which not only embodies the notion of a continuum of provision but is much too simplistic to help us in our understanding of what children need in their lives. Yet the committee felt they had hit upon a truly heuristic notion for they said:

> The concept of these three characteristic forms of integration – locational, social and functional – sharpens discussion of its meaning. Each element of the triad has a separate validity, although the functional element is perhaps uppermost in most people's minds when they speak of integration. Together these elements provide a framework for the planning and organisation of new arrangements for the education of children with special educational needs jointly with other children, and later for judgement of how effectively it has been achieved. (p.101)

During the deliberations of the Warnock committee, the Education Act 1976 set out the conditions under which integration would become the expected norm within the context of an overall comprehensive system of education. This Act was superseded by the 1981 Act, which embodied the spirit and many of the recommendations of the Warnock report but signally failed to make available the resources necessary to bring about the desired reforms.

The 1981 Education Act (which came into effect in 1983) proved to be a deeply flawed piece of legislation in that it placed duties upon LEAs which were simply too loose and vague, leaving their enforcement more a matter of goodwill than duty. The most important example of this is the qualified duty to integrate, which the Act said should be compatible with: (1) the child receiving the special educational provision that (s)he requires; (2) the provision of efficient education for the children with whom (s)he will be educated; and (3) the efficient use of resources.

Although the Act placed a duty upon LEAs to identify and assess children with special educational needs (SENs), it placed no time limit on the process and many parents were forced to wait for years for an assessment to result in a Statement detailing their child's needs and the provisions necessary to meet those needs. For many parents, further difficulties arose when they received the Statement and found that certain key provisions were missing or were described in such vague and non-specific terms as to be non-binding upon the LEA or Health Authority.

In 1983 the Independent Panel for Special Educational Advice (IPSEA) was established with the aim of providing free second professional opinions for parents who were unhappy with LEA accounts of their children's SENs. IPSEA is a limited company and a registered charity and still exists entirely on voluntary donations. IPSEA came about because of the continuing deep concern parents were expressing, throughout the UK, over their difficulties in having their children's needs met under the 1981 Act. The service provided by IPSEA was two-pronged: it provided telephone advice and also in-depth individual casework, which evolved into highly effective lobbying (Wright 1995).

In 1986 another voluntary organisation – Network 81 – was established to link up and support local groups and individual parents experiencing difficulty in achieving their children's entitlements under the Act. The main thrust of the work was to help parents in England and Wales through the process of having their child's needs recognised by her/his school and/or local education authority. Indeed, such was the level of concern over the way in which LEAs were implementing the 1981 Act that, by 1992, 50 per cent of calls to the Advisory Centre for Education (ACE) were from parents of children with SENs (ACE 1992). There were clearly problems to be addressed.

SPECIAL EDUCATION NOW

These, and other, difficulties for parents resulted in widespread dissatisfaction and led to an enquiry conducted jointly by Her Majesty's Inspectorate (HMI) and the Audit Commission (HMI 1992a). Their report confirmed what parents had long been saying and led to the introduction of a Bill which, in turn, produced a major revision of special needs arrangements – eventually culminating in the 1993 Act. In spite of its apparent ground-breaking provisions, this Act remains a flawed piece of legislation which will, in my view, not stand the test of time – for a number of reasons which are argued elsewhere in this book.

It is useful to look at the process which led up to the passing of the Act and, in so doing, to identify the major obstacles facing parents as they strive for a valued education and an honest Statement for their child. It is only through having a better understanding of the causes which lie behind their frustrations that it will become possible for parents and willing professionals to find ways of dealing with the widespread injustices in special education services.

In its White Paper, *Choice and Diversity* (HMSO 1992, p.40) the government made the following statement of its intention to build upon what it saw as the achievements of the 1981 Act:

> The Education Act 1981 is one of the important landmarks of education legislation in this century. The Government remains firmly committed to the general principles enshrined in that Act – the emphasis on the needs of the individual child; the duty on LEAs to identify, assess and provide for special educational needs; the right of parents to be involved in that process as partners; the requirement that pupils with SEN should be educated alongside their peers in ordinary schools to the maximum extent practicable; and the need for current arrangements to be kept under review so that provision remains sensitive and responsive to individual children's needs and parental wishes.

The White Paper then went on to acknowledge 'that there are widespread concerns about the way in which the Education Act 1981 is working, particularly in respect of parents' access to the present arrangements for assessments, Statements and appeals' (40,9.2). An additional stated intention in this document was to build the administration of special needs education into the new Grant Maintained (GM) sector: '…the Government believes it is in principle right that, once special schools have delegated management, they should be given the choice to ballot their parents on the case for GM status' (42, 9.7).

Also in 1992, the Audit Commission and HMI jointly published two documents on special needs education: *Getting in on the Act* (HMSO/Audit Commission 1992a) and *Getting the Act Together* (HMSO/Audit Commission 1992b). The former was a searing critique of the way in which special needs services were being mismanaged nationally and the latter, which is a management handbook, provided guidance on practice to remedy some of the problems identified.

Getting in on the Act identified some serious deficiencies in the way in which children with special needs were identified and provided for and highlighted five main problem areas:

- lack of clarity about what constitutes a special educational need
- uncertainty over the respective responsibilities of the school and the LEA
- lack of clear accountability by both school and LEA for pupil progress
- lack of accountability by the schools to the LEA for the resources they receive
- lack of incentives for the LEA to implement the 1981 Act.

These broad conceptual, management and administrative problem areas were resulting in a host of difficulties for parents in their dealings with their LEA over Assessment and Statementing, which included:

- the Statements taking far too long to produce (up to three years instead of the recommended six months)
- unsatisfactory time delays in processing appeals
- a steadily increasing volume of appeals over the period 1983–1991
- an increasing number of complaints to the Ombudsman 1987–1991
- unsatisfactory descriptions of needs and provisions
- marked inconsistency between LEAs in their placement of children in special schools, leading to wide variations in the proportion of pupils in such schools
- a failure to move children from special to mainstream schools (less than 2% of pupils move annually onto the roll of an ordinary school)
- failure by LEAs to take account of parental wishes in respect of mainstream school placement (36% of parents with a child in a special school wanted a change of school, and most of these wanted a mainstream school).

Faced with such a catalogue of problems causing mounting anger and frustration for parents because of the inadequate provision for their children, the government was forced to act. In July 1992 the DFE produced a consultation paper entitled *Special Educational Needs: Access to the System* (DFE 1992) which set out the government's proposals to:

- extend parental rights over the choice of school
- reduce the time taken by LEAs in making assessments and Statements of SENs
- make parents' rights to appeal more coherent, and to extend those rights
- establish an Independent Tribunal which would replace the jurisdiction of both the Secretary of State and appeal committees to hear appeals under the Education Act 1981
- issue further guidance for authorities on the criteria to be used for making assessments and issuing Statements.

Clearly there was to be an attempt to redress the balance of power between the parent and the LEA. The 1993 Act, along with its regulations and Code of Practice, was intended to do just that.

THE 1993 EDUCATION ACT – PART 3

The 1993 Education Act (HMSO 1993) represented the largest piece of educational legislation ever enacted in Britain. Part 3 of the Act dealt exclusively with SENs. The 1944 Act had previously been the foundation upon which the British education system was based and it had less than half as many sections (122) as are contained in the 1993 Act (308). Part 3 of the 1993 Act is *the law* on special needs education. This quite major revision of the 1981 Act took ten years to formulate and it seems unlikely that significant new SENs legislation will appear for some years to come.

Such an extensive overhaul of the flawed 1981 Act was necessary because there had been so much dissatisfaction expressed by parents and some professionals. It was in this special education part of the Bill which preceded the Act that many of the hardest battles had been fought, although much of this struggle took place in the Lords rather than in the Commons. The government was forced to concede a small number of amendments and the Act itself contained two major innovations: 1. A *Code of Practice*, by way of guidance to LEAs on how they should conduct the assessment and Statementing process; and 2. an *Independent Tribunal* to adjudicate on parental appeals.

The Act also increased, and greatly clarified, the role of the school in educating children with SENs and, in so doing, placed significant responsibilities upon governors. It also attempted to clarify the respective duties of the school and the LEA. There was, however, a weakening of the duty to integrate – which was created by the introduction of a virtual parental veto on an integrated placement, irrespective of the perceived needs or the expressed wishes of the child.

Because the 1993 Act is such an important piece of legislation in the lives of children with significant SENs, its provisions will be dealt with in greater depth in Chapter 2.

SEGREGATION – STILL ALIVE AND WELL

Midway through the 1990s, we find 'special' education alive (though distinctly unwell) and growing with a burgeoning professional structure – albeit one that has recently been somewhat trimmed at the LEA centre. The belief that integration is now the norm is not supported by the statistics produced by the Centre for Studies on Integration in Education. Earlier, CSIE had reported 'a disturbing increase in the segregation of children in special schools in some parts of the country' (Swann 1991). Over the period 1982 – 1990, 15 LEAs in England (the statistics did not cover Wales and Scotland) had become significantly more segregated with dramatic national variations – such that, in one LEA, a child was four-and-a-half times more likely to go to a special school than would have been the case if he had lived in an LEA in a different part of the country (although this was the most extreme variation, the overall picture was one of wide disparities throughout the country).

CSIE also conducted research into the level of Statementing for children in special schools and found that, in 1986, 26 LEAs failed to Statement 10 per cent (range 11.0 – 97.2%) or more of their segregated pupils. This was contrary to the requirements of Section 7(1) of the 1981 Act, which placed a duty on an LEA to make a Statement for a child it had assessed under Section 5 of the Act if, having made an assessment, the LEA had determined that special educational provision should be made for that child.

The Audit Commission published a report, entitled *The Act Moves On: Progress in Special Educational Needs* (Audit Commission 1994), in which it reported on the results of 'value for money audits' conducted in nearly all LEAs in England and Wales during 1993. Although this work cannot be seen as a judgement on the effectiveness of the working of the new Act (whose provisions did not come into force until September 1994), it did serve to underscore the seriousness of the problems the Act was intended to address. The report found that:

- requests for pupils to be assessed were increasing
- LEAs should define when a special need warrants a Statement, otherwise inequities will persist in the way help is targeted
- most LEAs take much longer than the statutory time of six months to make assessments and issue Statements
- up to £30 million could be released from special schools with falling rolls for pupils helped in mainstream schools.

As regards LEA efficiency/inefficiency, the report found the same pattern as outlined in the 1992 study – which included:

- poor framework of policy and strategy
- lack of clarity about the roles and responsibilities of LEAs and schools
- lack of monitoring and accountability
- poor targeting of resources
- poor management and administration of the assessment process
- lack of delegation of learning support services.

Clearly LEAs have work to do, and the Act and its Code of Practice should provide some of the help they will need to achieve more efficient and coherent special needs provisions. However, the Act and successive government circulars will not solve the problems alone, and parental pressure will need to be maintained with the support of the various voluntary organisations which provide the advice, guidance and the essential encouragement to keep battling in the face of apparently overwhelming LEA resistance. Whilst the legal framework of special education is extremely important, it is not the whole story and there are many other issues which serve to define the current context of special education. Much of what is relevant here has to do with the service structure and its professional staffing arrangements.

LEAs have a good deal of discretion as to how they plan and manage their special needs services and we have already seen that this is reflected in the sometimes extreme variations in both the numbers of Statements they produce and the proportion of children they send to segregated schools. This local variation is difficult to explain and probably results from complex historical factors which might, at a later stage, be difficult to identify. Sometimes the way a service develops can be due to the values and drive of a single individual who may no longer be around, but whose mark has been left as an indelible imprint on the pattern of local services they left behind. Such was the case in the London Borough of Newham where the parent of a child with SEN became chair of the education committee and began to formulate a strategy which was to have a powerful influence on education policy for many years to come.

Linda Jordan and her partner, Chris Goodey, were determined that their daughter, who has Down's syndrome, would remain in the educational mainstream. When Linda was elected chair of the education committee, she was well-placed to help the authority pursue an integration policy. In 1987, Newham produced a policy statement outlining its intention to provide special education only in mainstream schools and, in so doing, firmly nailed its colours to the mast of what it later came to call 'inclusive' education. In its statement it said:

> The London Borough of Newham believes in the inherent equality of all individuals irrespective of physical or mental ability. It recognises, however, that individuals are not always treated as equals and that people with disabilities experience discrimination and disadvantage. The council believes that segregated special education is a major factor causing discrimination. We therefore believe that desegregating special education is the first step in tackling prejudice against people with disabilities and other difficulties. They have been omitted from previous Equal Opportunities initiatives, and it is now obvious that our aim of achieving comprehensive education in Newham will remain hindered while we continue to select approximately 2% of school pupils for separate education. (Lockhart 1987)

This momentous step by Newham began with the determination of Linda and Chris that their child would not be sidelined, and the certain knowledge that many other parents felt the same way. In the struggle which ensued, many good and supportive professionals weighed in to try and make the policy a living reality in Newham schools – and that struggle continues today. To date, as far as I am aware, Newham is still the only LEA in Britain which has taken a clear policy stand on the integration/segregation issue and, within Newham, the battle is still far from won. It is worthy of note that many professionals were eager to implement an integration policy in Newham because the initiative came from the top. This was also the case with the Catholic Separate School Board in Kitchener, Ontario, where all segregated classes were eliminated by a decision of the Director of Education and his Management Committee. This should lead us to be optimistic that real change might be achieved through a top-down policy initiative.

At the other extreme, some LEAs are still building new special schools and planning to increase the number of children who must be educated outside the mainstream. Here again local tradition may have been created by the influence of a particular individual – elected member or professional – who believed that the special school provides the best conditions for some children to learn.

Yet another variation is the LEA which sees itself as committed to 'integration' and embarks on a programme of special school closure in favour of mainstream unit provision. In one authority this policy was conceived some 20 years ago. In 1995 it had just a handful of, mostly small, special schools and a large, and still growing, number of special classes and units in mainstream schools. This authority has not seriously revised its view as to what may count as 'integration' over the 20 years in which the policy has steadily grown and it looks set to end up with few, if any, special schools and a very large number of largely segregated units attached to ordinary schools. Integration? Such a policy does little more than shift segregation to the site of the mainstream school.

Clearly the current context of special education in Britain is a very mixed picture with LEAs pursuing their own policies on such important matters as Statementing and integration within a legislative framework which, whilst being progressively tightened, remains loose enough to allow individual authorities a considerable degree of free rein. Many would see this freedom as a prerequisite for experimentation and the development of innovative practice, and there is something in such an argument, yet within such freedoms the rights of the child should not be ignored and that freedom must be exercised within the tight framework of responsibilities laid down in statute. The correct balance remains to be struck.

Chapter 2

Special Education and the Law

THE IMPORTANCE OF UNDERSTANDING THE LAW

It may not appear immediately self-evident why a book on the integration and assessment of children with Special Educational Needs (SENs) should include a chapter on the law of special education. In fact, the law is coming to assume an ever greater significance for parents in their dealings with their LEAs, perhaps because parents have developed a stronger sense of their rights as citizens; or because they are coming to a better understanding of notions of social justice; or perhaps simply because our society is generally becoming more litigious.

Professionals in many human services interpret the laws, rules and regulations as though they were the embodiment of what clients need and what is morally right for them. Working within this limited legalistic perspective, rather than looking to provide what clients actually need, is at the root of much poor and inappropriate practice. This is as true in education as in any other human service area, so, whilst it is important to know and understand the law, it is certainly not sufficient to assume that the law reflects the real nature and extent of human need.

The 1993 Education Act (HMSO 1993) has given parents additional rights and powers, and that is to be welcomed; however, there is a serious question as to whether these are adequate to redress the imbalance between parents and the LEA which created the pressure for improved legislation in the first place. There is also a serious question as to how parents will be able to exercise those rights without support, because the law and its regulations are highly complex. Just where such support is to come from and what shape it might have is still far from clear – although the reader will find some suggestions and guidance on this elsewhere in this book, particularly in Chapter 8.

In what follows, account has been taken of the needs of parents and their advocates to have a fuller understanding of the law and of the way in which an LEA is likely to act in interpreting that law.

John Friel, a practising barrister, provides a truly authoritative and comprehensive account of the law as it relates to special needs education in the latest editions of his books *Children with Special Needs: Caught in the Acts* (1995a) and *Young Adults with Special Needs: Caught in the Acts* (1995b). Although Friel describes these books as practical guides rather than textbooks, they are quite comprehensive in their coverage and written in a language that non-specialists should not find too difficult. Two more explanatory publications on the 1993 Act, which both professionals and parents will find useful, are the Advisory Centre for Education (ACE) publication *Special Education Handbook: The law on children with special needs* 6th edition (1994) and the Independent Panel for Special Educational Advice (IPSEA) *First Step Guide* to solving problems facing parents whose children have SENs.

THE EVOLVING LEGISLATION

The children's parents and their LEAs have basic legal duties towards the education of children, which were enshrined in the 1944 Education Act and later elaborated in the 1993 Act. The 1944 Act states: 'It shall be the duty of the parent of every child of compulsory school age to cause him to receive full-time education suitable to his age, ability and aptitude and to any special educational needs he may have either by regular attendance at school or otherwise'. (DES 1944, Section 36)

The primary duty of the LEA is found in Section 8 of the 1944 Act. The LEA must ensure that there are sufficient schools available for its area, the schools are sufficient in number, character and equipment; and educational provision is made for the different ages, abilities and aptitudes of pupils.

The general duty of the LEA has been underpinned by more specific duties in respect of children who have SENs, which have been elaborated in subsequent legislation – most notably the 1981 Act, which came into force in 1983, and the 1993 Act, which states:

> A local education authority shall exercise their powers with a view to securing that, of the children for whom they are responsible, they identify those to whom subsection (2) below applies.
>
> (2) This subsection applies to a child if –
>
> > (a) he has special educational needs, and
> >
> > (b) it is necessary for the authority to determine the special educational provision which any learning difficulty he may have calls for. (HMSO 1993, Section 165)

In Chapter 1 we saw the extent of the concerns over special education which resulted in a commitment from the government (Department for Education 1992a) to redraft the 1981 Act. The chapter also summarised the joint research and recommendations by the Audit Commission and Her Majesty's Inspectorate (HMI) (Audit Commission/HMI 1992) which provided a damning indictment of current practice. All of this activity led to Part 3 of the 1993 Act, which basically *is* the law on special needs education.

The following account of current special needs legislation is selective in that it deals with the law specifically as it relates to the two central themes of this book: integration and assessment/statementing. The treatment of these two issues will not be comparable in terms of the space allocated since the Act has much more to say about the latter than the former.

It is important to note that the 1981 Act was repealed from September 1994, thereby leaving Part 3 of the 1993 Act, Schedules 9 and 10, The Education (Special Educational Needs) Regulations 1994 and The SEN Tribunal Regulations 1994 as representing the law on special needs education. Although much of the 1981 Act was simply carried over and incorporated into the 1993 Act, the latter contained some completely new elements including:

- a *Code of Practice* for schools and LEAs

- a new appeal system in the form of an Independent SEN Tribunal

- time limits on LEAs completing assessments and issuing Statements

- a parental right to express a preference for the school to be named in their child's Statement.

INTEGRATION AND THE LAW

The 1981 Act (Section 2) attempted to enshrine one of the three key principles of the Warnock Report (1978): that there should be maximum integration of children with special needs into the lives of their mainstream schools and their communities. The Act itself stated that:

(2) Where a local education authority arrange special educational provision for a child for whom they maintain a statement under Section 7 of this Act it shall be the duty of the authority, if the conditions mentioned in subsection (3) below are satisfied, to secure that he is educated in an ordinary school.

(3) The conditions are that account has been taken, in accordance with section 7, of the views of the child's parent and that educating the child in an ordinary school is compatible with –

(a) his receiving the special educational provision that he requires;

(b) the provision of efficient education for the children with whom he will be educated; and

(c) the efficient use of resources.

These three key qualifications of the duty to integrate were carried forward and incorporated into the 1993 Act virtually unamended. The Act restates them in Section 160 as follows:

(1) Any person exercising any functions under this Part of this Act in respect of a child with special educational needs who should be educated in a school shall secure that, if the conditions mentioned in subsection (2) below are satisfied, the child is educated in a school which is not a special school unless that is incompatible with the wishes of his parent.

(2) The conditions are that educating the child in a school which is not a special school is compatible with –

(a) his receiving the special educational provision which his learning difficulty calls for,

(b) the provision of efficient education for the children with whom he will be educated, and

(c) the efficient use of resources.

One difference between the 1981 and 1993 Acts on integration is that the latter introduces the right of the parent to relieve the LEA of its duty to consider integration under Section 160. What this would mean in practice is that the LEA would not have to consider whether the three conditions can be fulfilled. However, the LEA would still be at liberty to conclude, after assessment, that a mainstream place is appropriate and name such a school in the final Statement. A further difference contained in Section 160 of the 1993 Act is that a duty is placed on 'any person exercising any functions' and not just the LEA as in the 1981 Act. It is not clear just what this might mean in practice although it could be seen as referring to the SEN Tribunal.

Commentary

Since it is a central thesis of this book that integration is *the* major issue in special needs education, both from the ethical and the educational/organisational standpoints, it remains to be explained why so little attention is paid to it in the Act (one section out of 35, or less than 3% of the whole of Part 3 of the Act).

Integration is either a big issue or it is not and it is clear that educationalists devote a great deal of time to talking and writing about integration, even if they, typically, put little effort into bringing it about. That it is dealt with so peremptorily in the legislation might be because, as a quasi-human rights issue, it has been difficult to pin down procedurally. Alternatively, it might be construed as unwillingness on the part of the government to dictate to LEAs on the issue – relying on the law establishing the value of integration as a principle; the approach therefore being *enabling* rather than *enforcing*. There is also, of course, the question of cost, and no government would happily write a blank cheque to implement a rights issue – especially if they thought the costs would be prohibitive.

That such an important and vexing matter can be dealt with so summarily is, perhaps, due to the inherent simplicity of the intrinsic issue – a child is either integrated or segregated. However, to have reduced this to a checklist of three items is inevitably to engage in over-simplification. In straightforward language, the test of whether a child *may* be integrated involves asking three simple questions:

1. Will the child receive the educational provision *(s)he* requires?

2. Will the other children receive the education *they* require?

3. Is it a sensible (prudent, cost effective or whatever) way to spend money?

That the law is able to deal so succinctly with the issue of integration is testimony to the amount of work remaining to be done to educate government, as well as professionals and the general public, about the importance of this issue in the lives of children.

ASSESSMENT AND STATEMENTING AND THE LAW

Most of what was new in Part 3 of the 1993 Act reflected the widespread concern described in Chapter 1 over the failings of the 1981 Act. It is important, therefore, to describe these changes in the context of the shortcomings of the 1981 Act, which mainly concerned the requirement for LEAs to identify children with SENs, assess the needs of such children and describe each and every one of the child's needs and specify and arrange the necessary provisions to meet those needs. These responsibilities had been focused in Section 7 of the 1981 Act through the requirement to make and maintain a *Statement* of SEN.

The Statement was seen as necessary for only about 2 per cent within the approximately 20 per cent, of children who might have a SEN at some time. The intention was to provide for those children experiencing the greatest need. The remaining 18 per cent of children were seen as a continuum whose needs could be met without the requirement of a Statement. In addition, the system for appeal (first to a local Committee then, if necessary, to the Secretary of State) by a parent who was unhappy with the way in which the LEA discharged its duties was put in place in an attempt to protect parental rights. However, this system found little favour with parents.

The key provisions in the 1993 Act to meet the widespread concerns voiced over the operation of the 1981 Act will now be dealt with in turn. These are covered sequentially as they appear in the Act, but also under the relevant topic headings. An attempt has been made to provide a relatively *Plain English* interpretation of the necessarily legalistic language of the Act itself.

Identification and assessment of children with SENs

The arrangements for the identification and assessment of SENs are contained in Sections 165 to 176 of the 1993 Act and largely repeat the arrangements which had stood under the 1981 Act. However, an important difference lies in the introduction of a limit on the time allowed to the LEA to complete the process. The following are the duties that the LEA must, by law, discharge in addressing a child's SENs.

GENERAL RESPONSIBILITY FOR SPECIAL EDUCATIONAL NEEDS

Section 165: The LEA retain a general responsibility for identifying and assessing the SENs of children in their area between the ages of 2 and 16 (up to 19 if registered at a school).

DUTIES TO CONSULT WITH DISTRICT HEALTH AUTHORITY AND LOCAL AUTHORITY

Section 166: The LEA also has a duty to call upon the District Health Authority and the Local Authority Social Services Department to assist it in carrying out its duties and that authority must comply. Here the request is likely to be for advice on the child's need for speech therapy, physiotherapy, or occupational therapy, or for advice on the social needs of the child and family.

DUTY TO INFORM PARENTS

Section 167: Where the LEA believes a child has SENs for which it is necessary for them to determine the provision, it has a duty to inform the parents of a proposal to initiate an assessment. Provisions for carrying out this assessment are described in *Regulations 5–11*, which cover medical and other advice and the time limits to be observed.

DUTY TO MAINTAIN A STATEMENT OF SPECIAL EDUCATIONAL NEEDS

Section 168: Once an assessment has been undertaken under Section 167, and if the LEA have found it necessary to determine the special educational provision a child requires, it then has a duty to draw up a Statement of the child's needs. This statement *must spell out each and every need identified and specify provision to meet such needs.* In conjunction with the parents, the LEA must also identify a school which can meet the child's needs. *Schedule 10* deals with the making and maintenance of Statements under Section 168 of the Act. The most important duty, at the end of the day, is under Section 168 (5) (a) (i): 'the authority...shall arrange that the special educational provision specified in the Statement is made for the child'.

RIGHT OF PARENT TO APPEAL AGAINST A DECISION NOT TO MAKE A STATEMENT

Section 169: If, after making an assessment under Section 167, the LEA decide **not** to make a Statement, the parent may appeal to the SEN Tribunal. The Tribunal has the power to:

- dismiss the appeal
- order the LEA to make and maintain a Statement
- remit the case to the LEA asking them to reconsider their decision.

RIGHT OF PARENT TO APPEAL AGAINST THE CONTENTS OF THE STATEMENT

Section 170: If, after receiving the Statement conducted under Section 167, the parent is not satisfied with the way in which the needs have been described and/or the provisions outlined, the parent may appeal to the Independent SEN Tribunal. The Tribunal has the power to:

- dismiss the appeal
- order the LEA to amend the Statement
- order the authority to cease to maintain the Statement.

RIGHT OF THE LEA TO MONITOR THE SPECIAL EDUCATIONAL PROVISION

Section 171: The LEA has the right to inspect any school (maintained or grant maintained – GM) where they maintain a Statement for a child.

DUTY TO REVIEW EDUCATIONAL NEEDS

Sections 172 and 173: The parent has a right to request that their child's SENs be assessed, whether or not the LEA currently maintain a Statement for the child. However, there should not have been an assessment within the preceding six months. The LEA should comply with such a request if they consider such an assessment necessary but, should they decline to do so, the parent has a right of appeal to the Independent SEN Tribunal. The Tribunal has the power to:

- dismiss the appeal
- order the LEA to arrange for an assessment to be made.

The LEA also has a duty to review a Statement made under Section 168 within a period of 12 months of the Statement coming into effect, and annually thereafter. The procedure for such reviews is detailed in Regulations 15,16 and 17, Education (SEN) Regulations 1994. This guidance places a duty upon the headteacher of the child's school to submit a review by a specified date having consulted a number of key professionals and agencies. It also prescribes a procedure for collating information for the review which must include: convening a meeting to which parents and relevant staff are invited, preparing a review report and requesting written advice from the child's parents and certain key professionals.

RIGHT OF A GM SCHOOL TO REQUEST AN ASSESSMENT

Section 174: Where a GM school has been directed (under Section 13 of the Act) to admit a child without a Statement, the governing body can make a request to the LEA to assess the child's SENs. The LEA then has a duty to propose an assessment. Such an assessment should not have been made within the previous six months.

ASSESSMENT OF EDUCATIONAL NEEDS OF CHILDREN UNDER TWO YEARS

Section 175: Where the child is under two years of age the LEA may, with parental consent, make an assessment of the child's educational needs. The LEA must make an assessment at the request of the parent. Having made an assessment, the LEA may make a Statement detailing the child's SENs and may maintain that Statement in such a manner as they consider appropriate.

DUTY OF THE DISTRICT HEALTH AUTHORITY TO PROVIDE INFORMATION FOR THE LEA AND PARENT

Section 176: The District Health Authority must notify the LEA of any child under five years it considers may have SENs. It also has a duty to inform the child's parents and to provide an opportunity for the parent to discuss the matter with an officer of the health authority. It should also put the parent in touch with any relevant voluntary organisation.

Such are the duties, responsibilities and rights of the parents, the LEA and the other statutory agencies over the assessment and Statementing process. From the parental perspective it would appear that significant new parental rights are conferred under the 1993 Act, over and above those parents enjoyed under the 1981 Act – in particular, the right of appeal to an Independent SEN Tribunal.

The special needs tribunal

Section 177: The Special Educational Needs Tribunal (SNT) was established to exercise jurisdiction over the workings of Part 3 of the Act. The Tribunal has a President and a panel of persons, known as 'the chairmen's panel' who may serve as chairman. There is also a panel of persons who may serve as the other two persons on each of the Tribunals. Hence there will be a three-person panel for each hearing. The President and the members of the chairmen's panel are appointed by the Lord Chancellor and the panel members by the Secretary of State.

Section 178: Qualification for appointment as President or member of the chairmen's panel is a minimum of seven years relevant legal experience. Lay panel members must meet requirements as prescribed, which at the present time is that they should have: (a) knowledge of one or more areas of SENs and/or (b) knowledge of the workings of local government.

Section 179: The Secretary of State has the power to defray the expenses of the Tribunal to such an amount as he may, with the consent of the Treasury, determine. At present, parents may claim travel expenses and a contribution towards loss of earnings of £23 for an appeal lasting up to four hours and £44.80 for one lasting over four hours. They may also have reasonable travel costs reimbursed. This also applies to witnesses but *not* representatives.

Sections 180 and 181: The Tribunal procedure is defined in *The Special Educational Needs Tribunal Regulations 1994*. Membership of the Tribunal will be as described above, that is one chairperson plus two lay members. The procedures of the Tribunal include provisions which are important changes to the appeal scenario:

(g) for granting any person such discovery or inspection of documents or right to further particulars as might be granted by a county court, Part 3, Section 22 of Regulations

(h) requiring persons to attend to give evidence and produce documents, and Part 3, Section 23 of Regulations

(i) for authorising the administration of oaths to witnesses. Part 4, Section 30(4) of Regulations

Further information on the procedure for mounting an appeal with advocacy support is provided in Chapter 8. The grounds for appeal are as follows:

SUMMARY OF PARENTAL RIGHTS OF APPEALS

Parents are able to appeal against the following:

- refusal by the LEA to a parental request for an assessment or re-assessment (Sections 172 and 173)
- refusal by the LEA to make a Statement having conducted an assessment of a child without an existing Statement (Section 169)
- parental disagreement with the description of the child's SENs or the provisions outlined in the Statement or where, having conducted an assessment under Section 167, the LEA determine not to amend the Statement (Section 170)
- parental disagreement with the LEA's decision not to name a school or change the name of the school (Schedule 10 Para 8)
- parental disagreement with the LEA's decision to cease to maintain the Statement (Schedule 10 Para 11).

It is *not* possible for a school to appeal to the Tribunal if the LEA turn down its request for an assessment. An appeal form is included at the end of a booklet for parents entitled *Special Educational Needs Tribunal: How to appeal* (DFE 1994)

APPEAL PROCEDURE

It is absolutely crucial that once the parent has decided to appeal against a decision of their LEA on any of the above grounds, they have access to truly independent advice. The issues and the law are complex, and officers of the LEA will know precisely what the rules of the game are and how they should conduct themselves. (It is fair to make this generalisation at the time of writing, although when the Act first came into effect LEAs were clearly very unsure of what they should do and many mistakes were made.) I take the view that parents need independent advice and advocacy support of the type described in Chapter 8.

Whether these newly acquired legal rights genuinely strengthen the hand of parents in their dealings with their LEAs will, in large part, be determined by the way in which the Tribunal does its job. It is too early to make any generalisations about this. A summary of the work of the Tribunal in its first year of operation is provided in Chapter 8.

The code of practice

Sections 157 and 158: The Code of Practice published in 1994 (DFE 1994) (which will be subject to amendment from time to time) gives practical guidance to LEAs and governing bodies in respect of the discharge of their duties under the relevant sections of the Act. The Act says:

> It shall be the duty of (a) local education authorities, and such governing bodies, exercising functions under this part of this Act, and (b) any other person exercising any functions for the purpose of the discharge by local authorities, and such governing bodies, of functions under this Part of this Act, to have regard to the provisions of the code. (Section 157 (2))

This statement is not intended to imply that those with a duty to make provision for children with SENs should merely have to look at what the Code has to say and then decide what *they* wish to do. The requirement is very much stronger than that; a duty is laid upon those concerned to act in accordance with what the Code requires – if they don't, they will be in breach of a duty. At the Lords Committee Stage of the Bill, Baroness Blatch said quite firmly that

> any departure from the Code will, if challenged, require justification – to parents in the first instance and then, depending on the circumstances, to the Secretary of State if the matter at issue is the subject of a statutory complaint, or to the new Special Needs Tribunal if the matter at issue is the subject of an appeal'. (Hansard 1993, col 487).

In plain language, this means that those concerned should act in accordance with the Code or otherwise explain why they have not and if they cannot give a satisfactory explanation, it will be open to the Secretary of State to direct them to behave differently. Whether the Secretary of State will use this power has yet to be established. The Code itself provides detailed guidance on the following:

- school-based stages of assessment and provision
- statutory assessment of SENs
- drawing up Statements of SENs
- assessments and Statements for children under five
- procedures for the annual review.

Some key issues for advocates

It is rarely self-evident from a straight reading of a particular piece of legislation just what the law actually is. This is certainly true of the 1993 Act and its schedules and regulations. If this is a problem for professionals working in the field, it will certainly be so for parents – who need to understand the law in order to be able to pursue their rights. To help clarify matters, the various issues of concern to parents and special needs professionals are now highlighted with suggestions as to how an individual's needs might be safeguarded.

THE DUTY TO INTEGRATE

In English law there is only a qualified duty to integrate a child with SENs in an ordinary school. We have already looked at the three clauses of the Act which mitigate this duty as far as the LEA is concerned. In practice it has proved very easy for a reluctant LEA to invoke one or more of these 'let-out clauses' to duck their 'duty' to integrate. It is difficult to see how the government is able to maintain that LEAs are under a *duty* to integrate children whilst, at the same time, offering such convenient caveats on that supposed duty in the way they did in the 1981 Act, and then again in the 1993 Act.

The government speaks of the duty to integrate 'provided certain reasonable conditions are met...' but then offers no criteria to test 'reasonableness', so any LEA may invent their own criteria and then move the goal posts as they please, and this is indeed what happens. Also, within an authority, the individual teacher, headteacher, adviser, psychologist or administrator may all take different views on what is reasonable or unreasonable. In such circumstances it is hard to see how a parent could expect the test of reasonableness to produce even a coherent response, let alone a positive one.

Advice on how to achieve an integrated placement is not easy to come by and it may well mean a protracted and bloody battle with the LEA up to a Tribunal appeal. This is because, in the author's opinion, many professionals employed by the LEA will have only a half-hearted commitment to integration. It will, therefore, be important for the parent and any positive professionals to get as many allies as possible to support their case, and if the headteacher of the chosen mainstream school is prepared to accept the child then that is a great help. However, pressure may then be exerted on him/her to review their decision. Sadly, many heads feel unable to stand firm against such pressure.

As soon as there is resistance from the authority, parents should consider finding an advocate who is able to offer support in subsequent negotiations and in the writing of letters (see Chapters 6 and 8 for guidance on the type of person required). It would also be helpful to obtain an independent psychological report stressing the importance of an integrated education. In the Tribunal hearing, the

to be able to reach an informed and balanced view of what the child needs.

THE DUTY TO ASSESS AND STATEMENT

By comparison with the matter of integration, issues around assessment and Statementing represent a very much more fruitful area on which parents might seek to challenge their LEA because the law is so much clearer in specifying the duties and responsibilities of the various parties (HMSO 1993, Sections 165–168). The following is an outline of these various duties commencing with the very young child.

ASSESSMENT OF THE VERY YOUNG CHILD

The duty of the various authorities to identify and make provisions for children under two need apply only with parental consent. If the LEA believe a child has SENs which would call for them to make special provision, they may assess the child only with the consent of the parents. If, on the other hand, the parent requests such an assessment, the authority need only comply if it is 'of the opinion' that the child has, or probably has, a SEN (HMSO 1993, Section 175).

ASSESSMENT OF THE CHILD OVER TWO YEARS OF AGE

For children over two, the full requirements of the Act come into force in respect of the involvement of parents and the right of appeal. LEAs have a duty to assess a child who they believe may have SENs which call for the LEA, rather than anyone else, to determine the provision necessary to meet them, with or without going through the three school-based stages in the Code of Practice (HMSO 1993, Section 165). This duty to assess and identify possible SENs is one which they may enforce irrespective of the wishes of the parent, and a parent who fails to produce their child for an examination may be prosecuted (HMSO 1993, Schedule 9 Para 5).

COLLECTION OF INFORMATION

The Act lays duties upon the relevant statutory services to cooperate in the investigation of a child's SENs. The Health Authority have a duty to cooperate with the LEA (HMSO 1993, Section 166) if they have been asked for help with a child who may have SENs. The Health Authority must also inform the parents and advise them of any voluntary organisation that may possibly be of assistance (HMSO 1993, Section 176). The Social Services Department and the Health Authority are always asked for reports when a child is assessed for special education (1994 Regulations 6 (1e)). The LEA have to obtain medical advice irrespective of whether the child has a medical condition.

FOR EVERY NEED A PROVISION

The provisions set out in Section 3 of the Statement must meet the needs set out in Section 2 (1994 Regulations 13 and Schedule Part B, Statement Part 3). This has been built into the law following the court judgement in the case '*Ex parte E*'. There is also a requirement that the Statement specify the objectives for non-educational provision (1994 Regulations 13 and Schedule Part B, Statement Part 6).

As for the teaching and non-teaching provisions, there is probably a requirement under the law that these be quantified (1994 Regulations 13 and Schedule B, Statement Part 3 says that the Statement in Part 3 (titled 'Special Educational Needs') must: 'Specify the special educational provision which the authority consider appropriate to meet the needs specified in Part 2 and to meet the objectives specified in this Part, and in particular specify – (a) any appropriate facilities and equipment, staffing arrangements and curriculum...' The Code interprets the duty to specify, saying that this means provision should 'normally be quantified in terms of hours' (Para 4.28).

RIGHT OF APPEAL

The LEA has the power to finalise or amend a Statement without written consent from the parent. The parent may appeal against the provisions set out in the Statement on any one of the grounds cited above (HMSO 1993, Section 170 (1)). Also, it is not necessary that the LEA undertake a complete review of the Statement before amending or ceasing to maintain it (HMSO 1993, Schedule 10 Paras 10 and 11). Parents can appeal against the proposal to cease to maintain the Statement (HMSO 1993, Schedule 10 Para 11).

THE STATEMENT MUST BE REVIEWED

The Statement must be reviewed annually (Section 172 (5) b) in accordance with Regulations 1994 (15, 16 and 17), and the headteacher can invite reports from anyone he or she chooses (1994 Regulations 15 (3) c and 16 (2) c).

THE LEA DETERMINES PROVISION

In the end it is the LEA which determines the provision a child requires, irrespective of the professional advice it might receive (HMSO 1993, Section 168). The role of the professional then is to provide advice which the LEA may accept or reject. However, some professionals provide the advice their employers *require* them to give, rather than the advice they feel would support what the child needs, so it is hard for these individuals or the LEA to sustain an argument that their advice is independent. This is a source of puzzlement to many parents who tend to start out with the belief that when a local authority or health authority professional assesses their child, they will be acting in an objective and independent manner concerned only with the needs of that child. When the parent later finds out that this is not the case and the diagnoses and recommendations may be heavily constrained by resource-led policies, frustration and anger may come to replace respect.

Yet the law is on the side of the professional who wishes to make an honest and independent contribution to the Statementing process: (HMSO 1993, Regulation 6)

(1) For the purpose of making an assessment under Section 167 an authority shall seek –

(a) advice from the child's parent;

(b) educational advice as provided for in regulation 7;

(c) medical advice from the district health authority as provided for in regulation 8;

(d) psychological advice as provided for in regulation 9;

(e) advice from the social services authority; and

(f) any other advice which the authority consider appropriate for the purpose of arriving at a satisfactory assessment.

(2) The advice referred to in paragraph (1) shall be written advice relating to –

(a) the educational, medical, psychological or other features of the case (according to the nature of the advice sought) which appear to be relevant to the child's educational needs (including his likely future needs);

(b) how those features could affect the child's educational needs; and

(c) the provision which is appropriate for the child in the light of those features of the child's case, whether by way of special educational provision or non-educational provision, but not relating to any matter which is required to be specified in a Statement by virtue of section 168(4) (b).

The regulations go on to say that the person asked for advice may consult anyone they feel may have information relating to the child. So the law clearly expects professionals to provide *relevant inde-*

pendent advice and this should sustain any particular individual who may feel under pressure from their employer to tailor their advice to fit policy when this is not in the best interest of the child in question.

An additional requirement in connection with the advice of the educational psychologist (EP) states that:

(2) the advice sought from a person as provided in paragraph (1) shall, if that person has reason to believe that another psychologist has relevant knowledge of, or information relating to, the child, be advice given after consultation with that other psychologist (HMSO 1993, Regulations 9 (2)).

Some general points

LEA RESOURCE PROBLEMS

LEAs are increasingly strapped for cash and so have to juggle budgets in an attempt to balance their books. Special needs is seen by some as a prime target for retrenchment and the Audit Commission/HMI reports (1992 and 1994) may be seen to provide LEAs with ammunition to do just that, whereas a more careful reading of these reports reveals a wish to see resources *re-allocated* as children move from segregated to mainstream schools. But this does *not* mean an LEA can choose not to issue a Statement because it feels it does not have the necessary resources, and this is not an argument that any professional or parent should accept.

Likewise there is no 'Statement quota' which the LEA may not (or choose not) to exceed. The Audit Commission/HMI (1992) cites the LEA range of Statements as having been 0.8 per cent – 3.3 per cent and the mean is probably around 2 per cent, but this represents nothing more than general practice and an LEA may set itself a target. This implies nothing in respect of any particular child whose needs may require the protection of a Statement, however.

WHO SHOULD ASK FOR AN ASSESSMENT?

It is better that the parent, rather than the headteacher or another professional, asks for an assessment because there is no time limit on the LEA response, other than in the case of a parental request. Also, only the parent has a right of appeal against refusal. Where the parent asks, the LEA must respond within 6 weeks (1994 Regulations (11)3) and, if refused, parents may appeal (HMSO 1993, Section 172 (3)b and Section 173(2)b).

WHO MAY APPEAL A STATEMENT?

Only a parent or legal guardian may mount an appeal over a Statement, or against the refusal by their LEA to issue a Statement. The child's school is not entitled to appeal, nor is any other professional involved with the child.

APPEALS AND THE CODE OF PRACTICE

Parents have no right to appeal to a Tribunal if they believe that the school is acting contrary to the Code of Practice (HMSO 1993, Sections 172/3 and Schedule 10 Paras. 8,10 and 11). The appeal procedure, on the grounds outlined above, is solely concerned with the Statement or the lack of a Statement, or the refusal to assess.

WHO MAY BE A TRIBUNAL WITNESS?

The LEA will decide who is to appear as a witness in their defence, and it may decide to call any of its own employees or those of another statutory agency or even some quite independent expert. Likewise, it might use one of its own staff – an officer or a lawyer – to present its case. The LEA cannot, however, forbid a teacher or headteacher from appearing as a witness at the Tribunal if they have been summonsed (1994 SEN Tribunal Regulations 23). It may, though, try to deter such an employee from attending as a witness for the parent through bringing pressure upon them. The author has himself been subjected to quite extreme pressure because he wanted to represent parents at Tribunal Hearing, and IPSEA (The Independent Panel for Special Educational Advice) has had a number of similar reports. Indeed the president of the Tribunal raises just this matter in one of his progress reports (SEN Tribunal 1994–95) when he says: 'It turns out that in some cases local education authorities are reluctant that any of their employees, and this particularly applies to teachers, should give evidence 'for' parents and 'against' the authority. This takes a confrontational approach to the Tribunal which seems unfortunate.'

It is perhaps understandable that an LEA would not wish its employees to support parents by supporting their position, and once again the probably unavoidable issue of conflict of interest raises its head here. If the child's teacher, headteacher or even the EP are asked by the parent to be a witness and agree, they may be refused leave by the LEA or they may be given leave without pay or pension rights. In the final analysis, however, if they are summonsed by the President of the Tribunal to attend, they must do so or pay a fine of £1000. In such circumstances it is unlikely even the most resistant LEA would act in a punitive way towards one of its employees.

PARENTAL RIGHT TO CHOOSE A SCHOOL

Much is made by the government of their commitment to the right of parents to choose the kind of education their child has and the school (s)he might attend. Yet a parent of a child with special needs has no right to express a preference for an independent school to be named on their child's Statement (HMSO 1993, Schedule 10, Para 3 and 8). The parent has a right to express a preference when the Statement is first issued and later to ask for a change of school, but the LEA's duty to comply is qualified. Hence there is no *absolute* choice. Also, transport costs will not necessarily be met by the LEA if the school the parents have chosen is further away than another that the LEA believes can meet the child's needs.

If a parent wants a school outside their county and the authority refuses, it is incumbent upon the parent to prove that the school(s) proposed by the authority cannot meet their child's needs. Hence it is not a simple matter of which school *best* meets the child's needs but for the parent to show that the school offered by the LEA does not.

PARENTAL DUTY TO CO-OPERATE WITH AN ASSESSMENT

The LEA can assess a child without the parent's permission (HMSO 1993, Section 167) and the parent can be prosecuted if they fail to produce their child for examination without a good excuse (HMSO 1993, Schedule 9 Para 5).

POWER OF THE LEA TO PLACE A CHILD

An LEA can insist that a school takes a child without a Statement (HMSO 1993, Section 168 (5) b), but if the school is Grant Maintained, it can then ask that an assessment be undertaken (unless one has already been completed) within six months. This provision does not relate to LEA maintained schools.

WHO MAY WRITE EDUCATIONAL ADVICE?

It is not just the headteacher of the child's school who has the right to write the educational advice (HMSO 1993, 1994 Regulations 3). The advice must be sought from the child's school or one which (s)he has attended during the preceding 18 months or, if the child is or has not attended school, then 'from a person who the authority are satisfied has experience of teaching children with SENs or knowledge of the differing provision which may be called for in different cases to meet those needs'. The person providing the educational advice must, however, be a qualified teacher.

It has recently been ruled in the High Court that a child cannot be party to an appeal on a point of law arising out of a decision of the Tribunal. Such an appeal would have to be made by a parent, as a party as defined in the 1993 Act (Section 181) and Section 11 of the Tribunal and Enquiries Act 1992. The upshot of this is that fewer appeals to court will be possible than under the previous appeal system as it is more difficult for parents to obtain legal aid than it is for children (who usually have no savings and income).

CONCLUSION

Parents and professionals with a concern for children with significant SENs must have a grasp of the fundamentals of the relevant legislation if they are to be able to serve children effectively. This is so because of the conflict of interest which besets professional agencies and individual service workers as they strive to meet an ever expanding range of needs from a steadily decreasing annual budget.

Many of the parents and colleagues I work with and I myself, take the view that the law on special needs education is still deeply flawed and most obviously so in respect of integration. Yet the law as it stands today is far stronger and more supportive on assessment and Statementing than it was prior to the implementation of the 1993 Act which largely came into force in September 1994. There is, unfortunately, still widespread ignorance of what might be achieved by parents and their advocates if they were to start using this – albeit still inadequate – legislation to the advantage of the child who is the focus of their concern.

One of the main objectives of this book is to try and show how much more can be achieved for vulnerable children through invoking the law whilst continuing to press for new laws which will guarantee rights which remain unprotected.

On November 1st 1996 the 1993 Education Act was repealed. The law on special education has, from that date, been incorporated into the 1996 Education Act which is a consolidating Act which pulls together, among other Acts, the whole of the 1944 Education Act and the 1993 Education Act. Although this consolidation involved no substantive changes to the 1993 Education Act, there were consequences for that Act arising out of the Disability Discrimination Act 1995 and the Nursery Education and Grant Maintained Schools Act has also been incorporated.

Table 2.1 The 1996 Education Act

Content	Before 1/11/96	After 1/11/96
The law on special educational needs	Part III, EA 1993	Part 1V, EA 1996
Definitions of 'special educational needs' and 'special educational provision'	Section 156	Section 312
Duty to 'have regard to' Code of Practice	Section 157	Section 313
Issuing/revising the Code of Practice	Section 158	Section 314
LEA duty to review arrangements for special educational provision	Section 159	Section 315
Duty to educate children with SEN in ordinary schools	Section 160	Section 316
Duty to educate children with SEN in ordinary schools	Section 160	Section 316
School Governors' duties towards children with SEN	Section 161 (1) – (5)	Section 317 (1) – (5)
Annual reports and arrangements for disabled pupils	Section 29 (2) Disability Discrimination Act 1995	Section 317 (6) (7)
Grants for Nursery Education	Schedule 3, para 2, Nursery Education and Grant Maintained Schools Act 1996	Section 318 (3)
Provision 'otherwise' than in school	Section 163	Section 319

Table 2.1 (continued)

Content	Before 1/11/96	After 1/11/96
Definition of children for whom LEA are responsible	Section 165	Section 321
Duty of Health Authority or local authority to help LEAs	Section 166	Section 322 *Change in terminology re local authority and health authority*
Provision of goods/ services re SEN (4)	Section 162 (1) (2) (3)	Section 318 (1) (2)
Assessment	Section 167	Section 323
Statement of Special Educational Needs	Section 168	Section 324
Appeal against LEA refusal to issue Statement	Section 169	Section 325
Appeal against contents of a Statement	Section 170	Section 326
LEA access to schools	Section 171	Section 327
Parental request for assessment of child with a Statement and right to appeal if LEA refuse	Section 172 (1) – (5)	Section 328 (1) – (5)
Annual Review	Section 172 (5) – (6)	Section 328 (5) – (6)
Parental request for assessment of child with a Statement and right to appeal if LEA refuse	Section 173	Section 329
Governors' right to request assessment of child with SEN	Section 174	Section 330

Table 2.1 (continued)

Content	Before 1/11/96	After 1/11/96
Remuneration and expenses	Section 179	Section 335
Assessment of children under 2	Section 175	Section 331
Health Authority duty to inform LEA of child with SEN	Section 176	Section 332 *Change in terminology re health authority*
Constitution of the SEN Tribunal	Section 177	Section 333
Membership of the SEN Tribunal	Section 178	Section 334
Tribunal procedure	Section 180	Section 336
Making of assessments	Schedule 9	Schedule 26
Making and maintenence of Statements	Schedule 10	Schedule 27

Those sections of the **1944 Education Act** relating to making formal complaints against LEAs have been relocated as follows:

Table 2.2 The 1996 Education Act (consolidation of the 1994 Education Act)

Content	Before 1/11/96	After 1/11/96
Complaints of LEAs acting unreasonably EA 1996	Section 68 EA 1994	Section 496
Complaints of LEAs failing to fulfil their legal duty	Section 99 EA 1994	Section 497

The author is grateful to John Wright of IPSEA and Richard Poynter for permission to reproduce the above tables which appears in their book Taking Action – Your Child's Right to Special Education. (Pub. Questions Publishing).

Chapter 3

Rethinking Special Education

WHICH IDEOLOGY FOR SPECIAL NEEDS?
'Special' children?

That special education is not working and needs to be thoroughly re-examined is no longer seriously in question. We have seen that successive amendments to the legislative framework have been necessary because parents are still very unhappy with what schools offer their children. The 1993 Education Act, whilst being a genuine attempt to redress the balance in favour of children through increasing parental rights, remains a deeply flawed legal framework. This is so because it still fails to confer the necessary basic right to a socially valued education for children with special needs alongside, and on an equal footing with, their peers.

The process of rethinking special education is something that needs to be undertaken as an urgent priority by special needs professionals, because they have no coherent paradigm to guide their actions. In this they should seek the advice of parents and their advocates who, for some years, have been quietly and patiently insisting that things must change.

Having to go away to a residential school hundreds of miles from home, family and friends and only come home for school holidays; having to travel for up to an hour in a bus to a segregated day special school and lose touch with the children in the local neighbourhood; having to be shut away in the special unit across the playground and only see your peers at lunch and playtime; having destructive and demeaning labels heaped upon you until you lose track of who you are; being told you cannot go on the school trip because it would not be safe; having people constantly talk about your 'problems' in front of you as though you had no feelings – this is what is wrong with special education and it is going to have to change.

For too long the child with special needs has been seen as 'the problem', not the inadequate teacher or the unwelcoming school. Schools exist to teach children, not to label them as ineducable, and parents of children with additional needs would like them to attend their local school with their neighbourhood peers if the school would offer a welcome.

The real problem with special education is that it is 'special'. Special is a funny, but deceptively lethal, little adjective which seems to confer privilege but actually creates misery. The Oxford English Dictionary (OED 1989) says something (or someone) is 'special' if it is *of such a kind as to exceed or excel in some way that which is usual or common; exceptional in character, quality or degree.* Many people, including far too many professionals, speak condescendingly of children with additional needs as 'our *special* children' and you can usually tell what they mean by this because their voice may take on a softer tone, along with a slightly pained expression, conveying sympathy and understanding for the inevitable suffering that is accompanied by being 'special'.

I understand this to be one of the most difficult burdens disabled people have to bear – along with the denial of their basic human rights in so many areas of life. They also have the burden of being patronised by people who carry in their heads a stereotype of who or what disabled people are and what their impairment must mean to them. As a non-disabled person I cannot know what this feels like, yet I can try to imagine what it would be like if, at every turn, people treated me as though my life were nothing more than a tragedy; if they patted my head and addressed their questions and comments to those accompanying me rather than to me directly. I know this would cause me pain and being 'special' would be a burden in my life; I am sure I would yearn to be 'normal' (ordinary or typical).

Some people really are special

Yet for most of us there is a way of being 'special' which makes us feel good, and this feeling enhances our self-esteem and happiness. Having a talent to do something well or to get on with others are positive qualities because they enrich our own lives and the lives of others and, in so doing, foster an enhanced sense of the self. Who would not wish to be thought of as a 'special' person? Such people give us hope that as human beings we can transcend the petty, the mean, the selfish, the egotistical; to begin, that is, to be truly human and to help give meaning and dignity to the lives of others. Special people are pretty thin on the ground but when they touch our lives a curtain lifts and we see all too fleetingly what we might have been, or even what we might yet become; then the curtain falls again and we continue as before but with a lingering sense of unease.

Is this really what we mean when we say a child with an impairment is 'special'? Do we mean we would like other children to be like that or even that we would have liked to have been like that ourselves – special, that is? I think not. Or perhaps making children 'special' is really another form of positive discrimination to compensate for their perceived disadvantages, like spending more money on their education, giving their parents mobility allowance or sending them off to Disneyland for the 'holiday of a lifetime'? Does that show how special *we* think they are, and does it make them really feel special?

Special people need special places?

One of the corollaries of being thought to be so special is that you will have the opportunity to go where the other special people go – to 'special land'. It has been this way since we decided to provide services to special people. Services such as mental handicap and mental health institutions, training centres and special schools have been our response to the needs of special people because they need to be together, somewhere away from the rest of us. In these places it is possible to give them the special services they need to meet their special needs, such as trained medical staff to look after them, teachers and instructors to educate and train them and therapists to treat them. It would not, of course, be possible to provide these things in ordinary places where the rest of us go and, anyway, it can all be achieved so much more efficiently and cost-effectively under one roof.

Such remains our rationale for educating some children with additional needs and it all starts with someone noticing how 'special' they are. Being noticed as special has the almost magical effect of instantly closing some doors while others simultaneously open. The door of the local nursery or primary school closes while the door of the special school swings open, along with the door of the bus that will take you there; the door of the dentist your family uses may slam shut while the door of the special mobile dental unit that visits the special school is opened wide; the door to the local theatre remains shut because there is no ramp access, yet flies open when the Variety Club provide a free pantomime showing for all the handicapped children at Christmas – sometimes it is possible to do things if somebody really important wants it to happen.

So what's wrong with special places?

There is nothing wrong with special places if they really are *special* places. Places like Disneyland, the Great Barrier Reef, The Natural History Museum, Glyndebourne, Rio during Carnival, any theatre, any time when Billy Connolly is performing – these really are special places. Yet it can be confusing because some places are ordinary one minute and special the next, like the theatre which cannot admit disabled children all year round because of the supposed danger but which can cope with 300 of them for one special Variety Club showing of the pantomime every Christmas. Or like the shopping mall which has a special exclusive evening for disabled shoppers during the run-up to Christmas. Then there is the lecture theatre in the Further Education (FE) college which has classes especially for people with learning difficulties only on Thursday afternoons and is used by other students for the rest of the week.

It seems that some places are special all year round while others switch between being special and ordinary depending upon who is there. This connection between places which are intrinsically special and places whose 'specialness' is a function of who is present can be very confusing. The theatre is special while Billy Connolly is telling his stories but becomes a shabby down-at-heel barn when everyone has gone home, while the Grand Canyon remains special whether or not anyone is present.

If the child with an impairment is special like Billy Connolly is special, then when he goes somewhere it will become a special place, but the problem is that we do not really think they are both special in the same sense of *special* – so when the child goes to his special school it does *not* become a special place but remains a place where children with special *needs* have to go.

'Special' really means having special needs

So the truth of the matter is that when we say a child is 'special' we do not really mean he is a special *child*, all we really mean is that he is a child with special *needs*. How does it come about that we equate being special with having special needs? Is there really an identity here or is something else going on? It really depends on what is meant by 'special' needs.

When we talk about needs in the same breath as talking about human beings, we should be talking about human needs. This is because the thing human beings have in common is their human nature (and occasionally their humanity). Talking about one person's needs ought to be the same as talking about another's. Here we are not talking about 'wants', which are a different kind of thing altogether; wants vary between people, but needs do not – at least not the kind of fundamental needs we are talking about here. The fundamental needs people have in common are for nourishment and shelter, to love and be loved, to grow in relationships in community with others, to have challenge in one's life and receive respect for who and what one is. These are the essential prerequisites of a worthwhile life, and unless our lives are marked by these opportunities and experiences we are unlikely to develop self-respect.

Common and uncommon needs

If these are our *fundamental human needs*, then how do they relate to what we call the 'special' needs of disabled children (people)? Perhaps we mean the *additional* needs these children have for such prosthetic devices as a wheelchair, standing frame, computer switch, individual educational programme – things which their impairment dictates as necessary and which function in a compensatory way. This is certainly part of what we mean by 'special needs' but it is wrong and dangerous to speak of these things as needs when they are not really needs at all but *solutions*. It is dangerous because it leads us to think that if these things are needed and they are certainly special, then the children who need them are in some sense special. It is so easy to progress from 'this child has the need for special solutions' to 'this child is special'.

In reality, these things are not needs at all but *responses* to needs or attempts at *solutions* which may or may not be helpful, and that is a quite different thing. A prosthesis is not a need but a provision. This is a difficult distinction even for many professional workers to understand but it is a very important one if children and their particular needs are not to be misconstrued. It is too often the case that the child becomes identified with the need – 'a wheelchair child' – with a consequent loss of perspective on his or her real identity. This point deserves further elaboration.

It is perfectly all right to say a child needs a wheelchair because we understand that if he does not have one then things will not go the way we would like them to. However, when we say he needs a wheelchair what we are really saying is:

(1) that (s)he has a physical impairment such that (s)he cannot walk around like other children; and

(2) that (s)he needs something to compensate for his or her lack of mobility and that a wheelchair will fit the bill quite nicely until something better comes along.

Hence the need is for *mobility*, and, until we find something better, a wheelchair will meet that need, but the wheelchair is not of course *identical* with the need.

All of this is quite straightforward and unproblematic as far as wheelchairs are concerned, but not so when it comes to things like schools. The problem is that we carry over our talk of needs and solutions from wheelchairs to schools without noticing they are not the same kind of thing. When we notice a child has great difficulty in understanding, we say (s)he needs a special school. But this, unlike the case of the wheelchair, is a *non sequitur*. Let me explain.

Proposition 1. Factual statement: *Gareth has a severe learning difficulty.*

Proposition 2. Factual statement/recommendation: *Gareth needs some additional/different help to learn.*

Proposition 3. Recommendation: *Gareth needs a one-to-one classroom support worker and an individual educational plan which takes account of his learning difficulties.*

Nowhere up to this point does there need to be mention of a *location* where Gareth's needs must be met, because it is not intrinsic to the meeting of a need that it should have to be in a particular place. Not that there are not traditional ways of meeting needs – there certainly are – but these are little more than conventions which may, and in some cases should, change while the need remains the same.

As a child like Gareth is processed through the assessment and Statementing procedure the third proposition would probably not appear, but, in its place, would be the recommendation that he attend such-and-such special school for children with severe learning difficulties (SLDs). Thus the *placement* comes to stand in for the *need*. The problem is that, through habit inculcated by tradition, we conflate needs and solutions and fail to notice we have done so. This is part of the reason why there is still so little professional questioning of the role of segregated schools and classes, in spite of the fact that they may damage the children who attend them.

THE SEARCH FOR A NEW IDEOLOGY

Conceptualising another person

The problem for the professional human service system is that it does not know how to conceptualise the people it is designed to help, and we have seen that this is, in part, through miscasting them as having 'special' needs. This happens because the service system tends to operate with a mish-mash of conflicting and incoherent ideologies. Whether the client group be disabled or learning impaired children or adults, those with a mental health problem or the elderly, the situation is exactly the same – there is confusion as to *who* is to be served *where* and in *what* way, by what *means* and towards what *end*. This comes about, in large part, because our confused thinking leads us to develop the wrong concept of *who* the individual is that we are trying to serve.

To conceptualise or construe another person is to make all manner of judgements about that person. George Kelly (1955) developed a theory about how, as individuals, we go about the business of trying to make sense of the world in which we live and, most importantly, make sense of one another. His approach is based upon trying to put oneself in the position of the other person so as to see the world *as he sees it* and, through seeing it from *his perspective*, to be able to make better sense of his actions.

Very briefly, Kelly's theory is known as the *psychology of personal constructs*, which has as one of its core premises that there are always alternative ways of looking at events; hence he coined the term 'constructive alternativism', which really only means that when faced with a typically complex social or other situation we operate so as to test out our predictions about events. Kelly says of this process 'that a person's processes are psychologically channelised by the ways in which they anticipate events'. He used the term *construct* to describe the process of anticipation or prediction that we employ as we go about trying to make sense of the world. He said that all such *personal constructs* or *predictions* are bi-polar or dichotomous – by this he meant that we can only make sense of reality by making judgements which imply another judgement which is its exact opposite; hence 'cold' only has meaning in relation to 'hot', 'tall' in relation to 'short', 'clever' in relation to 'stupid' and so forth. All such construing, according to Kelly, is individual and personal.

It is only by gaining an understanding of both poles of a person's constructs, and the way in which their constructs interrelate, that we can gain insight into their personal view of the world. There is, of course, no total world view just a number of ways of viewing different aspects of reality. So, Kelly's account of how people function is as hypotheses-testing *personal scientists* – which complements the model provided by Wolfensberger (1992) (see Figure 3.1), which he offers to show that the ways in which we make sense of another person or group is a multi-level process with elements largely acquired from our culture and our own personal past experience.

Wolfensberger's schematic model of the psychological process of judgement formation attempts to portray the deep complexity of the usually entirely unconscious process of judgement formation which takes place when we encounter another person or group. It will be clear from this diagram that most of the factors relevant to a judgement about the other are characteristics already present in the observer when he comes to the situation. So perception is, in large part, *projected expectation* and not the passive process it subjectively feels when a judgement is made. It is helpful to think of those characteristics of the individual which, on the basis of the particular ideas and assumptions held, predispose him towards a particular type of judgement. We may characterise these as his habitual ways of thinking and responding, or his 'ideological set'.

The real difficulty is that knowing how to conceptualise another person is not something anyone thinks they have a problem with because it is not an issue that is likely to be addressed other than in a training situation, and even there (Normalisation and Disability

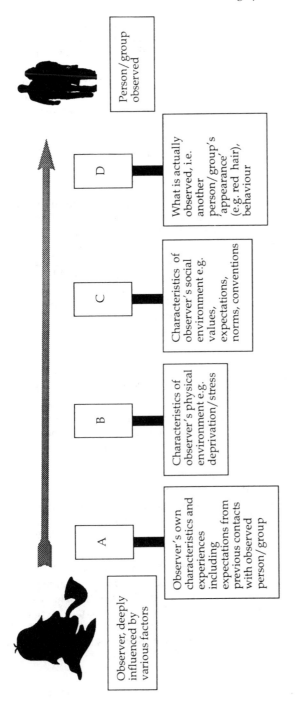

Source: Wolfensberger (1992)
Figure 3.1 Wolfensberger's model of the psychological process of judgement formation

Awareness Training aside) it is not likely to be addressed formally. Yet it is clearly a problem, if only because of the history of inappropriate societal responses and those of the service system to its most vulnerable members (Wolfensberger 1975).

Making sense of another person is a complex process and one which it is important to bring into conscious awareness since, without an opportunity to subject the process of decision-making or judgement formation to conscious reflection, it is impossible to know what is going on and, most importantly, to know whether we are operating with a realistic appraisal or a dangerous stereotype.

Basing services on misperceptions

Basing services upon erroneous and potentially harmful misunderstandings of people and their needs reflects the possession of a bad ideology. Whilst there is no agreed definition of ideology, it is, nevertheless, useful to think of it as implying a view of certain relevant events characterised by a set of values or beliefs underpinning societal practices. Any social practice is susceptible to such an analysis, whether it be the provision of social welfare benefits, health services, education or whatever. One can look at the ways in which such services are organised and make a judgement about the values and beliefs to which its architects and managers subscribe.

The power of ideologies

Wolfensberger (1972) describes the source, scope and power of ideologies quite succinctly when he says:

> Man's behaviour is in good part determined by what I want to call his ideologies. By ideology, I mean a combination of beliefs, attitudes, and interpretations of reality that are derived from one's experience, one's knowledge of what are presumed to be facts, and above all, one's values. Ideologies can be thought of as being 'big' or 'little'. Religions, political systems, philosophies of life, etc. these are all big ideologies, or conglomerates of ideologies. Little or at least medium-sized ideologies deal with a wider range of our functioning in our private and professional lives. (p.7)

Here the term 'ideology' is used as the 'manner of thinking characteristic of a class or individual...the science of ideas; that department of philosophy or psychology which deals with the origin or nature of ideas' (OED 1989). As far as the individual is concerned, the first part of the definition is most applicable while the latter part relates to any formal attempt to systematise ideas or a set of such related ideas.

When an ideology is expressed as a set of concepts, assumptions and practices in the management of a certain group of people and becomes widely used, this is referred to as a service 'model' or 'paradigm'. If one looks very closely at a number of services which operate on the same set of assumptions, that is services which are run in accordance with the same model, then one can identify features which those services have in common which relate back to the meanings which the assumptions of the model embody.

As well as distinguishing between big and little ideologies (more as against less inclusive belief systems) Wolfensberger makes a distinction between 'good' and 'bad' ideologies. Bad ideologies tend to contain a number of assumptions which are held unconsciously, and remain unconscious because they conflict with the holder's own higher order ideologies.

Many professionals, not unsurprisingly perhaps, reflect the extremely negative view of the potential of profoundly handicapped children (and adults) held by the wider society. This view may include such entirely conscious judgements as that the individual:

- is genetically deficient and hence unable to change
- is so low functioning as to be incapable of participating in any ordinary setting
- can never be acceptable to others because (s)he has so little to offer
- will only be further demoralised by being amongst 'normal' people
- may distract others from getting on with what they are supposed to be doing.

The view may also be held, but almost certainly unconsciously, that the individual:

- does not have the same feelings, needs and sensibilities as others
- is so damaged as not to be fully human – more like a vegetable or an animal
- is really not worth trying with because (s)he can never really amount to anything
- no great effort should be expended to resuscitate him/her should the situation arise.

Taken together, these conscious and unconscious assumptions/beliefs provide a highly unpromising basis for planning and managing a service for people who, more than anything, need positive support and encouragement to grow and develop in community with others.

Ideologies can get stuck

In the context of the human service system, the working ideology (or paradigm) which most professionals share evolves dynamically – or at least that is the theory. Initial training, and the individual's own prior personal beliefs, are shaped by the daily activities of providing the service, the outcomes of which feed back to reinform those beliefs. This process produces in the mind of the service professional a service 'model' which, in turn, informs daily practice, and so the cycle continues. This cycle of belief – model – activity – outcome – belief is described by Peter Ritchie (1995) and may be seen as the process for the development of a paradigm (see Figure 3.2).

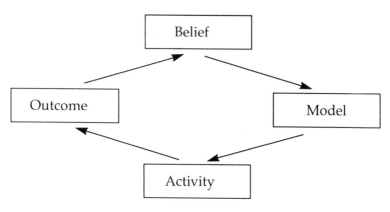

Source: Ritchie 1995

Figure 3.2 The developing paradigm

A paradigm can get stuck, however, if those running services, and society itself, are indifferent or immune to what is going on around them – if the outcomes of practice no longer shape belief. This has, for quite some time, been the case in special education, and the most conspicuous evidence for this is in the continuing practice of segregation. Special education continues to segregate when other services long ago learned that it is harmful – the best examples of this are that the health service no longer places children in residential mental handicap institutions and social services are highly reluctant to use children's homes. Family foster homes are now the placement of choice when the natural family is not an option. The roots of this problem go very deep but a major contributing factor is the negative attitude held by educationalists about children who cannot learn more or less autonomously in a class size group.

Holding negative beliefs about the potential for profoundly handicapped children to be accepted by others in society, for whatever reason, is likely to lead to the development of services which hide such children away in remote institutions, and this has been the historical pattern since services were first provided.

Death-making ideologies

The huge mental handicap hospitals are one expression of the desire to put devalued people at a distance, although there is no guarantee things will end there – as was so tragically the case in Nazi Germany in the run up to, and during, the Second World War. At the end of the 19th century, *Social Darwinism* was a fashionable theory in academic circles. Theorists tried to reapply the principle of the development and survival of the fittest from nature to human society and it was thought that, in the competition between the quickly developing industrial societies, only the strong, the sane and those able to work should be allowed to live. In 1920, eminent scientists called for the killing of mentally ill and mentally handicapped people because they felt they had a duty to eliminate the bad or sick blood from the gene pool. In some quarters vulnerable people were not only seen as not valuable to society but also far too expensive to keep, on account of their unproductivity. So, a programme to eliminate them was thought to be essential by way of speeding up the process of natural selection.

The programme began with the enforced sterilisation of 300, 000 disabled people and, in 1939, all mentally handicapped children had to be registered. Doctors were under orders to report handicapped people to the authorities. There followed the programme known as T4, which was designed to eliminate mentally handicapped people in places known as 'clinics' which were managed by doctors and other professionals. There were six such clinics – Hadamar, Bemburg, Brandenberg/Havel, Hartheim near Lindz, Sonnestein-Perna and Grafenech – which together killed over 70,000 people, mostly through gassing.

Euthanasia of people with severe handicaps is not something which arises only with brutal and totalitarian regimes. Rationalisations for allowing certain people to die seem to be ever-present (Lusthaus 1985). Wolfensberger is also deeply concerned about the resurgence, especially in Holland, of 'voluntary' euthanasia. Wolfensberger sees 'death-making' as the logical end point of the societal desire to distance those it devalues.

So, the ideologies we hold have a powerful influence, not only on the way we behave but also on the way we conceptualise the needs of others, yet the interventions we make in line with what a particular ideology dictates may have little or no empirical basis which demonstrates its efficacy. Such is now recognised to have been the case with the big mental handicap hospitals and the junior and adult training centres, and we await a similar dawning of awareness that the special school is also an unhelpful way of serving children. Because this book is concerned primarily with the dominant societal response to what is characterised as 'educational disability', we shall now draw out the implications of the dominant societal and professional ideology for children who are labelled *educationally disabled*.

By citing some of the most extreme consequences of socially-devaluing ideologies in this context, it is not the author's intention to suggest that segregated schooling is simply an expression of a parallel modern day desire to suppress and ultimately to liquidate those who are seen as different or in some way threatening. No such interpretation is either warranted or intended. Rather the point is that we must never allow ourselves to become complacent about society's potential for (even unwittingly) doing harm to those upon whom it places a low value. Also that individuals are likely to be at greater risk once they are labelled and separated from the societal mainstream and this typically means becoming institutionalised. The progression from initial separation to eventual maltreatment or worse is not inevitable but history offers us innumerable examples of how things may go terribly wrong.

It is extremely difficult for any of us to face our own worst impulses towards those we do not like, place a low value upon or simply fear. When we are paid to work on behalf of individuals who fall into these categories we are likely to face a personal conflict.

The meaning of educational disability

The notion of 'educational disability' has meaning only by reference to 'educational ability'; hence the, now officially discarded, notion of certain children as 'ineducable' implied that while the majority of children were clearly able to learn, some were not and, failing a formal rationale for what 'ineducability' was, it was convenient to define the condition by reference to an IQ test score.

It is interesting to reflect that although professionals no longer openly refer to children as being ineducable, their practice reflects a continuing attachment to the idea that some are; hence, for the children who are the main focus of this book, we find services which provide low intensity Individual Educational Plans (IEPs), low expectations, negative labels, short hours, segregated settings and so forth.

Being educable means having the potential to eventually become self-sufficient, employed, supportive of others and all those things defined as desirable elements of citizenship in an industrialised economy and, conversely, to be ineducable means to have none of these potentials. The notion of educability, therefore, does not stand alone as a discrete characteristic of typical children unrelated to the linked notions of social participation and productivity; it is merely one of a complex set of notions which together comprise a particular ideology.

Special education as a discrete provision

Part of the problem of special education is that it is provided on the mistaken premise that it is a stand-alone construct with no implications beyond school and college, and this is simply not a helpful state of affairs for those children (perhaps 2%) who are segregated. Most segregated schools and classes deal only with the child's learning-related needs and, although this will certainly encompass his physical care and paramedical needs, the school is unlikely to ask larger questions about the relevance of the education offered to the child's broader life outside school. Nor is the school likely to think too deeply about the child's likely life circumstances once schooling is over. Teachers and classroom support workers in such schools are very unlikely to have visited social services or voluntary sector day and residential services and may not even know what happens in the FE college. This compartmentalising of special education inevitably produces such ignorance and insularity.

The problem is that exclusion from the preschool playgroup, the nursery, the school, the college or the workplace, and from the possibility of developing any kind of meaningful relationships or socially-valued roles during one's lifetime, is not merely a chapter of unfortunate but unrelated accidents, it represents a syndrome of treatment by the society in which one lives which, in turn, amounts to the expression of a set of values and beliefs about *who* or *what* one is and what place, if any, one should have in society. In short, an *ideology*.

This then, in my opinion, is the prevailing ideology of the service system (including the education service) and the overwhelming majority of professionals who work within it. It is the key to an understanding of why statutory agencies such as social services, health and education – though dissimilar in so many ways because of the nature of their tasks – are yet so alike in their response to disabled people. What they have in common is that they:

- offer a differential diagnosis of individuals perceived as 'deviant'
- label these 'deviant' individuals in ways which are image-mortifying
- tend to provide less well-qualified staff to work with those seen as 'deviant'
- provide separate services for those they have labelled

- group those served according to their perceived 'deviancy'
- mix 'deviancy' groups within a single service or programme
- segregate 'deviant' groups away from those who are non-deviant
- offer low-intensity programmes of 'treatment', occupation or education
- operate on the basis of a short day.

The practice of special education is largely atheoretical

Special education is an edifice completely lacking a foundation; it is an almost entirely theory-free zone. Theories as to how children learn abound, and research on the psychology of learning has a long and respected tradition. Since this research is rooted in child development, all of it is, of course, absolutely applicable to children with special needs. Yet special education services seem to reflect little or nothing of what is understood about the fundamental needs of children.

Special needs professionals must discipline themselves to be less precious about their skills and get back to some simple child development fundamentals. One useful starting point is a little book by Mia Kellmer-Pringle called *The Needs of Children* (1975) written when she was the director of the National Children's Bureau. In this book she said that all children share some very basic needs which are for: *love and security, new experiences, recognition and achievement,* and the *taking of responsibility.* She went on to say that:

> How well a handicapped child makes out in the long run depends far less on the nature, severity or onset of his condition than on the attitudes of his parents first and foremost, then on those of his peers and teachers, and eventually on society's. These determine how he feels about his handicap. (p.117)

If we can assume that the family provides the love and security, it is not unreasonable to expect that the school should provide a model of good educational practice. The task for the school should be that of developing the other key needs through its curriculum, whilst providing the family with an appropriate model for how this should be tackled. The segregated class or special school offers entirely the wrong model.

It may seem hard on that diverse group of individuals – the special needs professionals – to keep banging on about how badly they have got it wrong but I believe they really have, and this fact is not without consequence for many children and their families. For them to be able to start getting it right now would require a major perceptual shift of the kind described in the following pages.

How we got to where we are

The beginnings of special education were rooted in curiosity over how severely sensorily impaired and learning impaired children make sense of their world and, as we have seen, it was deaf and blind children who first attracted the attentions of educators towards the end of the 18th century. One of the earliest recorded reports of an investigation into how intellectually delayed children learn was the famous case known as the *Wild Boy of Aveyron* (Lane 1977). Itard was a French physician who, in 1799, became interested in a young boy of around 12 years of age who was found wandering in the country-side near Bordeaux. This boy, who became known as Victor, seemed to have developed a number of animal-like behaviours and the belief was that he had been reared by animals. He selected food by smell, walked on all fours and drank from pools on the ground.

Two very different views were offered to explain Victor's behaviour: (1) that he was an 'abandoned idiot', and (2) that he was a 'noble savage', that is he was an ordinary child who had grown up amongst animals and simply mimicked their ways. This divergence of diagnosis, and its implications for whether or not it was worth trying with Victor, reflected the then deeply held societal beliefs about the meaning of mental handicap. As an 'abandoned idiot', Victor would have been deemed a hopeless case; a boy forever damned by his irremediable condition and hence unworthy of effort because his retardation was intrinsic to his very nature and not merely a consequence of his lack of opportunity to learn. As a 'noble savage', on the other hand, he was presumed 'normal' but inexperienced in the civilised ways of human society, hence just in need of retraining. Itard worked with Victor for ten years and managed to teach him a number of basic skills – but not that of reading, although he could understand much of what was said to him.

Following on from this work, Seguin, a noted French education-alist, opened a school for children with intellectual disabilities around 1830. He published a book in 1846 on the theory and practice of his work entitled *The Moral Treatment, Hygiene and Education of Idiots and Other Backward Children*.

Such were the early beginnings of the scientific investigation of the learning characteristics of atypical children who hitherto had been assumed incapable of being taught. These early pioneers were to have a major influence on the much later development of educa-tion for children with all manner of 'special' educational needs.

As we have already seen, special education in Britain developed in a piecemeal and haphazard fashion, largely as a consequence of parental, public and some professional concern that children, what-ever their disability or learning difficulty, had a moral right to some form of training or education. It was this very slowly evolving sense of moral duty, linked to a dawning realisation that education can make a difference, that lead to the emergence of professional practice in what came to be known as *special education.*

However, it was not simply social conscience which brought about the extension of education to disabled children since, as Tomlinson (1981) has pointed out, there was a clear economic motive for all children to be educated so that they might escape poverty and dependence upon the state. Also, the way had to be cleared to release parents to work and the best way of achieving this was through universal compulsory education for all children, and eventually even for those who were at that time considered ineducable.

The advent of the special needs professional

Once education became compulsory and gradually increased in scope to eventually (in 1970) encompass *all* children, it was inevitable that there would emerge new groups of trained professionals to take on the more specific tasks involving children with special needs. An important distinguishing feature of professional practice is the presumed underlying knowledge base that informs their practice. Heraud (1970) puts this in the following way: 'A major condition for the distinction between professional and non-professional is the possession of knowledge and skill which is not generally available.'

A profession eventually emerged which was to displace the medical profession as the key decision-making group on the education of children with special needs – educational psychology. Until educational psychology came of age, it was the medical profession which advised such bodies as the Committees on Epileptic and Defective Children on the differential needs of children who were described as 'imbeciles' or 'feeble-minded'. However, once the provision of certain forms of special education was made compulsory under the 1944 Education Act, local authorities were required to ascertain the needs of children. This marked a major shift to the development of professionalised systems for doing so.

Cyril Burt was the first influential educational psychologist (EP) and played a major part in promoting the idea of the importance of standardised assessment through the use of tests such as that developed by Binet. This was later to become the Stanford-Binet. So it was through the medium of standardised IQ testing that the new profession of educational psychology emerged before going on to dominate the practice of special education. The medical profession had lost its grip because it had not managed to develop what were at the time seen to be powerful and objective tools for differentiating between different degrees of learning impairment. The emerging profession of educational psychology had truly arrived, as Quicke (1982) observed:

The diagnosis and treatment of handicapped children was the main point of intervention in the education system for educational psychologists...the educational psychologist had just claim to be the most likely person to develop services for the 'newer' handicaps of 'educational subnormality' and 'maladjustment'. Both handicaps could more easily be construed in educational/psychological than medical terms and it was educational psychology that provided the technology to enable concepts to be readily operationalized so that needs could be easily and 'objectively' identified...the traditional individual intelligence test was usually the centrepiece of the diagnostic and assessment process. (p.13)

Quicke's observations clearly reveal his own deeply-held reservations about the psychometric foundations upon which his own profession had been built and the implications this was to have for the development of special education, for he goes on to say:

It is no exaggeration to suggest that the development of special education was not only assisted by but in a sense made possible by the application of psychological techniques and findings. They served to legitimate diagnostic and assessment procedures and provided a rationale for the various definitions of handicap. (p.14)

Initially, the new profession of educational psychology by and large served a valuable purpose in the development of a social welfare policy which required that resources be directed to children on the basis of their clearly defined needs. Even the deeply flawed tools for psychological assessment were valuable in this particular sense for they provided a basis – albeit a pseudo-scientific one – for resource allocation. The rationale for this was quite simple. The tests were able to demonstrate that the needs of some children are clearly much greater than those of others because, on an IQ measure, the 'retarded' child scores much lower than the typical child and this score differential is the measure of their relative needs.

It is just this principle which is used in a more systematic way today as the basis for distributing special needs funds within LEAs on a formula basis roughly in line with government guidelines. Such funding might provide something in the region of £8000 for the education of a severely disabled child in a special school, which would represent something like five or six times the cost of educating a non-disabled child in a mainstream school. Of course this cost differential is almost entirely accounted for by the staffing costs.

The real danger of psychometrics

However, such relatively minor advantages of psychometrics are far outweighed by the socially destructive influence they exert through their historical association with the aforementioned 'Social Darwinism' (the view that social evolution is inevitably and rightly rooted in the biological process known as 'the survival of the fittest'). Although it is much less fashionable nowadays, some still take the view that it is possible to apply Darwin's theory to human affairs, as was the case with the eugenics movement earlier this century. The eugenicist believes it to be both possible and desirable to improve the gene pool of the race by preventing 'defective' individuals from reproducing by sterilisation and social segregation. This was part of the underlying rationale of the mental handicap hospital which was typically built far from centres of population and separated the 'patients' (inmates) on the basis of their gender. The history of the emergence of the eugenics movement and use of IQ testing in pursuance of anti-humanitarian social ideologies is described by Sarason and Doris (1979).

It would be a mistake to assume that the values and beliefs which gave rise to this system of human service management is disappearing with the demise of these institutions.

The genetic basis of much of psychometrics and its most influential product – the IQ test – have an influence which goes far beyond the oppression of those seen by society as 'defective', in that it is at the root of both racism and sexism.

The profession of educational psychology was, for many years, tied in closely with the work of Child Guidance Clinics, where the psychologist functioned as a member of a small team looking at individual child and family problems. The team was usually lead by a psychiatrist and included a social worker. This form of teamwork was an ambitious attempt to tackle problems on a truly interdisciplinary basis to the benefit of the client but there were inevitable stresses and power struggles and the model gradually changed, with psychologists working from within the education department providing a service directly to the schools.

This, then, is the role of the EP as we know it today, with a much less clinical approach and an emphasis upon helping schools to cope more effectively within their own resources. In the mid-1990s, the psychologist is very much the creature of his/her employer – the director of education – and required to implement departmental policy whilst trying also to recommend appropriate programmes and placements for individual children with special needs. This is not an enviable position to be in, but probably not too dissimilar to that of the school head or teacher required to work within a policy framework governed largely by resource limitations. Should either the psychologist or headteacher try to pursue the needs of the child when that involves challenging departmental policy, the potential for conflict of interest will become only too evident.

In such a sensitive situation, it is not just the fact that educational recommendations might be compromised, which is now a widely established and accepted reality, but the way in which the professional concerned deals with the situation which is at issue. Some will go ahead and honestly identify needs whilst reminding the other parties that his/her recommendations will not be adopted, while others will try to pretend (perhaps to themselves as well as others) that the needs are other than they honestly believe them to be.

We shall return to the role of the EP later but, for the present, it is enough to have noted that such credibility as the practice of special education has as a separate sub-discipline of education rests largely upon the development of the psychometric and diagnostic tests which psychologists introduced. This is not to say that the discipline of psychology is the only one which has made a contribution to the development of professional practice in special education, but rather that it is the one which has provided the tools of differentiation, which in turn open the door to the various 'treatment' approaches which have come to be known as 'special' education. Psychometric tools, like any other scientific methodology, may be used for good or ill, and it is largely within the structure of local government that the psychologist is required to use his technology to pursue local placement policies. There is nothing intrinsic to an instrument such as the IQ test which renders it oppressive, but, in the wrong hands, it may be used in such a way. Not all educational psychologists work within local authorities and it is falling more and more to independent psychologists working in support of parents to redress the damage done by those in local government.

The role of the independent psychologist

There is a growing body of independent chartered educational psychologists who may be used by parents to offer a second opinion on their child when the parent wishes to challenge the recommendations of the LEA psychologist. Their independent professional advice will not come particularly cheaply to the parent – a full assessment may cost between £150 and £400 – but the parent will receive a detailed report outlining the child's cognitive abilities and educational achievements. Such a 'second opinion' will frequently be used in a Tribunal hearing to counter the LEA psychologist's report. The independent psychologist is free to offer a completely objective and unconstrained view of the child's needs in a way which is no longer easy for the LEA-employed psychologist.

Such an independent opinion may be obtained from any one of a number of chartered psychologists in private practice. The British Psychological Society maintains *The Directory of Chartered Psychologists*, which contains details of several thousand practising psychologists in alphabetical order and by geographical location. Some independent psychologists work in a group practice or consortium with teachers and other special needs professionals to provide a service to parents, and such groups may also have available to them the services of a solicitor with expertise in special education law. One such practice, which operates in Wales, is called Class Consultants and offers a broadly-based special needs assessment, teaching, counselling and advice service. In addition to its multidisciplinary professional assessment service, Class Consultants will advise parents on their child's Statement and give expert evidence at appeal Tribunals. The address of Class Consultants may be found in Appendix 1.

IDEOLOGIES IN CONFLICT

Whither the medical model?

If psychologists believed they had won their battle with the medics for control of special education, then they had done so at a price. Whilst under medical domination, the process for distinguishing between different types and degrees of learning disability was quite naturally through the filter we have come to call the 'medical model' (see Figure 3.3).

The medical model emphasises pathology because the medical profession is essentially about healing sickness and mending that which is broken. The starting point, then, for the child psychiatrist or the school medical officer was (and largely still is) the identification and labelling of those parts of the child which were not functioning normally. Beyond this medicine had little of use to say. It was not that doctors were cruel and heartless individuals but that their professional contribution was limited to trying to deal with the broken bits, not the bits that worked. Having identified the parts which needed fixing, the psychiatrist had merely to attach an identifying label and place the child in an institution designed to deal with such children.

The educational psychologist as purveyor of the medical model

Psychologists were uncomfortable with what they saw as this negative and deterministic approach, feeling there is more to children than their impairments. However, in trying to break free from the (child guidance) system which tied them to such an analysis, they failed completely to notice the similarities between their own fundamental assumptions and those of the medics they felt the need to escape.

The medical model is only able to see the child and his impairments as *the problem* with the solution being to adapt the child and his circumstances to the requirements of the world as it is. All of the adjustments must be made to the lifestyle and functionality of the

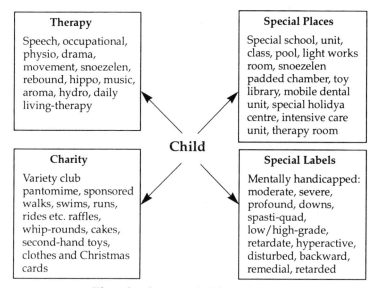

**The school system is life and image
defining for some children**

Source: Hall 1995
*Fig 3.3 The medical model of disability from the perspective
of a segregated child*

child. Hence a range of prosthetic devices will be offered, along with a separate educational environment and transport to facilitate attendance. The notion that the world might need to change hardly arises because the child *has* and *is* the problem.

Just as medicine pathologises through its exclusive preoccupation with brokenness, so educational psychology pathologises through being overly simplistic and reductionist. In terms of their education and social life, both professions have thus far, in large measure, failed disabled children. The reason for this is because they have embraced a paradigm of the human condition which is atomistic rather than holistic, that is one which seeks to deal with dysfunctional parts of the person without attempting to understand the person as a unified whole – as an individual. Indeed, many psychologists still work on a behavioural model which denies the existence of the individual as anything over and above a mass of complex sets of elicited responses, that is as a complex organism under environmental control without a central organising human core.

Because it has adopted a destructive paradigm I believe educational psychology as a profession has failed disabled children in a number of ways which we shall now examine in a little more detail.

The damage done by LEA psychologists

The original sin of the EP is not his allegiance to psychometrics, but to psychometrics in the service of the constraining policies of his local authority employer. The damage caused by the indiscriminate use of intelligence testing (and this in the face of quite an onslaught during the 1960s and 1970s from those who were concerned about the discriminatory use of such tests to prop up traditional ways of disposing of children) cannot simply be laid at the door of those who devised the tests. We have seen that the use of such tests has an extremely murky history, having been used to select children for what was known as the Tripartite system. The Tripartite system was a form of social engineering aimed at 'sorting out the wheat from the chaff' so that children would be properly prepared for their future role in life. It was, in fact, a system of educational streaming designed to facilitate and reinforce the dominant culture's desire for social streaming, ultimately for the 'haves' to retain their positions of privileged access to the good things in life.

The Tripartite system

Under the 1944 Education Act, LEAs were not legally bound to organise secondary education in a common format, although it was assumed that secondary education would take the form of a *Tripartite* system such that academically able pupils would enter the *Grammar* schools; other able children with a special aptitude for technical subjects would enter the *Technical grammar* schools and the masses, whom, it was thought, would be best served by receiving a practical and concrete education, would go to the *Secondary modern* schools. Selection depended upon performance in the 11+ examination. This exam was heavily dependent upon psychological evidence in the form of an *en masse* IQ test and it was assumed that the potential of the individual could be predicted at 11 years of age or even earlier. In fact, some schools sorted their children at seven years of age so as to prepare them for what was seen as an almost inevitable outcome at 11. This exam served to categorise children for the Tripartite system.

Giving the IQ test such a central role in determining access to the education system owed much to the then widely held belief that an individual's intelligence is largely determined by his genetic inheritance, and hence, to that extent, largely immutable. For the school administrator, the headteacher and the psychologist there seemed little point in trying to push square pegs into round holes since, if a child's human potential was pretty well determined at the point of conception, it made obvious sense to provide him or her with the education they would need to fulfil their role in later life.

However, it was concluded in the 1950s that the Tripartite system had failed because the secondary modern pupils were themselves seen as failures and evidence grew that the 11+ test itself was a poor predictor of potential. In fact, even within the limited assumptions of the system, the test failed 15 per cent of children who went on to the grammar school in that they could not keep up and a further 15 per cent of the secondary modern pupils could easily have coped with what the grammar schools offered. Such testing was supposed to be able to measure the individual's genetic potential to learn, which, it was assumed, was not only measurable but largely immutable. Beyond this, it was assumed by most psychologists that such a measure would be a good predictor of the likely success of the child in school – as well as of his achievements throughout the remainder of his life.

I was myself a victim of this system. Having been tested at seven years of age, I was placed in a class for children deemed unsuitable for training for the 11+. Those who tested positive at this time were placed in a class which was to be prepared for the 11+ on the basis that they were believed to have the potential to pass and then go on to the grammar school – in this, and other schools like it, they had engaged in a self-fulfilling prophecy known as teaching to the test.

This is not the place to comment further on the still ongoing nature/nurture debate and the foregoing is probably something of a caricature of the situation. Nevertheless, it contains sufficient truth to stand as a description of the kind of view held during the 1940s and for the succeeding two or three decades when the 11+ examination was almost universally practised. In fact, this system discriminated against working class children largely because the test was constructed so as to tap cultural influences with an emphasis on dominant culture values and knowledge, that is the middle class way of thinking and speaking. Such tests not only discriminated against the overwhelming majority of the indigenous population but also against those from ethnic minority backgrounds.

By the 1960s, the Tripartite system was recognised as having failed to provide equality of opportunity – which was worrying because there was a shortage of skilled labour. This, in turn, was placing pressure on the school system to properly tap the pool of ability of children, which was not then the case in respect to working class children. Such criticisms of the Tripartite system culminated in a concerted attempt to move towards a *comprehensive* system and, in 1965, the government issued Circular 10/65, entitled *Organisation of Secondary Education* (DES 1965), asking LEAs to submit plans for comprehensive reorganisation. However, it contained little detail on how this was to be achieved. The expansion of comprehensive schools did not lead to the elimination of private fee-paying schools, which still today cater for around 7 per cent of the school population. The process towards a comprehensive system was gradual such that even in 1986 there remained 155 grammar schools concentrated in a few LEAs alongside over 4000 comprehensives.

Some remained outside the system

None of this, of course, had anything to do with children with significant learning, physical or sensory disabilities, who were mostly assumed not to be able to benefit from any segment of the Tripartite system and hence to be in need of their own separate system of schooling. What actually existed at this time was not a Tripartite system but a Quadripartite system with the final party unacknowledged. It is interesting to note that in describing this period in the evolution of the education system it is very unusual for any commentator to mention the 'missing' children; it is almost as though they did not exist or that the places they were sent to were not really considered part of the school system at all.

A system in chaos

So the British education system evolved more as a kind of political football match within a still largely feudal society than as a rational exchange of views on what children need. This should not be surprising, although it is important to understand how our current system has evolved and why children with special needs are so poorly served by it. However, it is not just politics which drives educational policy development because there are deeper less obvious influences which play a key role in our understanding of what children need, and these have to do with the way we make sense of the world in which we live. In order to understand this better, we must look at the ways in which we make sense of experience. From perception through prediction to understanding there is a complex nexus of beliefs and assumptions which serve to orientate expectation and we shall now explore these a little further in order to try and make better sense of the plight of disabled children.

Knowing and believing

We have seen that perception is not a passive process, since the individual comes to each new experience with a wealth of experience which facilitates prediction – and such prediction is, in a sense, belief. At its most simple, my belief that the sun will rise tomorrow comes about through my observation of the constant occurrence of days dawning throughout the duration of my life. My mind set then becomes a prediction that the sun will rise. So it is, in less marked degree, with all else in our lives. Our assumptions about what the future holds are, however, firmly rooted not only in our own personal experience but in our shared understandings with others. We talk and exchange information – not all of which confirms what we already believe, so have to adjust and readjust our beliefs and expectations – and so our ability to predict grows as the years pass.

Paradigms and paradigm shifts

We have already, somewhat briefly, looked at the notion of a *model* or *paradigm* and it is now time to look more closely at the meaning which is to be attached to such notions within the human management context.

Another way of making sense of this pattern of human perception/ understanding development is to think of it as Thomas Kuhn has proposed in his book *The Structure of Scientific Revolutions* (1962). Kuhn suggests we look at the way in which scientific understanding evolves and then goes on to make a distinction between continuous and discontinuous scientific progress in the physical sciences. He says that normal science progresses by the gradual accumulation of knowledge that progressively elaborates, extends and articulates a paradigm that already exists. Here a paradigm may be construed as a set of presuppositions or basic beliefs which cohere to explain experienced events.

Although the work of Kuhn, from which the notions of paradigm and paradigm shift are drawn, was concerned with the physical sciences, the concepts are equally applicable to the social sciences. Whilst the application of this way of thinking (about our deeply ingrained beliefs and understandings) to particular areas of professional practice is far from unproblematic, it is nevertheless possible to discern certain significant core assumptions through the imposition of particular (albeit stereotypical) theoretical models on working practice to see whether their predictions are reflected in the day-to-day service practice we observe.

A topical, although somewhat simplistic, example of what is meant here concerns the French Cartesian view of animals: they are mere machines without feelings; mere objects. This national view (Brigit Bardot aside) strongly influences the attitude towards farm animals and the way they are transported for slaughter. Having made the mechanistic assumption, all manner of consequences follow which, for the typical Frenchman, seem perfectly logical and morally neutral. Had the alternative (typically British) assumption been made – that animals are sentient creatures and, as organisms, not entirely unlike human beings – then the French would be saddled with what they presently see as the hopelessly sentimental British approach, and along with it a moral dilemma over the treatment of such creatures. Paradigms are, therefore, powerful shapers of both belief and expectation and hence also strongly predictive of behaviour.

Beliefs shape experience

The point of all this is that in the social as well as the physical sciences people will inevitably operate within a paradigm, the assumptions of which will determine how they make sense of experience. The core ideas, values and beliefs implicit in that paradigm will also determine how they undertake their investigations and hence inevitably circumscribe what might be discovered.

An example of just how damaging it can be if the wrong assumptions are made is provided by the approach to meeting the needs of people with learning difficulties throughout the 19th and the earlier part of the 20th centuries. People with SLDs were generally assumed to be sub-human and hence not to possess the same feelings and sensibilities as other citizens. A consequence of this belief was that the vast mental handicap hospitals had no heating because it was assumed the residents would not feel the cold; a logical response had the original assumption not been totally incorrect.

Although it is perhaps too simplistic, it might help to try and see a paradigm as providing the setting conditions for the development of a *model* for making sense of clients and their needs within a social science context. So a paradigm is a shared perception of the world based on a core set of assumptions and expectations about how the world works. In this sense, our paradigm, in large part, both determines and rationalises our actions. The core set of beliefs implicit in paradigms tell us what is real and what we should expect, and this is what makes them truly normative 'because they conceal the very reasons for our actions in the unquestioned assumptions of the paradigm' (Patton 1975).

That the paradigms we operate within are largely unconscious makes them potentially dangerous, but it is in the nature of paradigms that they are only likely to become available for conscious reflection when they are in the process of changing. A further feature of paradigms is that they exist at varying levels of abstraction. Skrtic (1991) describes this in the following way:

> Thus, a scientific community engaged in normal science can be understood as operating on the basis of a hierarchy of implicit presuppositions, which from most to least abstract, include metatheories, theories, assumptions, models, practices, and tools, each of which are defined and subsumed by the higher levels in the hierarchy of abstraction, and all of which, ultimately, are defined and subsumed by the metaphysical paradigm. (p.9)

In looking at professional practice in the human service system, it is important to ask 'what is the hierarchy of implicit assumptions this individual professional (or group) is making in reaching their conclusions?' To get a handle on this it might be relevant to ask the following questions of the EP who has recommended that a child goes to a segregated school:

1. what is it about *this child* that made you think he would be best placed in a school like this?

2. what is it about *this segregated school* that makes you believe it will serve the needs of *this child*?

The answers to these questions will elicit explanations which will contain the key to an understanding, how this psychologist makes sense of his experience of children with additional needs, typical children, what ordinary schools can offer, what special schools can offer and so on. Asking specific questions about the child and school opens up a whole host of otherwise unexplicated assumptions about children and the system generally. Thus it is that we are able to pin down assumptions at the concrete level of tools, practices and models which are themselves only expressions of less accessible assumptions of a more abstract sort (theories, metatheories, etc.).

A placement recommendation is merely a *tool* which, if used repeatedly, becomes a *practice*; which in turn comes to be seen as a pattern; which implies a *model* in the head of the psychologist; which at root has to do with a number of things, including the needs of children. But the needs of children are not the sole consideration of the psychologist, however earnestly he or she might plead their case. Psychologists, like the rest of us, live and work within a society in which reality is socially constructed (Berger and Luckman 1966). This reality is essentially a reality of everyday life which is shared with others, and the sharing requires mutually agreed definitions of experience and some consensus about the meanings to be attached to such experience.

One way of conceptualising this process is as 'symbolic interactionism' which, according to Blumer (1969), involves three elements:

1. Human beings act towards things on the basis of the meanings the things have for them; also

2. That the meanings originate in social interaction; and therefore that

3. Meanings can be altered by interpretative processes as social action proceeds.

Any culture contains a whole host of meanings available to the individual which may be expressed in a number of ways, both linguistically and symbolically. In dealing with the events of everyday life, the individual will come to an understanding of the way in which others make sense of their experience and this will have an influence on their own judgement formation. Where they encounter a consensus on a particular matter, their own view will be influenced by this and where this consensus involves high status or credible individuals or groups, this too will be noted.

Returning to our example of the school psychologist, it is possible, through observing his or her day-to-day working practice, to identify a hierarchy of assumptions related to the subjects of their work. Given the relative uniformity of practice amongst psychologists, it would not be unreasonable to say that these amount to a working paradigm. This is not to say that all EPs work in the same way or share anything like an identical set of beliefs, yet there is enough uniformity in the way LEAs implement their special needs policies to ensure that practice is similar throughout the UK and the psychologist is a key member of the team required to adopt a certain working pattern.

The practice of educational psychology within the LEA must change

Having embraced the medical model and the use of psychometrics to justify the segregation of children seen as unwanted within the educational mainstream, EPs have implicitly chosen to deny the relevance of the broader discipline of psychology to education. Psychometrics clearly have a role in the diagnosis of learning difficulty, but it is an abuse of a valuable technology to use it to justify the segregation of vulnerable children. One valuable role for psychometric assessment is in the diagnosis of specific learning difficulty (dyslexia) and it is now widely accepted that this condition exists and can be identified by the judicious use of diagnostic tests.

It has been argued that the special education paradigm is still largely rooted in the medical model of disability which views the child or young person as sick or broken and hence in need of being made well or whole once more. Furthermore, from within the medical model, the disabled or learning impaired child is seen as the *problem* who must adapt or be adapted to suit the requirements of the world as it is for the non-disabled child. Linked to this is an approach to service development which sees the child as 'special' or 'different' since (s)he requires additional or different resources which are to be provided largely by specialist professionals in separate settings. It is this medical model view which created the large institutions and which still permeates much of the thinking and day-to-day practice of special needs professionals. It is also this same model which serves to maintain the special school and its various outposts of segregation in the mainstream.

The test of whether a particular professional or service is operating within a paradigm (of what it is to be human) which embodies the medical model is, at root, quite a simple one which concerns the perceived focus of the need to change. If it is being constantly suggested that the impaired individual must change, there is clear prima-facie evidence of a medical model assumption.

Many psychologists and other special needs professionals clearly hold this view because they support the argument for separation and preparation for advancement to the mainstream. This is the *readiness* model, which requires that the child remain separated until he has made sufficient progress to be able to function in the mainstream. This means, of course, that many children will spend their entire school careers 'getting ready' yet never be able to meet the criteria (for acceptance) which have been set way beyond their reach.

If we were to look for one piece of evidence that EPs are indeed locked into the medical model, we need look no further than the response of the Association of Educational Psychologists (AEP) to a request by the Centre for Studies on Inclusive Education (CSIE) that they sign the Integration Charter (see Appendix 5) which was published in 1994. CSIE had sent its Charter to a number of organisations asking if they would sign it. The response from the AEP was a resounding no, for the following reasons:

> Many members felt that integration with appropriate provision in mainstream schools should be a goal for the majority of children, but they did not support integration for all because:
>
> (a) some children's needs are too severe and/or specialised;
>
> (b) it does away with parental/pupil choice;
>
> (c) it devalues good work done by a number of special schools where skills and expertise are sharpened;
>
> (d) mainstream schools are not always the most 'effective environment' for pupils with special educational needs – we would need to be sure that they can offer *at least* the same opportunities as currently exist in special schools with the aim of offering more, if the charter were to hold up;
>
> (e) youngsters with Educational and Behavioural Difficulties (EBD) or those excluded from school also have rights (little mention in the Charter); and
>
> (f) there needs to be a continuity of provision to meet individual needs. (AEP: 14/94)

Apart from the solidly conservative view it takes on this issue, this response from the AEP is presented as a root and branch rejection of the Charter on the basis of just 15 replies, of which 11 recommended not signing, 3 who would have signed and one which expressed doubts. On the basis of this response, which the AEP described as 'most encouraging', this professional association was able to say the profession was against signing. It is perhaps a comment on the position of many other EPs who did not reply that the AEP was not inundated with letters of protest from their members on hearing this news.

So we can conclude that the profession of educational psychology has serious reservations about integrating certain children in the mainstream, irrespective of the level of resourcing and expertise that might exist there. Theirs is not the position that 'we would like to see all children included but at present the mainstream couldn't cope' because they make it clear that some children, by virtue of their severe and/or specialised needs, *need* to be segregated.

This response is somewhat at odds with an earlier working party report on integration entitled *Integration: Problems and Possibilities for Change* which was published by the AEP in 1989. In this report, in which it was acknowledged that the practice of segregation poses some very real dangers, it said:

> It may appear to be logical to attempt to meet the exceptional needs of individuals within a set-up which temporarily adopts the position of a protective environment with high levels of commitment and expertise. However, in reality, such settings can easily become permanent placements, having only marginal status and producing an environment where pupils can subsequently (if inadvertently) become devalued. Paradoxically, protection can create vulnerability for individuals by fostering high dependency.

It is interesting to speculate on why the position of the professional association of school psychologists should have effected such a volte-face on the integration issue. One cannot help but wonder to what extent this was brought about by the pressures that have progressively been brought to bear upon all LEA professional staff to fall in line behind more conservative policies in response to successive directives from central government. Certainly the greatly increased pressure on LEA budgets will have played a critical part.

So what are we to make of the position of EPs in relation to the two per cent of Statemented children? It is clear that many EPs are still locked into an 'individual', 'clinical' or even 'individual pathology' approach which is in tune with the medical model, and resolutely at odds with the analysis being developed by disabled people and their allies.

The need to rid ourselves of destructive paradigms

If the medical model is rooted in a paradigm that presents dangers to vulnerable children, we need to look elsewhere for a more positive characterisation of their circumstances and needs. In a complex social activity such as education a number of 'paradigms' may coexist. Education of children can be seen as primarily *economic* (the creation of a more skilled labour force), *social* (to reduce disadvantage and increase cohesion) or *cultural* (to inculcate dominant religious/ethical values). All of these belief systems continue to shape the model of education we have in the UK, although much of the current debate has tended to focus upon economic issues.

Our understanding of childhood is shaped by seeing it as a preparation for the first stages in life, yet this is absent in the way we see many disabled children. We have seen that the 'special education' paradigm draws on both 'education' and 'disability'. Ineducability is an 'economic' concept – is it worth educating this person as (s)he will not contribute to the workforce. Special education rests on a number of unhelpful (conscious and unconscious) premises:

- The greatest pedagogic effort (quality and quantity) should go to the children who are most able
- The presence of significantly less able children damages the learning environment for more able children
- The main way children learn is by being taught (rather than by discovery, collaboration, imitation or by teaching others) and this is done best if everyone is at the same page in the same book
- The presence of disabled children does *not* damage the learning environment for other disabled children
- There should be one teacher per class (in other countries, e.g. Italy, there are usually two)
- The assumptions about the nature of disability and what disabled children need.

The 'model' for special education based on these beliefs includes:

- The continuum – the more different in ability children are from the 'norm', the more different their learning place should be, and the more marginal those schools to the administrative mainstream (this is also true of course for the 'elite' schools)
- blurring of boundaries between care, therapy, occupation and education – for example, therapy intrudes on the school day and horse riding is seen as a school activity; nursery nurses are employed
- the negation of gender, age and culture in segregated schools – disability overrides everything, including parental choice

- the notion that 'moving up' to an ordinary school is a rare privilege and 'moving down' to a special school is a threat
- the absence of homework, pupil reunions, educational exchanges, etc.

The creation of a separate system implies a powerful judicial role to allocate children to this separate (and inferior) system. This is not voluntary – how many parents 'choose' to send their physically and intellectually able five-year-old to a special school, however intensive the staffing? EPs have assumed this role and we have seen that their development of psychometrics has legitimated their role as *the* special needs 'experts'.

AN ALTERNATIVE PARADIGM

The alternative paradigm – that education is a social issue; that disability is a social issue; that children are children and have a right to be included – is simply 'outside the frame' for most people working in special education. Instead, integration is seen as a privilege to be earned by the least disabled who can 'economically' be fitted into the existing model.

Although global costings of segregated and inclusive education have not been done in the UK, the argument put forward is 'it's too expensive'. In Italy and Norway, where there are no special schools, the costings have also not been done because it's seen as a simple matter of civil rights. Arguments about 'can *this* child be integrated', disputing a particular Statement, are crucially important for the families concerned but are bounded by the dominant paradigm of economic education and clinical separation of the economically educable from the rest.

The Social Model of disability

Thinking about disability is construed along a paradigm continuum from 'medical' (where disability is understood to be located in the individual) to 'social' (where it is understood as a feature of society) – a social construct. The social model is little known to most special education professionals, although it offers a more coherent analysis of the oppression disabled people experience.

Disability has both individual and social aspects and it is the different perceptions of the main locus of causality which gives rise to the different models for delivering services. The medical model, in its most extreme form, sees the impairment as equating the disability, while the social model sees disability as arising from social causes rooted in inappropriate (societal) responses to impairment.

The social model of disability takes as its starting point that serious illness and physical or intellectual impairment exist but only

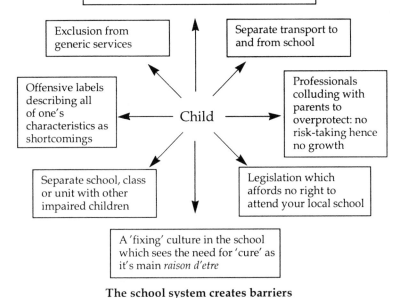

The school system creates barriers
which disable the child

Source: Hall 1995

*Figure 3.4 The Social Model of disability (informed by normalisation
theory) from the perspective of a segregated child*

become disabling because of the rejecting and oppressive response
to such impairments by the non-disabled world. Advocates of the
social model (largely disabled persons and their allies) argue that
the answer to the problem of disability lies in the restructuring of
societal attitudes and the physical environment. The social model is
best expressed by the statement that 'people with disabilities are
limited more by the attitudes of others than by their physical or
intellectual impairments'.

Figure 3.4 represents a social model perspective on the typical
response of the education service to a child with a significant impairment. The social model characterises such a response as oppressive, rejecting and essentially dehumanising, and evidence of
institutional discrimination not unlike racism and sexism. Understanding such oppression is a precondition for beginning the long

process of reversing it, which is not a task educationalists seem at all inclined to tackle.

The argument, then, is that special education is stuck within a completely inappropriate and highly damaging paradigm (or model) which has lead to a negative perception of the children to be served; also, that this has resulted in a variety of unhelpful, if not damaging, practices. It is, therefore, time for a complete rethink of the role of special education and a major paradigm shift. Such a major rethink should, of course, equally be applied to services for adults with impairments which result in their being socially devalued and distanced.

The social model has a number of profound insights to offer and provides a powerful analysis of what is wrong with society, but, in spite of containing major criticisms of normalisation theory, nevertheless draws very heavily upon that theory in terms of its major assumptions (see Figure 3.4).

Normalisation/Social Role Valorisation (SRV)

The principle of normalisation has become an important area of study for those working with adults who have learning difficulties. It is, first and foremost, a *values based* system in that it starts from the premise that services have failed miserably to acknowledge many of the fundamental human rights of those whose needs they are intended to meet. Wolf Wolfensberger has developed the theory into a highly systematised model for staff training and service evaluation, which has been seen as applicable beyond the field of learning difficulties for a number of groups who tend to be less highly valued in society (Wolfensberger 1975; 1983).

Normalisation is an 'interactionist' model which takes as its starting point that some people are different (in virtue of their impairment(s)) in ways which are negatively valued by society and that society then places these people in social roles which are highly damaging.

There are three main formulations of the normalisation principle, the first of which originated in Denmark in connection with the Mental Retardation Act 1959 and described the aim of services as being 'to create an existence for the mentally retarded as close to normal living conditions as possible' (Bank-Mikkelsen 1980, p.56). This definition referred to the general living condition of people in terms of their homes, education, work and social lives. The intention was that people with learning difficulties should be accorded the legal and human rights enjoyed by the majority of citizens; hence the term 'normalisation' was applicable to the relationship between the broader society and the individuals concerned. It was about trying to normalise the relationship between people and their society and not, as many have mistakenly concluded, about somehow making the people themselves 'normal' (whatever that might mean). The term later appeared in Sweden where it was redefined as 'making available to all mentally retarded people patterns of life and conditions of everyday living which are as close as possible to the regular circumstances and ways of life of society' (Nirje 1980, p.33).

What these early Scandinavian formulations of the principle have in common is their emphasis upon bringing about change in the living conditions of people with learning difficulties, so that they might begin to enjoy the benefits of citizenship which are valued by the rest of society. The emphasis was upon creating equality of opportunity for people who had hitherto been marginalised and extending to them the rights enjoyed by other citizens, but this did not explicitly extend to integrating them into the mainstream of community life.

These early formulations were also pointing to the need for people with learning difficulties to have available to them a life as much like that of other citizens as it is possible for society to provide, and contained within these recommendations was the notion that this is what social justice required. It was also being implied that the services which people had to rely upon could provide such conditions if they were organised differently, that is in line with the principle of normalisation.

At the time of these early formulations of the normalisation principle, it was assumed that an ordinary lifestyle could be achieved in the kind of segregated services then being provided, hence equal opportunity to an ordinary lifestyle did not require integration as a pre-condition. As a later commentator points out :

> the **'equal but separate'** approach encapsulated in the Scandinavian definition was reflected in the initial impact of normalisation in the United Kingdom which occurred largely in relation to the design of the physical environment of essentially segregated services.

> (Emerson 1992, p.4)

The work of the then Spastics Society (now Scope) reflected this view of normalisation in that it developed a range of very luxurious residential schools and colleges for children with cerebral palsy, such as Meldreth Manor school near Royston in Hertfordshire. I was once principal of this school and so was well-placed to vouch for the efforts expended by the Society to provide the very best services and facilities from the proceeds of the then huge income of that organisation. However, the philosophy of the Society at that time was that such children needed to be segregated, and looking at the provision now being made in its reincarnation as Scope it is, sadly, hard to detect a significant shift in ideology.

Following these early attempts to formulate the normalisation principle to reflect the aspirations of an egalitarian society, little further work was done to elaborate the theory until the early 1970s. Wolf Wolfensberger was born in Germany, but later migrated to the United States where he worked as a psychologist, clinician, researcher and teacher in the field of 'mental retardation' (this term does not have the negative connotations it would have if used in Britain) and published his seminal work *Normalisation: The Principle of Normalisation in Human Services* in 1972. In this book he extended the scope of the principle to encompass other societally devalued groups within the broader human service system. His formulation also shifted the focus to the desired *outcomes* as well as the *means* to be pursued on behalf of devalued people. Wolfensberger's formulation is not only the most highly elaborated, it is also the one which has become associated with our current understanding of what the term has come to mean. Since 1983, the term Social Role Valorisation (SRV) has come to replace normalisation in Wolfensberger's writing as his analysis of the difficulties faced by societally devalued people has evolved. However, in spite of this change of terminology by Wolfensberger, service workers still tend to use the term 'normalisation' and some remain to be convinced of the value of such a heavy emphasis on social role.

Wolfensberger initially defined normalisation as the 'utilisation of means which are as culturally normative as possible, in order to establish and/or maintain personal behaviours and characteristics which are as culturally normative as possible' (1972, p.28). He eventually offered an ordinary language version of this definition, saying normalisation is 'the use of culturally valued means in order to enable people to live culturally valued lives' (Wolfensberger and Thomas 1983). This meant that the normalisation principle should be seen as culture-specific, since cultures vary in their norms.

Wolfensberger's main work had been in the aforementioned field of mental retardation, but his formulation of the principle of normalisation is intended to embrace a wide range of individuals and groups who have one thing in common – their susceptibility to being socially devalued. This, according to Wolfensberger, includes those who are seen as deviant within a particular culture at a particular time. In most cultures this will certainly include those with a severe physical or sensory impairment, learning difficulty, physical deformity or speech defect and, perhaps a little more surprisingly, groups such as those with a mental health problem and the elderly. Although impaired children tend to elicit more sympathy from the public at large, they are by no means excluded from this dynamic of social devaluation.

It is important to understand, though, that the term 'normalisation' is not a part of the lexicon of most educationalists – although it has become a byword for the development of community-based services for adults with learning difficulties. People who work in education will probably not have encountered the theory, and that is surprising given the widespread exposure to the ideas which has occurred in adult services. Perhaps this once again highlights the insularity of service workers who seem to be unaware of professional practice with similarly disabled people across service phases. This is certainly a problem between the special school and the FE college, but is even more marked between education and social service provision.

The historical oppression of devalued people

The starting point for normalisation is an understanding of the historical position of people who have a learning difficulty or physical disability or who, for some other reason, have suffered social rejection and isolation. Within the theory, such individuals or groups have been seen as having low social status through having had a negative value placed upon them because of their possession of characteristics – which are themselves devalued within their society.

Human characteristics likely to be societally devalued are many and varied and may also differ between societies or cultures. Likewise, a particular characteristic might be valued at one time and devalued at another. Here the spectrum of characteristics likely to be devalued range from severe physical, sensory or learning impairment through to physical disfigurement and atypical patterns of behaviour. Such relatively trivial characteristics as the size of a person's nose or feet or their general bodily shape, or even the colour of their hair (the redhead syndrome), may also, in a minor way, mark them out as 'different'. It is certainly the case that the more severe forms of impairment tend to be universally devalued, although even here there are differential tolerance levels across cultures.

Following a period during which a number of misunderstandings became attached to the term 'normalisation', Wolfensberger was also developing his understanding of the key elements of social devaluation. He came to see that the essential defining characteristics of social acceptance and high social status were concerned with the individual's ability to fulfil a variety of valued social roles. The reverse of this was, of course, that those individuals who had few or only lowly-valued social roles were placed at far greater risk of social rejection, physical isolation, exploitation and, possibly, even physical harm.

THE NOTION OF DEVIANCY

A person is seen as deviant if he is perceived to be sufficiently different to others in respect of a characteristic which is itself significant within the particular culture. Not all deviancy is construed negatively, only those observable aspects of a person's appearance, performance or behaviour which are negatively valued.

For the purposes of the present analysis, it is important to understand that characteristics of individuals are not in, or of, themselves deviant. They become so only through the judgement of another person; hence *deviancy is in the eye of the beholder* and, as such, is a 'social construct'. Such deviancy stereotypes as surround disabled or learning impaired people are socially transacted and hence open to reinterpretation.

Deviancy projections become self-fulfilling

Being perceived as deviant also means being cast into a role which creates strong expectancies in others, so that they behave towards the 'deviant' individual in ways likely to elicit responses in line with their deviancy expectations; this in turn becomes self-fulfilling because the individual learns to respond in accordance with what is expected so as not to disappoint or thwart such expectations. All this means is that people learn to *play the roles* they are assigned.

The problem with this is that the roles thrust upon people seen as deviant are deviant roles and, as Wolfensberger observes, 'the way in which these roles transcend time, distance and culture is remarkable' (1972, p.16). The major historical roles he identifies include those of the deviant person as: sub-human, a menace, an object of dread, a diseased organism, an object of ridicule, an object of pity, an eternal child and a holy innocent – quite a catalogue, and one which we need to look at briefly because it is central to our understanding not only of the normalisation principle but also of what is wrong with our current paradigm for special education. In doing this we shall look just at the roles which have a particular significance for children, that is the deviant child characterised as: sub-human, diseased organism, object of ridicule, object of pity and eternal child. The child as 'object of charity' is subsumed within many such roles.

The child as 'sub-human'

We saw from the work of Itard that there was a question as to whether the 'wild boy of Aveyron' was indeed a human child or an animal who just happened to have the physical characteristics of a young boy. Other cases, then and later, aroused the same speculation and the term 'feral children' was used to describe such children whose behaviour was animal-like in spite of their obviously human appearance.

Vegetable concepts have also been applied to children with profound disabilities and the medical concept is still applied to people who, having sustained a severe trauma to the central nervous system, are described as 'brain dead' and existing in a 'vegetative state'. The medical profession recognises that the essential bodily functions which keep us alive are mediated by the autonomic nervous system of the lower brain – so even when the cerebral cortex is catastrophically damaged, life may continue without the possibility of higher thought processes. People existing in such a state are seen to have lost all of their distinctively human attributes and abilities and hence may be deemed 'no longer human' and more 'vegetable-like'.

It is, sadly, still common to hear profoundly handicapped children referred to as 'vegetables', with the implication that, because they lack certain distinctive abilities, they are not truly human. Sometimes such children are also referred to as 'low grade', which is a term used to describe certain sorts of fuel ranging from high through medium to low grade; certain sorts of naturally occurring mineral aggregates are similarly described depending upon how much metal (e.g. gold) they yield.

The child as 'diseased organism'

An enduring role perception is that of the deviant child as sick. For anyone who has worked in a segregated school for severely impaired children this will be only too familiar. Whatever the disability of the child and whatever his/her life expectancy, those who do not know the child may well equate impairment with extreme illness and, possibly, imminent death. This misperception by outsiders has an effect on schools in much the same way that parental over-anxiety does; both collude to create an over-protective ethos which, in turn, serves to reinforce the impression that the child is indeed sick.

A macabre extension of the perception of the disabled child as 'sick', and not having a future worth planning for, is that of the child as 'soon dead'. Wolfensberger's main preoccupation currently is with what he describes as 'death making' in society, which he sees as increasingly embracing euthanasia as a means of ridding itself of troublesome individuals. This ideology embraces abortion of the foetus when it is known to be impaired.

The medical model in which special education still languishes reinforces this sick role by describing all of its interventions as 'therapeutic', hence physiotherapy, speech therapy, occupational therapy, aromatherapy, etc. Teachers and others mimic this medicalising approach by tacking *therapy* onto their own interventions, hence hippo-therapy (horse riding), rebound therapy (trampolining), hydrotherapy (swimming), music therapy, and so on.

Once a person is conceptualised as primarily sick, this role permeates the way in which services manage every aspect of their life, and for a child in education this not only distorts the way in which education is conceived, that is primarily as 'treatment', but also ensures that it takes place in a segregated setting away from the child's typical neighbourhood community and peers.

The child as an 'object of ridicule'

This is the 'village idiot' syndrome in which the individual is cast into the role of inconsequential fool or clown so that their whole status is trivialised. This, of course, happens with children too and many will be familiar with the way in which some children with Down's syndrome are treated in their mainstream schools, which may at one level be good natured teasing, but at another is damaging to the child's sense of self.

The child as an 'object of pity'

Everyone must be familiar with the style of media reporting of stories about disabled children. The headline 'tragic *palsy sufferer* rejected by her local school' or 'Down's *victim* takes leading role in school pantomime' will be all too familiar to the reader who is sensitised to the issues. The pity offered may be rooted in genuine compassion, but that does not detract from the fundamentally disrespectful and devaluing impact of the sentiments expressed.

It hardly needs to be said that disabled children do not need pity. Pity is not only disempowering but fundamentally insulting since it tends to imply contempt through reducing the individual's humanity to the impairment they happen to have, that is it diminishes them.

The individual as 'eternal child'

To treat a person as though they are, and always will be, younger than their actual age is as potentially damaging as it is common in the world of disability. For severely impaired children, age-inappropriate management and forms of description and address tend to be the norm, not the exception. To be cast into the role of eternal child is to be denied the opportunity to grow up and, although the notion of becoming 'grown-up' might be a difficult one to grasp when applied to a profoundly handicapped person, it is nevertheless essential to provide every opportunity for the development of a true sense of the person's age and status. It is important not to create a climate in which the child or young person is always conceived as a baby because they happen to understand some concepts at the level of an infant.

For disabled children in school or college, this issue is really about being conceptualised as an 'eternal infant' and, once an adult, becoming an 'eternal child'. In this context, the psychologists' concept of a person's 'mental age' has done enduring damage to the way in which teachers and many special needs professionals conceptualise learning impaired children.

The concept of 'mental age'

One of the ways of expressing an individual's performance on an IQ test is as a *mental age*. This is typically done by giving a test to groups of children of different ages, converting the results to raw scores, working out a typical or mean score for a specific age group and calling that the norm for that age. Where such tests are believed to tap 'intelligence', this 'test age' would be called a *mental age*. According to psychometricians, the process can be reversed so that a *mental age* can be converted to an IQ by dividing the *mental age* by the chronological age then multiplying the resultant figure by 100. The following is the formula for achieving this: $IQ = MA/CA \times 100$. If we applied this formula to the assessment of a 14-year-old child with SLDs, we would get the following result: CA = 14 years, MA = 3.5 years, hence $3.5 / 14 \times 100 = IQ 25$ (this against an average IQ of 100).

It is fair to say that many psychologists no longer make these conversions, but it is equally true to say that many special needs teachers and other professionals still place great weight on what they understand to be the child's *mental age* in planning a programme and in addressing and describing the child. This practice does incalculable damage both to the child's self-perception and to his overall development because it casts him inappropriately into the role of infant or very young child when he is really now a young man.

Some years ago I was invited to join the management committee of a local society serving people with cerebral palsy. The age range of those using its various services was 18–60+ and the people spent their time in what was called a 'special care centre' or a 'workshop' depending upon the extent of their disability. Most of the people concerned with this service – parents, workers and management committee – had adopted the convention of referring to the people who used the service as either 'babies' or 'children'; those who attended the special care unit were the 'babies' and those in the workshop were the 'children'. It was not that any of these people were callous or uncaring, and indeed many were good, highly committed individuals, but they had fallen into a way of describing those they were striving to serve which could only have negative consequences.

The ghosts of roles past still remain

Many in special education remain highly sceptical of the suggestion that these sorts of ideas are still around in society and most will certainly categorically deny they form part of the unconscious processes either of themselves or their fellow professionals. I have some direct experience of the use of such dehumanising language by some fellow professionals and even of a case where a member of Her Majesty's Inspectorate (HMI) of schools asked about a passing child with Down's syndrome: 'is that child a lower grade or not?'. There was also a most distressing incident in which a driver, who had come into a school to find out why his escort was so long collecting a child, suddenly exclaimed very angrily: 'I'm only paid to transport the vegetables, not to wait around for them'. The only thing that marked off this individual from a number of others was that he was sufficiently insensitive and stupid to say openly what he believed. Training is needed for such groups of workers so they may develop a better appreciation of the needs of disabled people. There is also room for the adoption of much more rigorous selection procedures by those responsible for the delivery of these auxiliary services.

Another role in which children perceived as 'deviant' tend almost universally to be cast is one which arises out of these sorts of role perceptions and the service system response to their need: that of 'object of charity'. Children with special needs – whether educational or not – are, and have for long been, the focus of an enormous amount of highly organised charitable fundraising. All the major children's charities, and such annual extravaganzas as the BBC Children in Need appeal, are very much part of the way the British like to see themselves, that is as generous, humane and caring towards disabled children.

Much good comes out of all of this and many valuable facilities and opportunities are created, but it has also caused a great deal of harm, for two reasons. First, the way in which much of this fund raising takes place is demeaning to the children who are supposed to be the beneficiaries – because it tends to present an image of them which serves to cast them into one or more of the roles described above; second, it creates a climate in which they are seen only to be deserving of that which is given charitably and not necessarily to have a *right* to it based upon their evident need.

Wolfensberger (1987) cites four main societal responses to deviancy. The deviant is: (1) destroyed, (2) prevented from acting deviantly, (3) supported to have the deviant condition reversed or (4) segregated. Fortunately, children who are perceived as deviant are usually only dealt with by methods 2, 3 and 4, although there is a growing body of evidence that some new-born children may be dealt with by method 1 in the absence of legislation allowing euthanasia.

So much for the important notions of deviancy and deviancy-making which are central both to the principle of normalisation and to the destructive dynamic inherent in much of the human service system. It is important to understand that normalisation is a well grounded theory or ideology which is firmly rooted in empirical research and not just a set of fine ideas. Indeed, Wolfensberger has described normalisation as a 'whole new ideology of human management' (1972, p.27) and it has certainly provided a new impetus to the development of services for certain vulnerable groups in

Britain and other English-speaking countries. One of its major contributions is that it provides a valuable analysis of the historical predicament of devalued individuals.

Normalisation (and the later SRV) represents an attempt to develop an overarching theory to explain the predicament of devalued individuals and groups within society and, beyond that, to provide a basis for building services which reflect a more appropriate societal response. The theory draws upon a broad base of social science research in identifying seven core themes, which together form the theoretical basis of the theory.

NORMALISATION'S SEVEN CORE THEMES

The powerful role of unconsciousness in human services

Normalisation theory places a heavy emphasis on *societal unconscious intent* in the development of services for disadvantaged groups. This unconsciousness is said to pervade the whole area of social policy-making as well as particular areas of service, individual services and the thinking of those who work in services. According to Wolfensberger, what is unconscious is a *destructive intent towards service users*. This is probably the most controversial aspect of the theory in that it represents a damning indictment of the professional agencies and service workers, and it is largely this which has served to alienate many potential adherents to other aspects of the theory.

However, Wolfensberger claims that because this destructive intent exists only at the unconscious level it is not available for examination and cannot be dealt with. The answer must be that it is *made available to conscious awareness* and this can only be a painful process. Wolfensberger's identification of this destructive dynamic in society is expressed in its most extreme form in his analysis of the developing acceptance of euthanasia, and particularly in the Netherlands – which he describes as the 'death making capital of the world'. However, it is hardly appropriate to carry over this sort of analogy to the treatment of children with special needs – which is the focus of this book – and it is *not* being suggested that death-making is the underlying ideology of the special school.

The major issue in the dynamic of unconsciousness for the special school is that it has to claim publicly to be working towards a number of societally-valued ends for its learners whilst engaging in practices that patently cannot bring them to pass. Hence special schools say they are preparing children for a return to the mainstream, but hardly ever do so and have no plans to do so; they claim to respect learners, but treat them in demeaning and age-inappropriate ways; they claim to be striving to increase the competence of learners, but are content to provide low-intensity programmes and a short service day.

Because the destructive underlying social intent remains locked away in the individual's unconsciousness, it is impossible for him or her to realise that it exists and hence cognitive dissonance is kept to the minimum.

Role expectancy in deviancy-making

We have looked at some of the most common roles that children are cast into, and it is important also to understand the power of role expectancy on the behaviour of people perceived as deviant. This is linked closely to the processes of labelling and categorisation according to the way in which the particular form of deviancy is socially defined.

The basic premise is that the characteristics and behaviour of groups labelled as deviant by the culture play an important part in determining the societal response to their perceived deviancy. Put simply, if a 10-year-old child is treated as though he were a two-year-old because he has been assessed as having a mental age of two years, this will encourage age-inappropriate behaviour. The obvious danger of such labelling is that, as has been said, it can become a self-fulfilling prophecy. The notion of self-fulfilling prophecies is an important one for special needs education. Merton (1968) said 'if men define situations as real they are real in their consequences' and went on to describe a classic case of a self-fulfilling prophecy in which a perfectly sound, established bank became the subject of a false rumour that it was in difficulty and, as word spread, people rushed to the bank to withdraw their money, thereby causing the bank to fold.

Mere placement in a special school is sufficient statement of negative expectation to ensure the child internalises the idea that he is a failure and not expected to amount to anything. The culture of the school also ensures this message is reinforced.

The conservatism corollary

Where individuals are known to have one or more devaluing characteristics it is likely they will be assumed to have others. The dynamic here is that the more devalued a person is, the greater will be the impact of any further devaluing characteristic on the negative judgement someone else may make about that person. It is easy to test this part of the theory by getting someone to take you out in a wheelchair. You will quickly find that, having made the assumption that you have a physical disability, others are also likely to assume you have a learning difficulty and perhaps also that you are deaf or even demented. Questions or comments will not be directed *to* you even though they are *about* you and the person pushing your wheelchair will be assumed to be your mouthpiece and your keeper.

The implications of the conservatism corollary for the special education service is that it should *overcompensate* so as to try to minimise devaluing characteristics. This can be achieved in a number of ways. Most important, the child should not be placed in a segregated setting alongside other devalued children. In addition, the child should be presented in age- and culture-appropriate ways – this means dressing as typical children of the same age would dress and not going around with, for example, bibs and dummies. Beyond this it would be important to ensure the child was supported in behaving appropriately in any social setting in which they would meet others. All of this would be part of a strategy to try to create and maintain for the child a social identity which would be as age-appropriate and culturally valued as possible.

The conservatism corollary goes beyond trying to achieve what is standard or ordinary within a culture, since it is recognised that a person with an already devalued identity will need to compensate by the addition of some highly culturally valued elements. Association with valued others is an obvious strategy.

The importance of competency enhancement

Normalisation theory places great stress on services making the 'developmental assumption', which means being committed to the belief that those being served do indeed have the potential to learn and grow. This is, of course, more important for a person during their childhood than at any later time in life – due to the relative plasticity of the central nervous system which enables children to learn more quickly and effectively than adults.

Schools *par excellence* are places which emphasise the importance of personal competency enhancement. If, as in the case of some special schools, there is educational nihilism because staff have no sense of purpose, seeing their role more as care workers in a day centre rather than as teachers in a school, the importance of the developmental assumption needs to be reinforced. It is because the education system places such a strong emphasis on enhancing the competency of learners which makes it all the more surprising that segregated special needs services are so desultory in their approach. The low-key, laid-back approach is just what Statemented children do *not* need. Normalisation stresses the need for programmes which are not only relevant but *intensive*.

The power of imitation

Modelling or imitation is an extremely important means by which children learn, and this is no less true of young children who are profoundly effected by the behaviour of other children. Although EPs do understand this principle, they do not for the most part seem to apply it when it comes to sending children to special schools and other impairment specific classes or units.

As those who qualify for admission have an inevitable homogeneity of difficulty, children who attend certain sorts of special schools are subjected to a constant stream of inappropriate and maladaptive behaviours and this is particularly true in the case of schools for children with SLDs, autism, behavioural difficulties and language disorders, where the last thing such children need is to be in one another's company. Such is the destructive effect of being surrounded by *inappropriate* models. Still worse is the effect of not having *appropriate* models which would be available were they in a mainstream school. We shall see in Chapter 4 that what children learn in school goes way beyond the formal curriculum and, for some children, it is this other curriculum – the *hidden curriculum* – which is what they need the school to provide. Learning by looking to see how other children communicate, interact, dress, etc., has a powerful influence upon personality development and there is a sterility about all of this in some special schools that must be seen to be understood.

The dynamics of social imagery

Through the unconscious association of devalued people with stereotypical negative imagery, their position in society has been rendered marginal. This is also the case with children who, as we have seen, have been cast into roles which ensure their continued separation as well as their dependency upon charity. Imagery common in special schools is typically of the age-inappropriate kind, reflecting the mistaken belief of most professionals in the importance of mental age as a guide to the appropriateness of forms of address, fixtures, fittings, decor and equipment as well as the content of the educational programme. There is also likely to be imagery which reflects an unconscious trivialisation of pupils, and the presence of clown imagery is much too common to be mere coincidence. Animal imagery also abounds, with the chimpanzee much in evidence – implying an (entirely unconscious) association of the profoundly handicapped as less than human or even non-human.

The importance of integration

Being fully integrated into the valued life of society is the major need which socially devalued people have, and the one need which their society could meet if it chose so to do. It is an almost reflexive societal response to place devalued people at a distance, but it is one which harms them in two main ways: it removes the opportunity to learn from the models provided by valued others and it denies the possibility of challenging the social stereotypes that grow up around such people through providing the opportunity to experience them directly. It is especially important for children not to be separated during their school years because this is the time for most effective learning and also because they need to know and be known by their peers.

These seven core themes are the theoretical basis of the principle of normalisation or SRV. Wolfensberger is in the process of broadening the empirical social science base of the theory and further core themes are beginning to appear. We shall see later how, through use of the PASS and PASSING instruments, services can be evaluated in terms of how they meet the goals of normalisation.

PROBLEMS WITH NORMALISATION

A root and branch criticism of normalisation would say that as a theory it panders to the value system of a WASP (White Anglo Saxon Protestant) society, but this is going much too far. Nevertheless, there are issues that need to be addressed.

Wolfensberger's most recent formulation of the principle (Wolfensberger 1985), with its emphasis on supporting the development of valued social roles, has raised the question of whether the theory places too great an emphasis on *valuing the role* at the expense of *valuing the person*. If true, this would be a serious flaw in the SRV formulation of the normalisation ideology. There is certainly prima-facie evidence of a problem here in that placing such a strong emphasis on the enactment of valued social roles seems inevitably to imply that the individual who is unable to enact such roles is less valued in virtue of that inability. This does not necessarily mean Wolfensberger and other SRV proponents are personally making such a judgement, but rather that it is implicit in the theory.

The danger is that placing too great an emphasis on supporting the individual to enact a role that is socially valued, whilst being a laudable objective in itself, should not be pursued at the expense of denying or suppressing the personal characteristics which make that individual the person (s)he is.

Alan Tyne (1995) says: 'Increasingly it seems to me there is less to SRV than meets the eye. If you wanted to hitch your wagon to a star, role theory would seem to be a rather dim one!' He goes on to say that there are, for him, three defining characteristics of the experience of disabled people: 'difference', 'dependency' and 'disconnection'; and that to emphasise 'role' is to give too much weight to *difference*. He also says that other movements too have a tendency to over emphasise the significance of a single factor, for example that disabled people assert the significance of power and rights whilst advocates of inclusion 'tend to elevate relationships to a mystical importance'.

These sorts of criticisms are over what has been seen as the theory's overly conservative nature. According to many advocates of the *social model* of disability, this is a fatal flaw because it seems to represent a denial of the very identity of disabled people. Certainly there would appear to be substance to this criticism in that normalisation lays heavy emphasis on changing the competency, appearance and social functioning of devalued people so that they will appear more like typically valued citizens. Some disabled people have seen this as a futile attempt to sanitise or hide their impairment as though it were something they should be ashamed of. For those who would see their impairment as intrinsic to their identity as people, it seems to be denying their essential humanity.

Normalisation/SRV has a dual focus

To be fair to the theory, it is two-pronged. Yes, it does seek to minimise the impact of difference upon the observer, but it also stresses the importance of working to change attitudes to achieve better acceptance of devalued people. It recommends advocacy at three levels: the individual, the organisational and the systemic. However, it is hard to ignore the theory's essential conservatism in its insistence that strenuous efforts should be made to support the devalued individual's social acceptance. This is, understandably, seen by some as pandering to the norms of a rejecting society rather than challenging societal insularity.

In truth, normalisation (or SRV) is a body of research which has done a great deal to highlight the underlying dynamic of social devaluation and rejection, but which needs to be treated with caution in respect to its recommendations for reversing this process. Its insights and (as we shall see in Chapter 5) the evaluation tools it has given rise to are extremely valuable in helping us to understand both what is damaging and also what is lacking in services. Therefore it is a case of taking what is helpful in the theory whilst recognising its shortcomings.

So what does all this depressing stuff have to do with the elaboration of a paradigm for special education? Just about everything, as we will see.

Deviancy making in special education

If a valued individual spends her time alongside other valued individuals doing socially valued things in valued social settings, the exact reverse is the case for those upon whom a low social value has been placed. To be systematically excluded from the company of socially valued others, and the places they inhabit, poses a very real danger for a person who possesses impairments or other observable characteristics which are known to be socially devalued.

This exclusion implies also that the individual is relegated to a social milieu which can only serve to compound the disadvantages (s)he already has.

To be removed from the mainstream of community life represents the most damning judgement of one's peers on one's individual's human worth, in that at root it represents a questioning of one's human value and status. As far as schooling is concerned, most parents choose to send their children to the local school to follow the curriculum alongside other children who share their local community. It would be fair to say that this is what we mean by a socially valued educational experience. The reason we say this is socially valued is simply because most people choose it for their children and the very act of making such a choice means that what is chosen is personally valued.

This model for schooling is very different to what the special school has to offer. The question we need to ask of the special school, class or unit is: *does it provide a socially valued education for the children it serves?* The answer is of course no. The reason for this is that it is not something which most parents would choose for their child were they to be offered a genuine choice. It is more likely to be accepted as the 'least worst' option.

If judged by the relevant criteria which concern such questions as does the school provide an opportunity to be with valued others and doing valued things in the course of developing a valued role, then the segregated school or class fails the test. Again it is important to stress that the model being used here is that for a child with a severe disability and complex needs such that, at present, (s)he would probably be placed in a segregated setting.

THE SHORTCOMINGS OF SPECIAL SCHOOL PRACTICE

Therapy not education

We have already seen that because special schools have historically developed their curricula within the medical model paradigm they have tended to pursue what might be called a 'therapeutic' rather than an 'educational' curriculum. This therapy orientation is marked by an attention to functional deficits in learners linked to a 'treatment' approach, which results in largely futile attempts to 'fix' that which is essentially non-fixable. In schools for children with severe and complex disabilities, this has involved the kind of speculative endeavours referred to earlier which may include such activities as: aromatherapy, Snoezelen therapy (multi-sensory stimulation), rebound therapy (trampolining) and horseriding (hippo-therapy), etc. which, because they are conceived as therapeutic interventions, focus attention upon the perceived need to 'cure' rather than to 'educate' (in the full sense of that term). It is not surprising that, within such a medically-orientated paradigm, the social aspects of education are relegated to a minor role. I believe that research would reveal a positive correlation between a therapeutic curriculum and a lack of concern for social integration.

Short, non-intensive school day

Special schools tend to have a shorter day than their mainstream counterparts and this is sometimes said to be due to difficulties over transport or to the lack of stamina of pupils. I believe neither argument holds water and it is simply due to an attitude amongst professionals that such children do not warrant a sustained and intensive programme. This shorter day, with low intensity programming, is also the norm for disabled adults and is, of course, convenient for staff in that they have to spend less time with their clients, whom they may find frustrating. This frustration is more a function of the job these teachers are being asked to do than any intrinsic slothfulness on their part. This is hardly surprising when one sees the difference in purposefulness of a mainstream class compared to that of a SLD school.

Loss of role models and damaging labels

Segregation brings with it a plethora of additional disadvantages for pupils including: poor role models, negative labelling, age- and need-inappropriate grouping, unnecessary travelling and social isolation. The most frequently cited justification for all of this is that separation is necessary if the pupil is to have his most pressing needs met. Here the reference is to the teaching expertise and the availability of paramedical staff offering speech, physio- and occupational therapy and so on, as well as the greater likelihood of there being a nurse on the staff who can liaise with doctors. That such supports could and should be made available in mainstream settings does not wash with those who see only the virtues of the segregated setting. This uncritical acceptance of a medical model solution to educating large numbers of vulnerable children is based on a major misunderstanding of the needs of those children.

The underlying problem

The problem with special education is that it has been hived off from general education *per se* to form a largely separate professional discipline within the broader field of education. It has spawned a range of career path structures, both within the LEA and in training establishments, and this has, in turn, created a vast body of knowledge on how to teach children with a diversity of learning difficulties. All of this effort has presumably been directed towards the development of what is seen to be the 'professional knowledge base' for the separate discipline of 'special education' as distinct from general education.

Special education is, therefore, seen as a sub-discipline of general education and, as such, it would not be unreasonable to expect that it would by now (special education has been around since the 18th century) have evolved its own distinctive knowledge base in allied disciplines such as psychology, social psychology, sociology, history, philosophy and so on. The only professional area of specialist professional knowledge which has developed is that of psychology – where the sub-discipline of educational psychology has been around since the early part of this century. There is, though, a notable absence of any social-psychological or sociological perspective on special education.

For many, educational psychology has become *the* area of relevant theory and EPs tend to be seen as the special education experts within the broader field of special education. However, this represents a very narrow theoretical base for a subject which is supposed to be a separate discipline in its own right and there seems little sign that this base is broadening to include worthwhile perspectives from other academic areas. This lack of an interdisciplinary perspective must cast serious doubt on the premise that special education is truly a separate discipline worthy of the professional structure and practices which it currently supports.

Another surprising feature of special education is that, viewed from within, it seems hardly to have suffered at all from the professional and public uncertainties which have afflicted general education during recent years. Yet from without – the parental perspective – the doubts have been legion.

THE BROADER EDUCATION DEBATE

Education in Britain during the 1980s and 1990s has become the whipping boy for the ills of the economy and central government has, from time to time, attempted, more or less successfully, to scapegoat the teaching profession and LEAs for its own failure to make the economy more competitive. Successive waves of reforming legislation seem, at this stage, to have done little to improve standards – but then these might be early days. That the teaching profession is in need of reform is hardly in question, but what has rightly been questioned is whether the current efforts to impose a uniform curriculum in the context of virtually privatising individual schools is really the right way to go about things. As has already been said, however, the broader public debate raging around general education has left the practice of special education virtually unscathed and the only serious issue has been whether parents and children have been well served by the system of assessment and Statementing under successive attempts to fine-tune legislation and regulations. The question of whether special education is effective or not has simply not arisen.

The catalogue of problems which surround the practice of special education persists because of systemic and individual professional complacency allied to the acceptance of a model of human need – the medical model – which utterly fails to address the real needs of children. The failure to recognise that it is their own belief system which is at the root of the problem is naturally not something special needs professionals will be likely to understand. The resolution of these problems must lie in finding ways of challenging that belief system and making clear its damaging implications for vulnerable children.

THE INSTITUTIONAL ABUSE OF DISABLED CHILDREN

While the majority of schools and other institutions for severely handicapped and mentally disturbed children at least take good care of them, there has always been a minority which descended to abuse and neglect. In just the first ten days of September 1995, reports appeared in the *Sunday Times* (3 September): 'Child carers in pin-down scandal', and in the *Independent on Sunday* (10 September): 'Boys in special school were at risk of Aids'.

The Sunday Times 'pin down' story concerned allegations that:

> mentally disturbed children have been routinely bound and tied to their beds in a new 'pindown' scandal at a children's home. An investigation by the Sunday Times has uncovered disturbing video footage revealing the scandal at the council-run Meadowdale home in Bedlington near Newcastle upon Tyne.

> The film shows Robert, a brain-damaged 10 year old who suffers from cerebral palsy, being strapped into a baby harness before being forced by a female care worker to lie face down on his bed. The harness was then secured to a thick belt tied round the mattress. Social workers have confirmed Robert was also restrained with leather straps binding both feet to the bed posts. A strap around his groin left him unable to move all night.

> Robert's 35 year old mother, who like her son cannot be named for legal reasons, claimed last week that sometimes staff put him into a cardboard box and shut him inside a cupboard. 'We noticed when Robert came home he would empty his toy box and sit in it. When I discovered about the cardboard boxes, I took all his boxes away. How could they have done this? These children are so vulnerable.'

The report went on to say that 'Parents and former employees claim dozens of other children were similarly abused between 1970 and the beginning of last year. Some may also have been sexually abused'.

The Independent on Sunday's Aids story recounted that:

> THEY were boys aged eight to 16 with learning difficulties, and what they needed from Knowl View special school in Rochdale was care. What they got, according to Phil Shepherd, a council HIV-prevention officer, was the risk of Aids.

> Mr Shepherd was horrified by the situation he discovered when he made a sex-education day visit to the residential school in March 1991. In a report he made within a week to the town's director of education, Mrs Diana Cavanagh, he set out a picture grimmer than anything Dickens imagined for Dotheboys Hall. He wrote 'One boy who is homosexual has contact with an adult outside the school. Several of the senior boys indulge in oral sex with one another.' Reputedly five of the junior boys have been or are involved in 'cottaging' in and around public toilets. Men as far away as Sheffield are believed to be aware of this activity and travel to Rochdale to take part.

Also, on 5 September 1995, HTV Wales screened a documentary entitled *The Old School Ties* in which eight disabled people recounted their experience of attending segregated schools and all claimed it had damaged them in one way or another. On 21 September, in the same series, there was an excellent account of the benefits of integration in the form of one of the best British documentaries on this issue.

The consequences of adopting the medical model and all this entails can be quite devastating for a minority of segregated children and these examples, drawn from a single week in September 1995, are by no means isolated cases. Children are clearly placed at greater risk by being sent to segregated institutions away from the public gaze, and we know it was this same pattern of abuse and denial of basic rights which led to the mental handicap hospital closure programme which is still ongoing.

We have seen then that many of the problems which afflict children with special needs are concerned with the way in which service professionals construe their roles and design services. We have seen also that these failures are, in large part, rooted in their having embraced an unhelpful ideology of who the children are and what they need in their lives.

THE PROFESSIONALISATION OF SPECIAL EDUCATION

The professionalisation of special education as a sub-discipline of general education has been paralleled by the development of allied sub-disciplines within medicine. Hence we have witnessed the gradual evolution of what have been described as ancillary medical services for people with impairments. Such relatively young disciplines as speech therapy, physiotherapy and occupational therapy have become an essential part of the contribution of the health authority towards meeting the non-educational – but also, very importantly, the educational – needs of many children with special needs.

An uneasy, and at times fraught, alliance has developed between these health-based special needs professionals and those based in education. Much of the unease that often lies close to the surface is rooted in the ongoing (but rarely discussed) struggle between health and education professionals for 'ownership of the client'.

The ever-increasing professionalisation of our lives, which has been an ongoing process since the middle of the 19th century, has resulted in the consolidation of the power of professionals over the way we think and act and has had profound consequences for our autonomy as citizens. As Skrtic (1991) points out:

> The professions extended their influence and consolidated their authority in society on the basis of two claims (a) that they had access to the scientific knowledge that society needed to achieve the good life, and (b) that they would release nature's potential in society in a disinterested way, in the interest of the common good, rather than for personal gain (Haskell 1984; Haber 1964). On the basis of these claims, advocates of professionalisation characterised professionals as the personification of the victory of science over traditional authority, and professionalisation as the institutionalisation of the ethic of service as a restraint on capitalistic self-interest. (p.4)

This rather grand claim on behalf of professionals has always been questioned, and particularly from a sociological perspective, in that it fails to take account of the inherently self-interested and bureaucratic way in which professional practice has evolved. Indeed, looking closely at services for devalued people, it is sometimes difficult to see how the benefits to the client even begin to match up to those enjoyed by the service professional. The cars parked outside the Adult Training Centre or the Community Home belong to the staff. The clients have to travel in a highly-visible social services bus or a vehicle labelled 'AMBULANCE', which is symbolically marked as a charitable gift from some worthy cause. Worse still is the increasing tendency for professionals to put their duty to their employer above all else, including the legitimate claim of their client for just treatment. Nowhere in the human service system is this tendency more evidently damaging than in the education service, where the compulsory segregation of vulnerable children remains a largely unchallenged institutionalised practice.

Professional practice in special education (as elsewhere) has tended to become more and more specialised with individual professionals learning more and more about less and less, to the point where each seems to have needed to take control of his/her own part of the child. Hence the teacher deals with the child's cognitive development, the classroom assistant with the care and self-help skills, the speech therapist with communication and eating, the physiotherapist with bodily posture and movement, the doctor with physical pathology and the occupational therapist with adaptation to the environment. There are, of course, many other slightly more peripheral specialists who all have their own distinctive contribution to make. These include: teachers of children with sensory impairments, sight and hearing, teachers specialising in dyslexia, teachers specialising in movement therapy, music therapy, etc., optometrists, opthalmologists, paediatricians, bioengineers (seating experts) and so on – so many people with a need to make their own particular highly specialised contribution and so much danger of fragmentation of the child's life and experience.

In special education we have also witnessed the appearance of new and somewhat questionable specialisms such as hydrotherapy, aromatherapy, rebound therapy and hippo-therapy, Snoezelen rooms and light-stimulation therapy. One segregated residential special school even offers what it calls 'daily living therapy' in which otherwise completely segregated pupils are taken out for forays into the community to see how regular citizens go about their daily routines.

PROFESSIONAL 'CURE' OR SPONTANEOUS REMISSION

Unscrambling what is actually going on within any human service is a complex process. Human nature is such that we are rarely able to stand aside from an activity in which we are engaged to reflect dispassionately upon what it is we are doing in relation to what we are trying to achieve. There is a deep-rooted tendency for us to assume that we are doing that which we aspire to and hence that we are achieving a measure of success in our lives and our work. The mission statement of any human service should be viewed with some caution since there is invariably a mismatch between what its high-minded aspirations describe (and what its high-flown phrases mean) and what is actually achieved on a day-to-day basis. This is particularly true where the service is for societally devalued people.

However much we might try to persuade ourselves and others, professional practice is not immune from this tendency and across the professional spectrum we see individuals, and sometimes whole service systems, struggling to project an image of their work which is consonant with its avowed aspirations. Hence the medical profession maintain the myth that they, by and large, 'cure' their patients and find it difficult to accommodate the notion that they may do harm. Yet there is a burgeoning body of evidence that mainstream professional practice may actually create dangerous conditions because of the way it treats its patients. There is even a term to describe these unwanted effects of treatment – iatrogenic (doctor-caused) illness. Similarly, psychiatrists, psychologists, social workers, special needs teachers and many other professional groups claim to alleviate the conditions of those they serve, but all too frequently fail to effect significant change – and in some cases do actual harm.

That some individuals are genuinely helped is not in question. It is, rather, the extent of the help which is claimed which concerns those peering in from the outside. What is true is that many conditions and symptoms undergo spontaneous remission over time, independently of any professional intervention, and this remains an utterly mysterious process. Not surprisingly, many such remissions will coincide with the individual receiving professional help – which is in itself unhelpful but which, with the benefit of hindsight, is seen to have 'effected the cure'.

None of this should be taken to imply that these professionals are acting in an underhand way to deceive their client, patient or pupil but rather that their desire to help, linked to a sometimes inflated view of the efficacy of their discipline, leads them to believe they have played a significant role in the process. There will be occasions when such professional confidence will also serve to engender a much more positive attitude in the person being helped, so that a claim such as 'I can cure you' becomes a self-fulfilling prophecy. We should here recall Merton's aforementioned dictum (p.???). Hence if a high status or otherwise credible person predicts an event, others will believe that the event will occur and behave in ways which are compatible with the reality of the event already having occurred. One would naturally expect that children with special needs would progressively overcome their learning difficulties in an environment of positive teacher expectations which would serve to increase self-belief, which in turn would promote greater effort and improved performance. Sadly, this is often not the case. Special education pathologises individual learners and so reinforces failure. It all too frequently does this by removing children from ordinary valued classroom settings to receive 'specialist' help in ways which are deeply stigmatising. This happens in a variety of ways in ordinary schools, but most damagingly when a child is removed to a separate 'special' school.

In Chapter 5 we shall look at the way in which services are presently evaluated and how alternative approaches may produce a very different picture of what segregated schools and classes can do for children.

Chapter 4

The Meaning of Integration

FOR SOME CHILDREN SEGREGATION IS THE NORM

Rejection is endemic

This chapter will explore our understanding of the meaning of integration and in so doing provide a critique of the arrangements typically made for those children not presently expected to be educated in the mainstream. The focus will be on trying to make sense of the linked notions of 'integration' and 'segregation' and so, I hope, provide a better understanding of what children need in their lives. Our starting point, then, is the assumption that the *status quo* means segregation for some children because they have additional needs which we would not usually expect to meet in an ordinary classroom.

Because the arrangements we make for children are largely determined by the way in which we make sense of our world, it is important that we try to understand why some ways of doing things are preferred to others. This requires us to look at the meanings we attach to certain key events and the language we use to describe those events. The kinds of events we shall be concerned with here are those involving the educational placement of children with significant additional needs. At present in the UK, as in most of the rest of the world where universal schooling is available, such children are almost certain to be placed in segregated settings. This, for the time being, is the almost reflexive response of the whole service system to the needs of these children. It is important to understand that although in Britain the LEA makes the placement decision, it is nevertheless, only the lead agency for children with severe and complex disabilities, and the health authority and social services departments also play an important part in providing services, and they too see segregation as the right response.

Beyond the service system, the general public also have a view and this, by and large, supports the way in which services operate. If asked for his view, 'the man on the Clapham omnibus' would be likely to say that it is only common sense that separate arrangements need to be made for *some* children and that the child needs to be educated separately for his education to be meaningful.

It is important to have an understanding of the depth of our societal conviction of the rightness of segregation if we are to have any chance of bringing about lasting change. To underestimate the societal forces operating to separate those who are seen as 'different' would be a serious and perhaps costly mistake. Too many of those who have attended an *inclusive education* event here in the UK have succumbed to the temptation to believe including disabled children is easy. To those who may currently be preaching the virtues of *inclusion*, I would just say that you may be in danger of raising expectations which will later be unceremoniously dashed against the rocks of societal prejudice. There is the potential for additional pain here for those parents who have already experienced the hurt of having their child rejected and misunderstanding the forces of societal resistance to including certain children is as dangerous as colluding unconditionally with those forces and never trying for something better.

THE PUZZLING LANGUAGE OF 'INTEGRATION/ SEGREGATION'

Our societal embarrassment about making separate arrangements for children is evidenced by the euphemistic language the professionals have evolved to describe the different kinds of placement arrangements they make for children with special educational needs (SENs). A place in a special school, special class or unit in a mainstream school is *never* described as a *segregated* placement. We are relatively content to engage in practices which are segregative but shrink from talking about them as such. The problem here is that there is no real possibility of attaching a positive meaning to such a term because it violates our most basic social instincts. The opposite is of course the case with the term *integration*, which has a warm and positive glow – embodying as it does all of what we like to think of as our humanitarian and essentially accepting instincts towards our fellow human beings.

At the other extreme, and under the slightest pretext, an arrangement will be described as *integrated* even when the child spends his or her entire time in a disability-specific isolated setting. Some special schools too play this language game when, for example, they arrange sessions for pupils in the special needs class to join other more able groups elsewhere in the school. Such an arrangement will usually be described as 'integration'.

Since the language of special education is confusing, it is as well to resort to the arbiter of common usage – the dictionary. According to the Oxford English Dictionary (1989), the definition of the verb 'integrate' is:

> to render entire or complete to make up, compose, constitute (a whole): said of the parts or elements...to complete or perfect (what is imperfect) by the addition of the necessary parts...to put or bring together (parts or elements) so as to form one whole; to combine into a whole...to bring (racially or culturally differentiated peoples into equal membership of a society or system; to cease to segregate.

and of the adjective segregated:

> separated, set apart, isolated...separated (wholly or partially) from the parent or from one another; not aggregated...to separate or isolate (one thing) from others, or one portion from the remainder; to place in a group apart from the rest...the enforced separation of different racial groups in a country, community, or institution (Apartheid)...the isolation or separate confinement of dangerous or troublesome prisoners.

Implicit in these common usage definitions is the idea that to integrate is to *improve* or *perfect* and to *make whole*, whilst to segregate is to isolate that which is seen as troublesome or a threat. It may be seen as pedantic to resort to the dictionary in order to clarify the meaning of our language but, in the case of the terms concerned, it is clear that over the years of their use within the special education context they have suffered from a degree of semantic drift. Some will argue that such terms have acquired their own meaning within education which is separate from that which the same terms will have acquired in other contexts, so the resort to root or core definitions is irrelevant. That is precisely what has happened, and just as no group can use language in a way which is at odds with the rest of the linguistic community, neither can they highjack particular words and impose their own idiosyncratic semantic straightjacket upon them. It is completely wrong, therefore, for educationalists to continue to use the language of segregation/integration in the way they have because they do both themselves and their pupils/students an injustice. The injustice to themselves is the relatively inconsequential one of self-deception, whereas the injustice to those learners who are segregated is a grave one – that of denied opportunity.

Some in special education will not accept this analysis, arguing that it wholly misrepresents their position because, in the social context, the notions of integration and segregation relate to whether or not children are grouped or kept in individual isolation, not whether children with particular disabilities are separated from non-disabled children. Their argument might even be extended to become an attack on their critics for seeming to imply that it is not worth spending time with disabled children.

Again, this is a distortion of the position of those who criticise special education and who would point to the consensual definition of the terms (integration and segregation) which embrace the notion of groupings within society and not merely the separation of individuals from their natural peer groups. Because we use language in this way, we clearly mean to invest it with notions of social oppression (by one group against another) as well as the oppression of an individual by his or her peers, or by the system.

Integration – high and low definitions

The so-called *Great Debate* on integration (organised by the then British Institute for Mental Handicap) which took place in Manchester in May 1992 during National Integration Week addressed the motion that 'special schools should be abolished' and was criticised by some at the time for polarising views and 'undermining constructive debate'. This criticism itself is interesting because it seems to imply that the answer to the problem probably lies in a service continuum, since neither end of the spectrum is likely to be viable for every child. If those on either side of the debate are using the same words but with very different meanings attached to them, it is hardly surprising that communication is so poor. One possible explanation might be that it is these usually unexplicated, implicit meanings which are at the root of the problem.

Because the integration debate continues to generate so much heat with little or no enlightenment amongst the protagonists, we need to look for some – perhaps less obvious – explanation than has emerged hitherto. One possible source of confusion might be due to those on either side of the divide operating with very different constructs of what is to count as 'integration' and 'segregation'; more specifically, that the critics of segregation subscribe to a 'high definition' while the defenders of segregation have a 'low definition'. Leaving on one side for the moment the possible grounds for an individual holding a high or low definition, the following may be taken as a rough illustration of each.

INCLUSION – A HIGH DEFINITION

A high definition may be equated with what some are now describing as *full inclusion*, which contains a number of key requirements concerning the desirable daily experiences of the child in question. These are that the child attend his *local mainstream* school, that he be in an *age-appropriate* class and that he *share the majority of the class lessons* with his classmates. An additional requirement would be that the school expend some effort to ensure that he is *socially integrated outside school hours*. Such a definition of integration would be called 'high' because it contains a demanding (its critics might say impossible for some children) set of criteria which need to be satisfied before the child may be said to be truly 'integrated'.

'TASTER' INTEGRATION – A LOW DEFINITION

Alternatively, a 'low' definition may only require that a child have one or more other children with him throughout the day in any setting, which might include a quite separate school. This would be the lowest possible definition and most would not find this acceptable. The more typical version of a low definition would be that offered by the special school, or special class in an ordinary school, in which the child spends most of his time pursuing his lessons in a disability-specific separate group with some limited opportunity to be with other typical children, albeit not those children who come from his own home community. It would be fair to say that many defenders of this 'low' definition example of integration would not so much wish to claim that it represents integration as that it is *not* segregation. This is an important distinction and brings us back to the earlier point that some words just stick in the throat because they have connotations which we find morally objectionable. This is undoubtedly the case with the notion of segregation.

There is a further paradox in the thinking of those who attempt to justify segregation, which it concerns their differential attitude towards the separation of an individual from a group. It is never argued that a child should be individually isolated to receive his or her education, yet it seems to some that one only has to add one or two children and everything will then be fine. This situation may arise in a small special school for children with complex needs where groupings may occasionally be as few as three or four in a class. The point here is that teachers will not accept that it is right for a child to be educated entirely alone, although they will be happy if one or two additional children are introduced – even if those children are profoundly handicapped and unable to interact with one another. What this shows is that teachers (and others in special education) are in fact operating with a distorted notion of what counts as integration or segregation; in other words, the notion that a disabled child cannot be truly said to be segregated unless he is *completely alone* and that to introduce another child or two – even if they are unable to offer companionship – changes everything.

Current terminology

A not insignificant part of our current difficulty is that we remain trapped within a narrowly circumscribed range of notions of what might count as 'integration'. This is due in no small measure to the poverty of the language we have used to express our ideas. If language plays a crucial role in structuring perception, our current terminology would be unlikely to inspire subtle and insightful conceptualisation.

That language plays a key part in structuring the ways in which we make sense of the world is now well understood, and a language rich in its ability to identify and elaborate the more subtle conceptualisations of experience, and to differentiate between discrete elements of reality, will serve its users better than one which is cruder in its reference. That some Eskimos are able to distinguish between 20 different types of snow according to the prevailing conditions is important when the well-being of the individual or group depends upon making such fine discriminations.

Closer to home, I recently bought my first hi-fi system and, during the process of decision-making, briefly entered a whole new world of auditory discrimination and interpretation. For a person who had always judged the output of music systems on the spectrum 'loud' to 'quiet', it was temporarily disempowering to hear the qualities of sound emanating from the speakers described as 'stereo images which are quite well focused with fairly good depth in the upper range' and specific sounds described as 'warm', 'clean', 'smooth and balanced', with a certain amount of 'dryness' and 'transient attack', not too 'overdamped', 'foggy' or 'sibilant'. Such niceties are as far from my aural discriminatory capacities as are 19 out of the 20 grades of snow recognised by the Eskimo.

To understand a set of complex phenomena requires two things: (1) some familiarity with the events in question and (2) some form of language or symbolism for interpreting and describing those events. It is probably futile to ask whether the Eskimo would have been able to make the snow discriminations had he not created the language with which to describe the range of difference. Conceptual development, even if it does not entirely depend upon linguistic elaboration, is certainly aided by it, and that is all we need to know.

Our range of concepts for integration/segregation remain at a primitive level for two main reasons: (1) we have very little good practice and (2) we have a stunted vocabulary to describe even the spectrum of existing arrangements, let alone the totality of possibilities. It is important that we extend our vocabulary to alert one another to the possibilities we have yet to explore. The terminology we have had available since the Warnock Committee reported in 1978 (HMSO 1978) is limited to the following: *social, locational* and *functional* – integration. These are usually understood in the following way:

- *Locational* integration means no more than that children share the same school campus, that is their education is located in the same set of buildings. In reality, many children who are locationally integrated experience little or no curriculum integration and attend a mainstream school miles from where they live.

- *Social* integration is taken to mean children mixing outside lesson times, that is in the playground at play and lunch times and possibly also on trips out of school.

- *Functional* integration is taken to mean full integration as a member of the school community with as much time as is deemed possible in an ordinary classroom. It is true that functional integration could mean being treated in the same way as all other children in the school but this is rarely the case for the children who are the main focus of this book.

The Warnock committee dealt with the theory of integration in less than two pages (ibid.) commenting that:

> We have distinguished three main forms of integration. They are not discrete, but overlapping, and although each has a validity of its own they represent progressive stages of association. They provide a serviceable framework for discussion both of the nature of integration and of the means of planning its effective provision' and furthermore that 'The concept of these three characteristic forms of integration – locational, social and functional – sharpens discussion of its meaning. Each element of the triad has a separate validity, although the functional element is perhaps uppermost in most people's minds when they speak of integration. Together these elements provide a framework for the planning and organisation of new arrangements for the education of children with special educational needs jointly with other children, and later for judgement of how effectively it has been achieved. (7.6–7.11)

Warnock's contribution to the integration debate was helpful, if superficial, and, with the benefit of hindsight, we can now see that the committee should have drawn upon a number of strands of sociological and social psychological research to deepen their analysis of the meaning of integration/segregation. The report contains no such deeper analysis of the social meaning of segregation (although there was a rich source of literature on deviancy and deviancy-making in human services available (Wolfensberger 1975)) and hence was unable to move beyond a value-free description of what *integration* could mean. This failure to treat integration as one pole of a bi-polar construct is less surprising when we reflect upon the phenomenon of unconsciousness as a device for protecting us against moral dissonance. Clearly the committee members were either unfamiliar with this literature or could not see its relevance to the world of education; either way it was a lost opportunity. The only conclusion we can draw is that they did not see segregation as an issue to get all steamed up about.

North American terminology

In Britain we typically adopt terminology which has already gained currency in North America and particularly in the USA. This is as true for the world of education as for most other areas of our lives. That American English is becoming the lingua franca of most of the English speaking world makes it more or less inevitable that as the language migrates, so does the culture in which that language is rooted.

In special education in the USA, the term *mainstreaming* has come to be synonymous with the term *integration*. The term *mainstreaming* is used to describe the integration of pupils with disabilities into regular (ordinary) classes or schools. This means it is broad enough to encompass the child who is fully included in the ordinary class as well as the child who is in a separate class somewhere within the school. This is the equivalent of our *locational integration*.

In the USA, the term 'mainstreaming' is used about as broadly as is the term 'integration' in Britain, and this has generated heated debate about what it implies for children. Some have argued that it means merely dumping children to fend for themselves unsupported in a largely unwelcoming or even a hostile school environment, while others say it means carefully integrating pupils with extensive prior planning and appropriate supports. The reality is that *mainstreaming*, like *integration*, means hugely different things to different people and hence, as a term, is about as unhelpful.

American special needs legislation

Special education in the USA is dominated by the *Right to Education for All Handicapped Children Act* (Public Law 94–142 (Sarason and Doris 1979)) which was designed to provide equal access to education for disabled children as was already enjoyed by their non-disabled peers. The Act was rooted in a widespread belief that millions of disabled children were not receiving appropriate educational services and that many were entirely excluded from the public school community. The law itself embraced the following six general principles:

Principle 1.   All children have a right to a free and appropriate public education (the zero rejection principle).

Principle 2.   The consent of parents is essential in identifying and planning for a child's education and in making an educational placement.

Principle 3. The right to an individualised educational programme (IEP) which would define the educational service the child would receive.

Principle 4. The right to be educated in the Least Restrictive Environment (that the child be educated with non-disabled children).

Principle 5. The right to Non-discriminatory Testing and Evaluation (that the test used should be fair).

Principle 6. The right of parents to be involved in the whole process of assessment and planning.

The existence of such apparently empowering legislation has certainly strengthened the resolve of some parents to seek a more inclusive school placement for their child, but has by no means proved a panacea for all. A major obstacle has been the lack of an agreed definition of what 'mainstreaming' is supposed to be. The legislation does not define what is meant by the 'least restrictive environment' or 'mainstreaming'. As it is in Britain in relation to 'integration', so it is in the USA for 'mainstreaming': both have a legal basis, but one which is too vague and imprecise to guarantee a particular kind or quality of experience for a child. We are thus left with the reality that there are types of integration which may range from the virtually complete segregation of a child within a disability-specific special class in an ordinary school to the fully functional participation of a child in an ordinary classroom within that same school.

THE MOTIVATION TO INTEGRATE

This chapter is, in part, about the need to try to identify the meanings people attach to terms, and this is often determined by their relationship to the child. A parent may well attach a meaning which is different to that which is in the mind of the headteacher, administrator or school psychologist. The motivation the individual has may well be determined by such diverse factors as the need to:

- comply with the law
- feel that one's child will make friends
- appear to an inspector to be pursuing a progressive philosophy

- do what the headteacher says the school's philosophy requires
- appease a parent
- provide a basic right.

These divergent motivations to integrate or mainstream will in turn be determined by a number of other factors such as:

- the view taken of the meaning of disability
- the perception of how others might respond to our action
- the understanding of what education is in its very essence
- the view taken of the needs of typical pupils.

Whatever the underlying dynamics which result in different stances being taken in this debate, we are faced with the reality of services which continue to segregate children and groups of professionals who continue to offer justifications for supporting such a state of affairs.

THE UNDERLYING ISSUES

In his book *Behind Special Education* (1991) Thomas Skrtic outlines what he calls the 'grounding assumptions' of special education in the USA. He then goes on to summarise the debate between the Regular Education Initiative (REI) proponents and their opponents who support the Education for All Handicapped Children Act 1975 (EHA), the core principles of which we have already examined. What he calls the grounding assumptions of special education are the basic body of beliefs of professionals about the key constructs which give the whole notion of special education meaning. He says these are that:

1. Disabilities are pathological conditions that students have.

2. Differential diagnosis is objective and useful.

3. Special education is a rationally conceived and co-ordinated system of services that benefits diagnosed students.

4. Progress results from incremental technological improvements in diagnosis and instructional interventions.

He goes on to say that beliefs of this kind 'define and subsume the models, practices, and tools that special educators use to perform services to clients' (p.54). Put another way, it is possession of these core assumptions or beliefs which determine how the professions also organise and deliver a special education service. These beliefs are of two kinds: beliefs about human pathology and beliefs about the nature of the organisational response to such pathology.

One of Skrtic's main claims is that the debate has centred on the efficacy of the ethics and methods of special education and not on its assumptions and theories. Looking at the mainstreaming debate arising out of the EHA/REI debate, he says the EHA/mainstreaming model is based upon the same grounding assumptions, theories, etc., as the traditional special classroom /segregation model. As he sees it, the problem with the EHA/mainstreaming model is that it does not question the adequacy of the general education programme or the way in which schools have traditionally operated. The argument was simply for greater access to such a programme for children with disabilities. The REI debate, on the other hand, argues for a fundamental change in what typically goes on in schools because it is seen as unhelpful to students with disabilities. In taking this position, its proponents are saying that the problem lies largely outside the pupil in the organisation of the school and the wider system. The problem as Skrtic sees it is that those involved in the REI debate do not see where the source of the problem lies, which is in the failure to locate the connection between practices and assumptions. The REI proponents subscribe to a more socially inclusive school system which makes provision for children with disabilities and reject the notion of a continuum of provision, which is essentially the EHA position. Basically, the REI advocates have characterised their opponents as segregationists.

It is a central argument of this book that Skrtic's analysis is the right one if special education is to be able to address its own internal contradictions. This must involve professionals and policy makers in looking beyond the interminable and unproductive debate about practice to an analysis of its core beliefs and assumptions. This is essentially what is being said by the proponents of the social model of disability, along with those who use a normalisation perspective.

I would also like to endorse the REI proponents' thesis that, in proposing a mainstreaming model, the EHA advocates all too readily accept the *status quo* within the mainstream – which is essentially hostile to children with additional needs. The EHA position is remarkably similar to the position taken by the overwhelming majority of special needs professionals in Britain, which is the main reason for this book.

A SPECTRUM OF OPPORTUNITIES

That this debate is not merely an ivory tower exchange between academics and theoreticians, and that there are very real consequences for the daily experiences of many thousands of children, is not something over which there can any longer be any serious doubt. The data presented in successive reports by the Centre for Studies on Integration in Education provides ample evidence of both the extent of segregation and the degree to which it is still a function of geographical happenstance.

In its most recent report (Norwich 1994), CSIE provide segregation statistics for children in the age range 5–15 years in English schools (there is no comparable analysis for Wales and Scotland) and also information on pupils with Statements in ordinary schools for 1992. With a caution as to the accuracy of some of the Department for Education (DFE) data, they provide the following picture.

The proportion of pupils in special schools

In England, over the period 1988–1992, there was a small but gratifying decrease in special school placements (from 1.52% to 1.49%), although there was a worrying increase over the period 1991–1992 (from 1.47% to 1.49%). The overall context for these two comparisons is a decrease in special school placements over the decade 1982–1992 (from 1.72% to 1.49%).

Possibly the most significant comparison in these results is the most recent increase – which might turn out to be an inexplicable anomaly in a steadily decreasing pattern of special school placements, but might also reflect a dangerous dynamic in the system. The CSIE analysis suggests a possible influence of the ongoing impact of the Local Management of Schools initiative and the national testing programme introduced by the Education Reform Act 1988 – the suggestion being that mainstream schools are moving more children with difficulties into special schools 'because they represent too great a challenge to the new working arrangements' (ibid., p.10). The analysis also shows that the difference between LEAs in their segregating tendencies is as great as ever, with the least segregating placing just 0.45 per cent and the most 2.98 per cent.

These periodic reports from CSIE are to be welcomed because they serve the function of what might be seen as a 'public watchdog' on what LEAs are doing. However, valuable though these reports are, it would be even more helpful if CSIE began to think a little harder about the deeper meaning of integration/segregation and not restrict its analysis to the simple surface issue of the mainstream versus special school placement comparison, important though this is.

Segregation in the mainstream

Whilst many people quite understandably point to the injustice of separate school placement, a significant number of children are subjected to a similar human rights violation which, for CSIE, goes largely unremarked. This relates to the 42.1 per cent of Statemented pupils aged 5–15 years in the mainstream, nearly a quarter of whom are in segregated classes. A further hidden statistic here is that of the children who are in a mainstream school out of their own home area. That CSIE express no concern over segregation within the mainstream is surprising but may be due in part to the fact that the background of their workers is in journalism rather than education, thus making it difficult for them to grasp the full implications of educational segregation.

Long before the battle to end the segregated special school has been won there will be a dawning of awareness of the system of segregation that will take its place; indeed, the building blocks of that system are already out there in the educational mainstream. I am, of course, talking about the segregated 'special class'.

SEGREGATION BY ANOTHER NAME?

A small number of authorities are already quite well advanced with their programmes to eventually close all their special schools and replace them with segregated units and classes in ordinary schools. The tide of public opinion is turning (albeit painfully slowly) against the practice of segregation; although it might be many years before we see the demise of the special school, it will come. It will come because such a practice is at odds with our developing societal ideology which says it is wrong to segregate. The evidence for this is that we have now eliminated the system of placing children in large mental handicap hospitals which are also seen as equally unsuitable for adults. The *care in the community* programme is sweeping away a whole system of human management which is now understood to have been misconceived because it was based on a flimsy charade, that is that people who are sufficiently different are essentially sick and/or highly vulnerable and need to be kept apart in their own best interest. The charade was, of course, that their separation was mistakenly understood to be in society's best interest and not that of the institutionalised people concerned. What is breaking down, however, is not the fear and loathing of difference but our resolve as a society to continue with a contradiction which is so hard to sustain; we have understood the illogicality of our segregative practices but we have not yet overcome our revulsion for those we do not want to be around us. The response of the service system to this dilemma is the compromise of continuing to segregate whilst appearing to do the opposite, which for the education system means moving children onto the site of the ordinary school whilst maintaining social and educational distance.

One LEA is so far down the road towards this new model of segregation that it is able to proudly boast 'that they are amongst the top ten integrating authorities in Britain' which, on the criteria they cite, is a just claim. This authority cites a segregation figure of just 0.4 per cent of all pupils in segregated schools and on this basis claims to be just about the most integrated in Britain. On the face of it this is an astonishingly low figure when set against a national average for England of 1.49 per cent in 1992 (we have no more recent figures to hand) and with the 20 least integrated authorities within the range 1.93 per cent – 2.98 per cent. However, here as elsewhere, things are not quite what they seem.

It sometimes seems that our desire to appear to be pursuing integration is impelled more by a desire to appear 'ideologically sound' than to provide what children really need. Over the years this has created what I have called (Hall 1992b) an 'integration salad...a bewildering array of activities and organisational forms which are described as "integrated"' (p.21).

The new segregation

The reality, though, for the LEA with just 0.4 per cent of its pupils in special schools is that it maintains around 30 largely segregated units in its ordinary schools which lack expertise and draw children from a very wide area. The children who attend these 'special classes' will typically spend a very high proportion of their school day segregated within a disability group and have to travel to and from the school in special transport. One of the major obstacles to integration created by this system is that the children do not meet their fellow pupils outside school because they mostly live some way beyond the school's catchment area. So this is the 'new segregation' once again masquerading as a service which is able to meet the needs of the individual. Before long these special classes will have swept away most of the segregated schools and, in so doing, will have served to salve the consciences of those who, while having acknowledged the contradictions of the separate school, have failed to rise to the real challenge of integration.

Degrees of segregation

The range of possible forms of integration/segregation for children with the most challenging needs is depicted in Figure 4.1 below. This analysis is in terms of what is generally socially valued or devalued, which is discussed in Chapters 3 and 5.

Figure 4.1 attempts to describe the spectrum of possible placement arrangements for children who would typically have to attend a special school because the policy in their authority would not allow an ordinary school placement, even if that is what the parent had requested. The range of opportunities is described along a spectrum from complete (educational mainstream) *exclusion* to full *inclusion*, in which the former is understood to be socially devalued and the latter socially valued. The range of options described inevitably implies *social* as well as *educational* consequences, since, as is the case

- Attending a residential special school and going to an **institutional** 'home' for breaks
- Attending a residential special school and going to a **substitute** home for breaks
- Attending a residential special school and going to **one's own** home for breaks
- Attending a day segregated special school with no integration opportunities*
- Attending a day segregated special school and having **other pupils visit for lessons**
- Attending a day segregated special school and visiting **any ordinary school**†
- Visiting an ordinary school which is the child's **own neighbourhood school**
- Joining assembly/breaks/lunchroom from an **on-site special class** in an ordinary school
- Joining **selected lessons** from an otherwise separate special class
- Being a full-time ordinary class member but **age-inappropriately**
- Being a full-time member of an ordinary class **age-appropriately**
- Being a full-time member of an age-appropriate class but doing **one's own separate lessons**
- Being a full-time member of an age-appropriate class doing **the same lessons as the others** but in isolation
- Being a full-time member of an age-appropriate class doing the same lessons as the others **with** the others
- Being a full-time member of an age-appropriate class doing the same lessons as the others, with the others, and it **mattering if you are not there**

**Exclusion
(Socially devalued)**

Spectrum of social value/devaluation attached to school placement

**Inclusion
(Socially valued)**

The ultimate goal of integration – full inclusion

- Being a **full** member of an **age-appropriate** class in your own **neighbourhood school/college** doing the **same** lessons as the others **with** the others, and it **mattering if you are not there**. Plus you **have friends who spend time with you outside school/college**.

* The accepted situation for most children in severe learning difficulty (SLD) special schools.
† Typically the highest level of integration aspired to by special schools and LEAs for these children.

Source: Hall (1990)

Figure 4.1 Different forms of educational and social segregation/integration (Sixteen degrees of possible community involvement/separation for some children and young people receiving 'special' education)

with any educational placement there can be no educational arrangement which is entirely neutral in regard to a child's social life.

Within the range of options available, the current typical arrangements for such children are identified as lying largely toward the exclusion/socially devalued end of the spectrum. This means that, in spite of enabling legislation, LEAs in England and Wales are still failing to integrate the 106,000 children who must attend special schools (Audit Commission/HMI 1992a), well as a deceptively high proportion of the approximately 65,000 children with a Statement who do not attend a special school but who are segregated within the mainstream.

CAN THE SPECIAL SCHOOL DELIVER INTEGRATION?

Given the broad range of meanings which current usage allows, the answer to the question 'can the special school deliver integration?' has to be 'yes', and it can do so in two main ways. It can send children out individually or in small groups to mainstream schools to join in lessons and break times or it might import groups of children in from the mainstream to share the lessons in the special school. Such involvement may rightly be called integrative because there is nothing in the way this term is defined which would disqualify it from being applied.

The question of whether the special school can deliver 'integration' of the kind the parent *wants* and the child *needs* is a different matter. It is fair to say that some parents only want their child to make the occasional visit to a (any) mainstream school, and hence that such a parent would not be critical of such a casual arrangement. However, others desire a more intensive involvement and feel that this should be with the child's *local* mainstream school. Some of these parents would like their child ideally to be able to attend their local school for a significant part of the week, progressively building towards full-time attendance. In such a situation the parent may see the child transferring onto the roll of the school and severing all links with the special school. So the question 'can the special school deliver integration?' is one which admits of a variety of answers, dependent upon how it is interpreted.

The report of the professional Association of Educational Psychologists (AEP) working party on integration (1989), which is discussed in more detail in Chapter 8, refers to the 'good practice in many special schools', which, in some cases, is described as 'exemplary', but the report fails to define the standard by which such a description might be judged. This report also makes the point that segregation does not end at the gates of the special school since, within some special schools, organisational expediency requires the maintenance of a 'micro system of segregation' which, in the case of schools for children with severe learning difficulties (SLDs), tends to involve a segregated 'care' unit for pupils with exceptional needs. The Association rightly make the point that this renders such groups the most isolated in the entire educational system and hence vulnerable to the greatest level of marginalisation and social devaluation.

SHOULD THE SPECIAL SCHOOL DELIVER INTEGRATION?

This is a difficult question and one upon which there is little consensus. It is certainly an expectation built into the legislation (HMSO 1993) and successive Government reports that, where possible, children should be educated in ordinary schools. However, the fact that this is a duty which is heavily qualified within the law has not been helpful in promoting integration.

The question is also open to more than one interpretation. It could be taken to be a question about the fundamental purpose of the special school, perhaps as a place whose primary or even sole function is to prepare children for life in the mainstream. Alternatively, and perhaps more realistically, it could be a question about a possible role in providing some mainstream involvement as part of the special school curriculum.

Many special schools acknowledge their duty to provide their pupils with experience in a mainstream setting and this is likely to be in the form of a group or individual visit, possibly on a regular basis. One school, which I visited in the course of carrying out an evaluation, ran what it called a 'taster integration' programme. A teacher was employed full-time to take children to mainstream schools on a weekly basis to join in lessons with children of about the same age. This programme of visits was run as an adjunct to the special school curriculum, with no particular objectives in mind other than to give the children experience of a mainstream classroom. Few, if any, of the children visited what would have been their local neighbourhood school and in no case was there an intention to significantly increase the contact, let alone build towards full-time attendance. The staff in the special school were unclear as to what the school's 'integration' programme was supposed to be achieving and there was no evidence that the children involved were benefiting from the programme.

One of the original grounds for sending children to special schools was that such schools would be equipped to deliver relevant and intensive programmes designed to bring the child to a point where he could join or re-join the mainstream. The Warnock report (HMSO 1978, para 8.8) envisaged that special schools would have a role in taking children for short periods of time for intensive work then return them to ordinary schools. A recent Government report (Audit Commission/HMI 1992a) showed that this is not happening and that the only special schools that did so to any significant extent were schools or units whose primary function was the assessment of pupils. This report also noted that some special schools engage in 'outreach' work, in which the special school staff work to support pupils going to ordinary schools on a full or part-time basis, and also that some special schools took groups of pupils. A further finding of this most damning (of special education) report is that in a survey of 85 special schools, less than 2 per cent of pupils moved annually onto the roll of an ordinary school. The situation for a parent who would like to have their child moved to a mainstream school is that there is no incentive for the LEA – since it would have to fund the ordinary school place, plus the extra support the child would need, whilst also continuing to fund an empty place back in the special school.

If 'ought' implies 'can', it is important to ask whether the special school could, if it so wished, deliver some level of integration to its pupils. Some schools would no doubt argue that this would be difficult within their staffing levels, but it is always pertinent to ask how much effort the headteacher and governors have put into bringing about integration opportunities for their children; is there evidence of correspondence with the LEA to release additional resources and have they looked at the possibility of recruiting volunteers to work in the school so that experienced staff can be released?

There is also the issue of Statementing. Any child who is thought to be in need of integration opportunities should have that enshrined in his or her Statement as a specific need and as a quantified provision to match that need. Ensuring that this is achieved should be seen by the headteacher and governors as part of their responsibility, and failure to at least attempt this would once again indicate lack of commitment to integration.

FULL INCLUSION

I have already (albeit briefly) described the various forms of segregation that are practised within the British school system (Hall 1992a) but there is little in the literature which usefully develops the notion of integration in a way which would serve to illuminate current practice.

The term 'inclusive education' has been in use in Britain for just five years, having gained currency following the introduction of the annual inclusion conferences initiated by me in conjunction with Joe Whittaker of the Bolton Institute. It was Joe Whittaker's initial visit to Canada in the late 1980s that created the link with Marsha Forest, Judith Snow, Jack Pearpoint, George Flynn, John O'Brien and Herb Lovett, who were at that time involved in an annual international conference on inclusive education at McGill University in Montreal. At this conference in 1990, Joe Whittaker and I extended an invitation to the team to come to Britain the following year to speak at conferences in Cardiff and Manchester. These were three-day events and attracted parents and professionals many of whom already had a commitment to integration. Following these events, the term 'inclusion' began to be used as a more precise way of describing what British educationalists had called 'functional integration', that is integration which involved the child with special needs having a curriculum, rather than merely a social, involvement with his mainstream peers. The term inclusion, however, embraced a much deeper philosophical notion of what integration should mean and, in this sense, was truly prescriptive.

Perhaps the best way to characterise this difference is by recognising that in Britain commentators merely noted the various kinds of integration they saw about them and coined terms which served to describe what was happening; hence, as we saw earlier, the distinctions believed to be important were social, locational and functional integration. It was very different with the introduction of the term 'inclusive education', which was rooted in *prescription* rather than mere *description*. The North American proponents of full inclusion for all children took as their starting point that it is a matter of basic human rights that children should not be excluded from the educational mainstream; from the outset the meaning of inclusion is thus linked to notions of social justice and community presence and participation.

As for definitions, there is as yet no firm agreement, but taking account of the key elements of the social justice argument and linking this to the best practice that has emerged in North America, I would offer the following as the basis of a working definition. For the typical child to be fully included in the educational mainstream means:

> Being a full member of an age-appropriate class in your local school doing the same lessons as the other pupils and it mattering if you are not there. In addition, you have friends who spend time with you outside school.

If this is a definition of what being integrated (included) means for the typical child, it might still be inadequate for the child with a significant impairment because it makes the assumption that physical presence is sufficient. However, we know that individuals who do not have the skills to make the running in relationship-building often need help, so a better definition of full inclusion might be:

> Being a full member of an age-appropriate class in your local school/college doing the same lessons as the others with the others, and it mattering if you are not there. Also you have friends who spend time with you outside school/college plus others who care for you work hard to ensure that you are fully included

in the mainstream of community life and use generic services along with other citizens. (Hall 1992a, p.12)

Whilst any such definition is inevitably arbitrary, the key elements are nevertheless not negotiable. This definition makes it clear to the school that their role is much broader than merely ensuring the child has a programme of work in an ordinary classroom. It does this by highlighting the following key issues.

Age-appropriateness

This is indeed a key issue for people with learning difficulties, who tend to be treated age-inappropriately because it is believed that an individual's 'mental age' is measurable and furthermore that it provides a guide both to how they should be approached and how their time should be structured. It is important to relate to all children age-appropriately, otherwise they may fulfil what they feel you are asking of them, that is that they behave as would a much younger child.

Local school presence

Attending the school which serves the local community is, as we have seen, a socially valued thing to do. The value most people would identify is that it enables children to get to know each other and carry over those friendships into their lives outside school. Being included in school makes it less likely that a child will be excluded outside of school and vice versa.

Sharing lessons

Being accepted and included requires participation as well as mere physical presence and, contrary to the view of many educationalists, *any lesson can be interpreted for any child so as to make such participation meaningful.* Being physically present in the classroom creates the opportunity for interactions which would never occur if the child attended another school (perhaps a special school) in another part of town.

Making friendships and developing understanding

Getting to know others is not something thought worthy of planning for, or measuring, in our schools. This is what we have tended to call the *hidden curriculum,* which embraces those thousand-and-one interpersonal encounters, observations and other informal experiences that make up the typical school day. Learning what your peers wear, how they behave, what they like, what they aspire to; learning how adults other than your own parents relate to one another and to children; learning how to make and break friendships and what the power structure is within the school – these and many other learning opportunities are presented to children in school, but most are not on offer in a segregated special school.

Community competence

As well as denying opportunities to their own pupils, special schools serve also to undermine a key learning opportunity for all other children. They do this by ensuring that the minority of children spend their school years out of contact with their typical peers, who then cannot get to know them. That severely disabled children remain forever mysterious to most others in society is due, in large part, to the fact that they are absent from the places in which most people spend their time.

Getting to know how another human being without speech is able to communicate; learning how a child with little or no use of his limbs needs to be cared for and supported to learn; discovering how a person with a learning difficulty can begin to understand if taught differently – all of these opportunities are denied to children in mainstream schools. These lost opportunities to learn undermine the competence of whole communities to help vulnerable people. Perhaps most damaging of all is the lost opportunity for friendships to develop. If schools and colleges were to become inclusive they would set a better example to society of the way it should order itself.

So the main difference embodied in the North American term 'inclusion' from its closest (semantically) British counterpart – functional integration – is that inclusion embodies a range of assumptions about the meaning and purpose of schools which are not shared by most British educationalists. This goes to the heart of our continuing communication difficulty in that it reflects a different set of underlying grounding assumptions about the nature of education generally and not just special education.

WHAT ARE SCHOOLS FOR?

In Britain, as elsewhere in the developed world, education is seen largely as a process of formal knowledge and skill acquisition whereby children can be prepared for the job market. School attendance also serves as the means for releasing parents from their supervisory roles so that they can themselves go out to earn a living. Broadly speaking, within such a system, formal learning is the primary aim and the evaluation of progress of learners relates largely (although not exclusively) to measuring how much of this takes place. In Britain, there has been enormous controversy over the introduction, for the first time, of a National Curriculum as a means of standardising the subject matter of schools so that knowledge acquisition could be tested and comparisons of efficiency made between schools. The imposition of a curriculum for *all* children (except those in fee-paying schools, which are still free to choose their own curricula) probably represents a strengthening of the link between the school and the needs of the wider community.

To the question 'what is a school for?' the instinctive response tends to be that it is to learn to read, write, do arithmetic, and so forth. This is something of a conditioned response because this is our shared construct of the main purpose of schooling, but this is not the whole story. In some of the training workshops I and colleagues have run, we do a workshop exercise with groups of parents and professionals which is useful in eliciting some of the deeper understandings that most people tend to have about the meaning and purpose of our education system, which rarely surface in the normal course of discussions between parents and teachers. The exercise (which was designed by Peter Ritchie) is designed to help groups and teams make sense of their own core assumptions about the meaning and purpose of education.

The meaning of education

Bring together a group of 5–10 people and allow them an hour or so to discuss the following questions in sequence:

1. What are the ten most important things children should learn in school? Having decided, place them in order of priority.

2. What are the ten most important things children with disabilities should learn in school? Having decided, place them in order of priority.

3. For question 2 – how many of these things could the child with a disability learn in a special school?

People surprise themselves when doing this exercise in that they usually begin by listing such items as reading, writing, arithmetic, etc., and, equally inevitably, end up prioritising things like communicating with others, making friendships, co-operating, developing respect and so forth. It is not simply that the formal measurable knowledge and skill aspects are not seen as important, since the importance of the curriculum is usually given due weight, but rather that the personal and social development of the child is acknowledged as being of prime importance.

As has already been said, we used to call these informal (apparently incidental) *consequences* of schooling the 'hidden curriculum' but it remains the case that we still do not see any point in measuring them. It is almost as though they are things which we take for granted as a natural by-product of the child pursuing the formal curriculum, and if some of the elements are not developing in a child then there is little we can do about it.

Whatever the individual view of the relative importance of the explicit *formal* versus the implicit hidden *informal* curriculum, it is probably a matter of little consequence for most children who grow and develop in relationships without major difficulties. It is, though, a very different matter for children with significant additional needs, who may lack the ability to comprehend social situations or the interpersonal skills to make effective contact with others. If such children are ever to be able to develop such skills, they will do so much more slowly than their peers and so will need as much opportunity as possible to engage with others.

So, in response to the question 'what are schools for?', the typical considered response shifts from an initial emphasis upon the formal curriculum to an acknowledgement that relationship development is really the key purpose of schooling and that without this formal learning becomes largely meaningless.

The other inevitable outcome of the exercise is that the priorities identified for typical children are repeated in the case of children with disabilities. A further conclusion is that it is hard, if not impossible, for children to learn these things in a special school.

It is important not to try and claim too much for what, after all, is only a theoretical consideration of a rather abstract set of notions about the meaning and purpose of education in our society. It is perhaps easy for a group of people to come up with such conclusions when there are absolutely no consequences for them as individuals, because it does not commit them to any particular action thereafter. However, it is certainly worthy of note that many people, some of whom have a stake in special schools in that they earn their living from working in them, actually find themselves having to acknowledge that they may not be able to deliver some crucially important learning opportunities for their pupils.

The North American analysis

To describe a particular view about any aspect of education theory or practice as the *North American* view is likely to be misleading in that views on every aspect of education are as discrepant on that continent as they are in Britain and the rest of Europe. The term is used here simply by way of acknowledgement of the source of some important ideas which have come to us from that part of the world. That these ideas are held by a small number of evangelists gives testimony to their commitment and the power of their presentation, for they have certainly made an impact here in Britain – at least in the way we speak about integration.

In an important book, *Action for Inclusion*, written by some of the leading advocates of inclusive education (O'Brien *et al.* 1989), they summarise their beliefs as follows:

> Good schools get better when they include all the children in the school's neighborhood. Good teachers grow stronger when they involve each child as a member of a class of active learners by offering each the individualized challenges and support necessary for learning. Students develop more fully when they welcome people with different gifts and abilities into their lives and when all students feel secure that they will receive individualized help when they need it. Families get stronger when they join teachers and students to create classrooms that work for everyone. (p.1)

It is clear from this initial statement of belief about the meaning of education that it has a different starting point from that which professional educators usually take either in Britain or elsewhere. The use of such words as 'neighbourhood', 'gifts' and talking about 'classrooms that work for everyone' clearly betokens a different starting point in considering what schooling is for. They define inclusion as being 'for those who have been left outside' and so, from the outset, adopt a stance which acknowledges the reality of rejection for children who are denied access to their neighbourhood school. In offering a definition of the meaning of 'inclusion' which most appropriately describes the reality they address, they point to its Latin roots – which have to do with shutting the door after someone has come in. They take the view that it is not possible to speak about integration without speaking of inclusion, saying that 'integration only begins when each child belongs'.

They take issue with the whole paraphernalia of professional labelling of children, and Marsha Forest says: 'the only label we need is the child's name'. On the criterion for inclusion, Forest once again provides the answer – 'there is only one criterion for inclusion. Breathing, life itself'.

Action for Inclusion is a manual for bringing about inclusion for a particular child who has been excluded, and for helping schools to become inclusive communities. It stresses the importance of relationships and the key role both of the parent and of every member of the school community in making a child feel included.

PLANNING FOR INCLUSION

The circles exercise

In stressing the importance of relationships, Forest and others (O'Brien *et al.* p.40) recommend the use of a technique called the *circles* exercise. This involves bringing a group of people together to

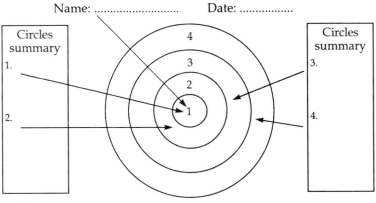

Key

Circle 1   People you love and count on
Circle 2   People you really like and count on
Circle 3   People and groups you know and like e.g. a club you attend
Circle 4   People who get paid to be in your life – professionals

Source: Hall 1992a adapted from O'Brien *et al.* 1989

Figure 4.2 Circles of relationships

look at who is involved in the life of a child and what that involvement means for them. The starting point is a sheet of paper with four concentric circles (see Figure 4.2) with the name of the child in circle one.

The first step is to put the names of the people closest to the child in the inner circle. These are the people the child *loves* and counts on most. The people the child really *likes* and counts on but not as much as those in the first circle are listed in the second circle. The third circle is for those people the child knows as acquaintances – people he might meet at a club or in the corner store. The fourth circle is for paid professionals such as the teacher or doctor.

This is a superb technique for getting a picture of what a child's (or in fact anybody's) life is like because it lays out before you a picture of *who* is involved and *what they have to offer*. The picture presented by this technique of the lives of disabled children is markedly different to that for typical children. The inner circle is the area of greatest similarity in that most children have parents, siblings and close relatives who care deeply for them. The differences begin to emerge when one looks at circle two (the people the child likes and really counts on – friends) where the typical situation for a child attending a school for children with SLDs is as depicted in Figures 4.3 and 4.4. The picture for such a child in terms of acquaintances (circle 3) is also likely to be as shown in Figures 4.3 and 4.4 and that,

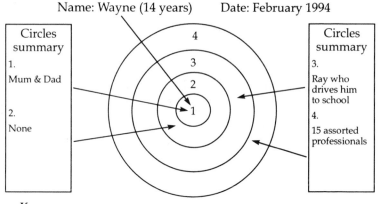

Name: Wayne (14 years)   Date: February 1994

Circles summary		Circles summary
1. Mum & Dad	4 3 2 1	3. Ray who drives him to school
2. None		4. 15 assorted professionals

Key
Circle 1   People you love and count on
Circle 2   People you really like and count on
Circle 3   People and groups you know and like e.g. a club you attend
Circle 4   People who get paid to be in your life – professionals

Source: Hall 1992a adapted from O'Brien *et al.* 1989

Figure 4.3 Circles of relationships – a child with SLDs

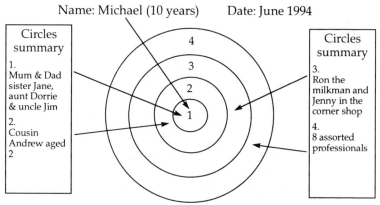

Name: Michael (10 years)   Date: June 1994

Circles summary		Circles summary
1. Mum & Dad sister Jane, aunt Dorrie & uncle Jim	4 3 2 1	3. Ron the milkman and Jenny in the corner shop
2. Cousin Andrew aged 2		4. 8 assorted professionals

Key
Circle 1   People you love and count on
Circle 2   People you really like and count on
Circle 3   People and groups you know and like e.g. a club you attend
Circle 4   People who get paid to be in your life – professionals

Source: Hall 1992a adapted from O'Brien *et al.* 1989

Figure 4.4 Circles of relationships – a child with SLDs

Name: Robert (aged 10 years)   Date: April 1994

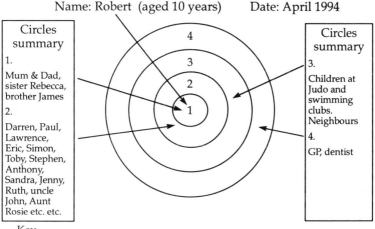

Circles summary		Circles summary
1. Mum & Dad, sister Rebecca, brother James 2. Darren, Paul, Lawrence, Eric, Simon, Toby, Stephen, Anthony, Sandra, Jenny, Ruth, uncle John, Aunt Rosie etc. etc.		3. Children at Judo and swimming clubs. Neighbours 4. GP, dentist

Key
Circle 1   People you love and count on
Circle 2   People you really like and count on
Circle 3   People and groups you know and like e.g. a club you attend
Circle 4   People who get paid to be in your life – professionals

Source: Hall 1992a adapted from O'Brien *et al.* 1989

Figure 4.5 Circles of relationships – a 'typical child'

for professionals, reflects the level of involvement for a child with physical, sensory and learning difficulties. A circle for a *typical* child is shown in Figure 4.5.

It is important to stress that this picture is not applicable to *all* children who attend special schools and might be markedly different for a child who attends a special school for children who have moderate learning difficulties. The point is, however, that attending a special school is in itself a risk factor for relationship-building because it separates children who would otherwise have spent their school years together and makes relationship-building very difficult. Most children make their strongest relationships with pupils they meet in school and encounter in the neighbourhood outside school hours.

The circles technique is used to identify any serious gaps in a child's network of relationships but also, to move on from that, to try to fill those gaps which are highlighted. Those who have used the technique find it helpful for the next stage in the process – that of *intentional relationship-building*. This involves bringing a group of children together to explore ways in which the child's peers might wish to spend time with him/her both within school and during out-of-school hours and holidays.

Having used the circles technique in segregated settings, I have found a grossly atypical pattern of relationships – especially amongst severely disabled children. It seems reasonable to expect that children who lack some of the skills necessary for making the running in relationship-building would end up with fewer friends than most other children, and this will very probably be the case for most such children. However, this probably does not explain why these children tend to have lamentably few friends and acquaintances or, in some cases, none at all.

REVIEWING FOR RELEVANCE

The circles exercise is a valuable technique for professionals to use when they review a child's progress or write professional advice for a Statement. Yet richer information becomes available if this technique is linked to an approach developed by John O'Brien and Connie Lyle called the *Framework for Accomplishment* (1986).

O'Brien and Lyle's Framework

O'Brien and Lyle's *Framework* is a strategy for making better sense of the life of a person who is likely to be seen as different in significant and negative ways and who is also dependent on services. The more the person is seen as different, the more the *Framework* applies. The primary goal in using the strategy is to improve the quality of services, and hence the quality of life, of those who use them. The *Framework* was developed to look at people caught up in the adult human service system but can be adapted for use in the school setting. The following is a very brief summary of the way in which the *Framework* can be used to improve the life of a child in a segregated school. The essence of the strategy is to describe the child's present situation and a desirable future and then agree how a special school might be able to help move the child towards this more desirable future.

Describing the child's situation

The starting point is to understand the child more systematically. This will require knowledge of the child's history and current situation. The exercise will involve looking at:

- the relationships the child has with his family and others
- the friends/acquaintances he has
- the range of professionals in his life
- what he likes and dislikes
- what he can and cannot do

- what he would like for the future, etc.

These areas of the child's personal life are embraced by the following key concepts:

- sharing places
- making choices
- developing
- dignity
- growing in relationships.

For each of these headings a number of questions are asked in order to build up a picture of the child's life, relationships and opportunities. By way of example, the following questions might be asked about the way in which the child is able to *share places*. It would be relevant to ask:

- Which community settings does he use regularly?
- To which of these does he go alone or at least without a family member?
- Does he experience problems in using any of these places?
- What other community settings might he benefit from using?
- What would it take to increase his opportunities to use places?

This strategy can easily be incorporated into the school/LEA review process and linked to the information made available through the circles exercise. This can be done in the following way.

A review strategy for the special school

What follows is a procedure developed by me for reviewing the progress of children in a segregated day special school. These children were described as having 'severe and complex learning difficulties'. The approach evolved over a period of some years, as other review strategies had been tried and discarded as failing to address the real and pressing needs the school saw in the lives of the children and their families. Given their increasingly anomalous status within the education system and society generally, special schools need to pay careful attention to the strategies they use to monitor their pupils' progress.

The strategy should not be seen as the sum total of what the school and the LEA need to do by way of reviewing and monitoring pupil progress since we are only here concerned with the broad sweep of the child's life. In what follows, we shall be mainly addressing the *big* questions which have to do with the overall meaning and direction of the child's life – what sort of education should he have? What kinds of relationships? What type of supports? What longer term aims should be entertained? Questions such as these will not cover the nitty-gritty of the school curriculum, integration arrangements and his health and care programmes, which should be dealt with in a different kind of forum.

It is also important to understand that the adoption of this (rather than some other) strategy is not prompted simply by the fact of the child's impairment(s) but rather through recognition of the fact that there is a *problem*. The problem is only in part to do with the impairment(s). It also has to do with the fact of the child's segregated schooling and life. This means that the strategy must be seen as a *strategy for change* and the change must be in the direction of bringing more *meaning* and *relevance* into the child's life. The procedure draws heavily on the ideas and techniques of Forest, O'Brien and Lyle described above but, I have interpreted the work of these authors quite freely and would not wish to attribute to them any of the flaws they might see in this particular application of their ideas.

The review

An independent facilitator – who is preferably not a member of the professional team – convenes a small group including two to four members of the child's family along with no more than two or three key professionals including the child's teacher or headteacher. The parents may choose to bring along a friend as one of their group if that person is closely involved with the child.

The facilitator first goes through the circles exercise, making it clear what each category means by giving examples of each which might relate to themselves or another child they know. Here it will be important to ensure that the participants understand that a 'friend' means friend in the conventional sense, and not in some special sense as this might be construed for a severely handicapped child. It is also important to establish clearly the status of relationships between the child and the various professionals in his life, stressing that these people are involved *because* they are paid and not for some other reason. The point here is that once they are no longer being paid, they will disappear from the child's life.

One of the important things about the circles exercise is that it clearly establishes *who* is involved in the child's life and the reasons *why* they are involved. Knowing who wants to (and can) stick around for the *long haul* is of the utmost importance because of the dangers that exist once the immediate family are no longer there to cope. Friends are, if anything, more important in the lives of children who are severely disabled, because they will need a high level of support – with much of the initiative being taken by others.

Once the pattern of existing relationships is documented, the process moves on to a consideration of *who* the child is and *what* he needs in his life. This is where O'Brien and Lyle's *Framework* comes into play. The broad strategy is illustrated in Figure 4.6 (*Planning a valued educational programme for a child or young person needing to be*

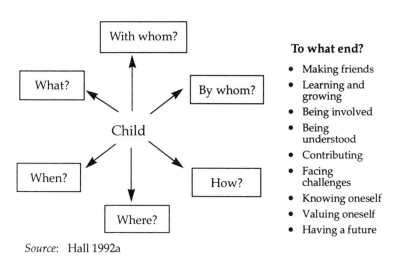

To what end?

- Making friends
- Learning and growing
- Being involved
- Being understood
- Contributing
- Facing challenges
- Knowing oneself
- Valuing oneself
- Having a future

Source: Hall 1992a

Figure 4.6 Making sense of the needs of a segregated child

included) and is my own interpretation of what I understand to be the intention of the *Framework* in the context of a child who has been segregated. The independent facilitator opens the discussion by explaining how the information provided by the circles exercise relates to what will now take place.

The facilitator then explains the procedure for the review saying that its purpose is to take a broad and longer-term look at the child's life to see whether everyone is on the right track, that is whether everyone knows and agrees what is important for the child and his family. The information elicited is put on a board for all to see. The questions to be addressed (as illustrated in Figure 4.6) are as follows:

- *Who* is this child?
- *What* does he need in his life?
- *When* does he need these things?
- *Where* should these things be provided?
- *How* should what he needs be provided?

- *By whom* should what he needs be provided?
- *With whom* should he spend his time?

These will now be dealt with in a little more detail.

WHO IS THE CHILD?

This is, at first sight, an odd question to ask parents and closely involved professionals, yet it is probably the most important question anyone can ask about a severely impaired person. We know from long experience, and of course disabled people know from bitter personal experience, that our fellow human beings have difficulty coping with human diversity. The attribution of valued status is important in direct relation to a person's competence and typicality, hence the more capable and 'normal' an individual is the more (s)he is valued, and vice versa.

Severely and profoundly impaired children tend *not* to be well-known, understood or sympathetically interpreted by professionals and others, but are, of course, much better known by their families. This lack of understanding of *who* the child is is not really surprising as many severely impaired children do not have sufficient skills to communicate their personality and their thoughts, desires, interests and aspirations – they remain enigmatic to all but the most persistent enquirer or befriender.

The evidence for this lack of knowledge of who the person is comes from two main sources. First, when professionals write reports on such children, they generally do so in highly impersonal terms, focusing almost exclusively on the nature of the child's impairments. Such reports tend to contain clinical labels and descriptions of the child's impairment(s), syndrome, incapacity, etc., and little by way of a description of *who* the child is as a person. This is, perhaps in part, a function of training rooted in the medical model. Second, when conducting reviews of the type described here, staff are forthcoming on *who* the child is in inverse proportion to the child's degree of disability; hence a profoundly handicapped child will elicit few personal identity observations or characterisations while a more able child is likely to elicit many more. Sometimes staff may become completely stuck for something to say about a multiply handicapped child yet produce reams on a more able child.

The facilitator's task is to gradually draw out what people understand to be the unique character of the child: his personality in terms of his likes and dislikes, his attitude towards people and situations, the things he finds interesting, pleasing, unpleasant and so on. Sometimes these contributions will be in the form of a summary observation such as 'he's a boy with a wicked sense of humour' or 'she's as stubborn as hell when she wants to be'. At the end of this first phase the facilitator will have a list of character/personality attributions or descriptions which embody the essential child as interpreted by those present.

WHAT DOES THE CHILD NEED IN HIS LIFE?

Here the purpose is to talk mainly about the big things like friends, self-respect, challenge, having others understand your needs, involvement with others, and so forth. It should also touch on those essential supports without which education and life generally would not be nearly so worthwhile or, perhaps, even a major obstacle to achieving what the child needs. For a severely disabled child this might include: one-to-one classroom support, a wheelchair, a standing frame, an adapted computer and switches, speech therapy, physiotherapy, etc.

WHEN DOES HE NEED THESE THINGS?

It is important to know *when* certain services and other provisions are required, both in terms of not missing a key period of developmental growth and also for ensuring that a provision does not clash with another pressing need the child may have. An example would be of speech therapy which the health authority say can only be provided at a distant clinic on Monday morning but which would clash with school lessons. Clearly such provision should be made outside school hours or in the school to avoid the waste of time travelling and disruption to the school day.

WHERE SHOULD THESE THINGS BE PROVIDED?

Given the history of inappropriate institutionalisation suffered by disabled people, the *where* tends always to be one of the central issues. Children are still far too frequently side-tracked away from generic education and health services.

HOW SHOULD WHAT HE NEEDS BE PROVIDED?

The *how* has to do with the *way* in which provisions are organised to meet needs, and here the emphasis needs to be away from 'special', more obvious approaches to a more low-profile style in which the child is seen as just another member of the class who has some additional needs.

BY WHOM SHOULD WHAT HE NEEDS BE PROVIDED?

The people who should meet the needs will, in the main, be teachers, classroom support workers, therapists and others who have specialist skills and training. However, there will also be a strong involvement with the whole school community – including teaching and non-teaching staff and, most importantly, other children.

WITH WHOM SHOULD HE SPEND HIS TIME?

This refers to the children who will share the child's school, leisure and social life, and here the strong emphasis will always be upon the same age peer group.

This exercise never produces a recommendation that the child should spend his time with others who have similar disabilities; in fact precisely the opposite is true, yet the reviews may well take place in a school in which children are so grouped.

Those most in need of integration are segregated

This *Review Framework* turns conventional wisdom on its head because it emphasises the pressing need for mainstream participation of those who have been segregated. It provides a clear account of what a vulnerable child needs in his life, then goes on to provide a stark demonstration of the damage caused by segregating him. It shows he has no friends, then highlights the fact that he is in a school which will not provide an opportunity to make friends; it shows he needs typical role models, then demonstrates he has none in his special school; it shows he needs services provided in a low-key way, then explains this is not the way special schools operate; it shows he needs to be where it is all happening, then emphasises the fact that the special school is just not that sort of place.

The ultimate logic of this analysis is that those who are at present most likely to be segregated are the very children who can least afford it because, lacking many of the skills important for relationship-building, they cannot make the running when an opportunity arises. Because they need more opportunities to observe and practice, they, *above all others*, need to be where such opportunities are present. An able child could probably survive the deprivation of a segregated schooling but a severely disabled child cannot.

The lesson here for the special school is that, in developing an integration programme, they have a duty to give priority to their *most disabled* children, but once again this turns current received wisdom on its head.

THE LIFE-DEFINING NATURE OF SEGREGATION

Some years ago the author had the privilege of spending two days with Peter Ritchie at a workshop for people working in special schools. The theme of the workshop was: *What is the problem that special education has been devised to solve?* After two days of intensive and stimulating group work the participants came up with the answer: *segregation*. This needs explanation.

During the two days, groups tried to agree answers to the following questions:

- What are the major life needs of our pupils (children in SLD schools)?
- What are the implications of these major life needs for the educational and broader social experiences that should be provided for them?
- What are the implications for the way we provide education and review pupil progress?

The conclusions reached were:

- Because the main issue (which professionals could do something about) in the lives of the children was that they had been rejected by society, then the problem special education was invented to solve is *rejection*.
- This rejection occurs at three levels:

  1. **Individual rejection** – by local children, siblings etc.

  2. **Organisational rejection** – by schools, youth clubs etc.

  3. **Societal rejection** – by being seen as different from, and not belonging to, society.

- That special education should tackle this rejection in the following ways:

  1. **Individual** – by providing guidance and practical help to parents and the school so that they are able to mediate social integration for their child. Also by helping the child to have a wide range of ordinary experiences inside and outside school.

  2. **Organisational** – by helping the regular education system to cope, that is by working to develop a mature mainstream.

  3. **Societal** – by improving the image of the service and of the users. Also by increasing opportunities for interaction with the public.

Since the problem that special education has been invented to solve is that of societal rejection, the focus needs to be upon *acceptance*. Acceptance is a notion that is not widely understood and discussed in special education but it has a number of important implications (see Figure. 4.7).

If the ultimate goal of integration is inclusion, the point of inclusion is acceptance. In fact the definition of inclusion offered earlier is intended to be nothing more than an operationalisation of what we mean by acceptance. A strategy for tackling this would be for the school to envisage some accomplishments for the child and gradually adapt the educational programme so that the accomplishments come to equate with an inclusive form of schooling.

It won't be easy

Whatever you the reader may have been told on an inclusion workshop, when the plastic hearts were doing the rounds and you were all clutching one another sharing a shower of mingled tears, *inclusion is hard, not easy*. The mechanics of the thing *are* easy and any child could be supported in any school tomorrow morning if everyone concerned wanted it, but the problem is they don't!

The danger with inclusion is that it is sometimes sold as a 'product' which will solve all of life's problems, so that all you need to do is get the child into his local school and life is suddenly rosy because *being there* will ensure your friendship circle grows and life will become a bewildering social whirl – how different to what it was like in the special school. Would it were that easy! Tyne's observation that some proponents of inclusion tend to elevate relationships to a mystical importance is a timely warning that serious planning and preparation is crucial if a child is to survive for long in a mainstream school.

PLANNING IS CRUCIAL

Planning for inclusion needs to be meticulous, irrespective of whether it is felt that few problems are likely to occur. Problems are very likely to crop up at some point. The planning should involve five stages: (1) the vision, (2) the needs, (3) the service, (4) the methods, skills and processes, and (5) the necessary safeguards (see Figure 4.8).

The diagram is pretty much self-explanatory and its different elements will be recognised as drawing heavily upon what has already been described. One point is worth stressing: the need for *safeguards*. If the reader takes nothing else from the earlier discussion of normalisation theory, it is important to understand the strength of societal and systemic pressures to keep disabled people from participation in the mainstream of life. This is why it is so important to try and ensure that there is no stinting of the effort to keep the child in his mainstream school, and this will mean constant preparation for each new teacher and phase of the system. For staff trying

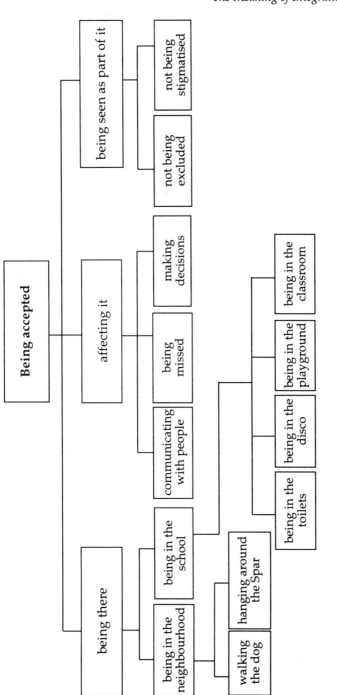

Source: Ritchie 1988

Figure 4.7 The deeper meaning of inclusion

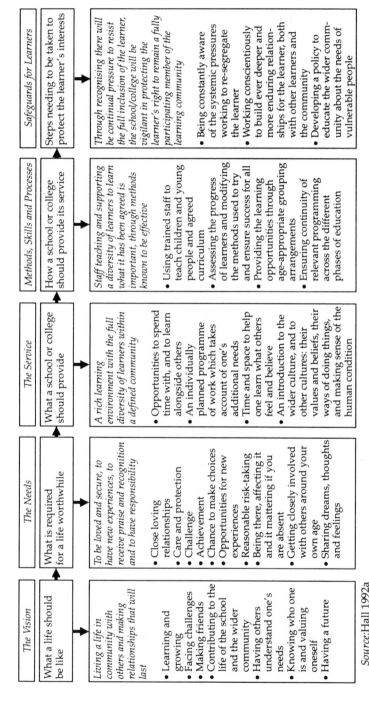

The Vision	The Needs	The Service	Methods, Skills and Processes	Safeguards for Learners
What a life should be like	What is required for a life worthwhile	What a school or college should provide	How a school or college should provide its service	Steps needing to be taken to protect the learner's interests
Living a life in community with others and making relationships that will last	*To be loved and secure, to have new experiences, to receive praise and recognition and to have responsibility*	*A rich learning environment with the full diversity of learners within a defined community*	*Staff teaching and supporting a diversity of learners to learn what it has been agreed is important, through methods known to be effective*	*Through recognising there will be continual pressure to resist the full inclusion of the learner, the school/college will be vigilant in protecting the learner's right to remain a fully participating member of the learning community*
• Learning and growing • Facing challenges • Making friends • Contributing to the life of the school and the wider community • Having others understand one's needs • Knowing who one is and valuing oneself • Having a future	• Close loving relationships • Care and protection • Challenge • Achievement • Chance to make choices • Opportunities for new experiences • Reasonable risk-taking • Being there, affecting it and it mattering if you are absent • Getting closely involved with others around your own age • Sharing dreams, thoughts and feelings	• Opportunities to spend time with, and to learn alongside others • An individually planned programme of work which takes account of one's additional needs • Time and space to help one learn what others feel and believe • An introduction to the wider culture, and to other cultures: their values and beliefs, their ways of doing things, and making sense of the human condition	• Using trained staff to teach children and young people and agreed curriculum • Assessing the progress of learners and modifying the methods used to try and ensure success for all • Providing the learning opportunities through age-appropriate grouping arrangements • Ensuring continuity of relevant programming across the different phases of education	• Being constantly aware of the systemic pressures working to re-segregate the learner • Working conscientiously to build ever deeper and more enduring relationships for the learner, both with other learners and the community • Developing a policy to educate the wider community about the needs of vulnerable people

Source: Hall 1992a

Figure 4.8 Planning a valued educational programme for a child or young person needing to be included

to gain a foothold for a child in his local school, it is important that opportunities are provided to discuss their experience and to problem-solve around issues *as they arise*. All the really big issues will have to do with the anxieties of adults.

A prediction I sadly feel confident in making is that parental appeals against the segregation of their child will not meet with the positive response they had hoped for from the SEN Tribunal. There is still a long way to go before we have a better societal understanding of the damage done by segregation and the members of the Tribunal are, at the end of the day, just ordinary citizens.

A MATURE MAINSTREAM – THE GOAL OF OUR WORK

Most of the problems likely to be encountered in trying to get disabled children into real schools are rooted in the irrational fears and deep-seated prejudices of other people – mostly adults. Although schools are the focus of our efforts, it would be wrong to assume that only teachers, governors, psychologists, advisers, officers, other parents, children, etc., are the problem – the problem exists in our society. Because we have an immature society (witness our continuing inability to cope with issues of gender, race and sexual orientation), we of course have immature schools. But what would a mature mainstream be like?

A mature mainstream school or college would be able to meet the needs of *all* the children within its catchment area, irrespective of the nature or degree of their disability. It would have staff and governors who did not question the right of a child to be present and adopted a problem-solving approach to any challenges a child might bring.

Individual stories are the key to understanding what children need and how we should go about trying to meet their needs and the following accounts of encounters with the system contain a number of important insights. Beverley's story is told by her parents and Martin Yates speaks for himself.

Beverley's story

The following story is told by Paul and Marion Burrows about their daughter Beverley's early schooling.

Beverley was just two when schooling became an issue. Her delayed development as a baby had become sufficiently marked by 14 months for a paediatrician to tell us she would need special schooling and she began receiving the Portage Home Teaching service. Marion had been ill and was finding Bev a handful (she was fitting a lot) and we were keen for her to start full-time schooling as soon as possible. We began the Statementing process with the LEA, whose educational psychologist recommended a choice of the nearest special school, the nearest special unit or a unit ten miles away.

In the meantime we had taken Bev to the weekly toddler group at our local nursery. As Paul was working away at the time, Bev and Marion made the visits to each of the schools suggested. Marion thought the nearest unit was very cramped and that the headteacher didn't like the look of Bev. The second unit seemed fine to Marion, but much too far away for a two-year-old.

When we went to the special school, the headteacher, John Hall, said 'this girl ought to go to the same school as her brothers and sisters' and Marion felt the world restart again (the real world had stopped for her when she had stepped into the special world merry-go-round of health visitors, therapists, psychologists, etc.). Marion thought it was a brilliant idea and, with Paul, became determined not to let Bev get sucked into the 'special whirlpool'. We enrolled her in the nursery school part-time and they said she would be welcome as long as she had one-to-one support.

We were told by the LEA that we were being used as political pawns and warned that children and parents might turn against us and Bev. So began our long battle for Bev to go to 'normal' school. We got the one-to-one and, at the same time as going to the nursery, Bev spent the other half of her day in the special school.

As she got near to full-time education, at four-and-a-half years, it became clear to us that there was little point in Bev spending time in the special school; all the gains she was making were being made in the mainstream. In fact, some good was undone by her going to a special school. Her confidence, her independence and her understanding of language and routine were all improving. But the LEA began to change their mind and refused an increase in support hours.

A meeting with an adviser, a psychologist and the head of the primary school (none of whom knew Bev) decided on two-and-a-half hours daily as an acceptable level of 'integration' in her new school. The LEA was adamant that mainstream for Bev was for purely social reasons and education for her had to be segregated. We were so outraged at this insensitive, random decision (Bev would have had to leave for her special school after morning playtime each day) that we collected a petition and kept her home for a month in protest. We also wrote to the Director of Education complaining about the heavy-handed way we were being treated by the educational psychologist.

Encouraged by John Hall, by mainstream parents and by Bev herself through the progress she was making, we persevered, and eventually, three years later, she started full-time at her primary school.

So now there are no taxi rides across town to school, friends call in the morning and she walks to school with them (luckily we are very close and Marion catches up when they reach the yard). In the afternoon, Marion waits for Bev at the school gate and gets her chance to chatter to other mothers instead of waiting for the dreaded taxi.

Everybody in our part of town knows Bev and greets her. Marion meets people in Sainsburys who tell her the latest Makaton signing system sign that they've learned from their children (Bev began to use her signing more when the other children began to use it with her). Her brothers have never minded her coming to football games, or taking her up to the park and having friends home, because they've not had to be shy about her.

Beverley, being a happy sociable child, helped enormously and almost everybody in our school has been very supportive – teachers, cleaners, dinner ladies – but best of all have been the children. Lots have been shy at first, a few have teased her, and the little ones have had to learn to duck when she flaps her arms about, and they all tell her 'round my waist Bev' if she squeezes them round the neck. But she's got lots of friends and they love her and love to help.

The one person we would never have managed without is Bev's brilliant, resourceful one-to-one, Sheila. Without her help, increasingly at a distance, Bev would not have managed nearly as well. Bev takes part in every activity in school – assembly, PE, Music, Science, Trips, Sports day, Carol concert, and so on – and when the class is quietly getting on with their maths or written work, where possible Sheila differentiates the class work or works with Bev on her Individual Educational Plan. Bev withdraws from Welsh lessons to follow her own speech and language programme.

We are very, very glad Bev has got the chance of a normal school life and hope we can carry this right through till she is 18. We cannot imagine anyone in their right mind trying to stop this now.

Martin Yates – A special school survivor[1]

Special schools providing 'education'! Well, that's a joke to start with, and as for it being the better way, well take it from someone who has been to a special school – it just does not work.

There is very little, if any, education at all in a special school and we should ask ourselves why special schools are called 'special'. Is it because they give special help to the children who attend the school or is it that they are special because they shut away and hide the children our society does not want to see?

---

1 Martin Yates is a Disability Consultant and can be contacted at 49 Gloucester Avenue, Blackpool FY1 4EH. Tel/Fax 01253 393650

Before I tell you my own story – a story of how I survived special school – let me explain a bit about my disability. I have the disability of cerebral palsy which, for me, means I have limited control over my leg and arm movements and this means there are things I cannot do for myself.

At the age of five, the normal age for starting school, I was not able to start along with all the other children as the school I was supposed to go to had no place for me. While I was waiting for a school place my LEA gave me some home tuition, wasn't that nice of them! Just wait until you hear the rest of it, it gets better. They gave me just two hours of home tuition a week! Every other kid of my age was getting 24 hours of education a week.

At the age of seven-and-a-half I finally got to go to school for the first time. I was really looking forward to going to school and being educated, what a joke that was, being 'educated' in a special school, what was I thinking of?

The first thing I learned was not how to read and write but how to fall over, and then how to walk. It was not until I went to Junior school that I saw any sign of anything that you might call 'education'. Please remember I only said 'might' call education and I did not say you 'would' call it education now did I? This so-called education included reading, writing and some basic maths. As I explained before, there are some things I am unable to do on my own, such as writing, because I am unable to hold a pen to write. To enable me to write at school I had to use a machine called a Possum which, in the 1970s, was the best thing – or perhaps it was the only thing – on the market.

The Possum was very slow when you look back and compare it to a word processor, but it was better than nothing, and at least I could get some stuff down on paper. Another problem with having to use a Possum was the fact that there were only two in the school and five children who needed to use them, which meant we had to take it in turns to use them. This went on for two years until my own education authority said they would buy me a Possum. The reason I mention my own authority is because I was being sent away to school in another authority.

It was only when I was in the second year of the senior school that my teachers worked out that I could not read. This had only taken them five years to work out. However, the only reason I could not read was because I could not see. The school optician did not want me to have glasses as he felt it would be dangerous for me since I might fall over and hurt myself. The fact that I could not see did not seem to matter to him. I must admit that I found it hard to understand that an optician was not concerned with the fact that I could not see. To cut a long story short, my teachers ganged up on the school optician and persuaded him to give me reading glasses. There was only one condition for him letting me have glasses: that my teachers put my glasses on for me at the beginning of the lesson and took them off again at the end.

Now that I could see, I had to brush up on my reading and for this I was given extra help within what was called the reading workshop. My reading then came on in leaps and bounds and, although I could not read as well as my classmates, I could read well enough to get by.

When I went into the fourth year I was put in for, and started to study for, my CSEs. I took five subjects: maths, English, history, science and geography. By this time I could use a typewriter. It was much quicker than the Possum but it still took me quite a long time to get things down on paper. With this in mind, my teachers applied to the Examining Board for extra time for the examinations.

After returning to school for the fifth year I was told by the head of department that I could not take my CSEs because I could not write and the Examination Board would not give me extra time. He went on to say that I could have taken 'O' levels but it was now too late. He said I would have to do the work but not sit the exams.

I left school in 1981 after spending nine years in the same school. During this time I gained no formal qualifications at all and my feelings about the time I had spent at school were that it had been a total waste of time. After leaving school I spent nine months at Banstead Place Assessment Centre, from which I gained a great deal. At the end of the assessment it was felt I would benefit from going to a college of Further Education. The college I chose was a mainstream college not far from my home.

The college had a special needs unit so I would be able to have the support I would need. I started at Blackpool and Fylde College in 1982 and, for the first year, was in the special needs unit full-time. This was like being back at school as the education was so basic – just like the work I had done in the Junior school. However, at least I got a formal qualification at the end of it.

After a year in the special needs unit it was time to move on to a mainstream course and also to move to the main campus of the college. During the second year there I took GCE 'O' levels in computer studies and sociology. Now, for the very first time in my whole life, I was receiving what I would call a 'real education'. Working alongside non-disabled students was a great feeling for me.

Although I was in mainstream classes within the college, I still had the support of the special needs unit – who made arrangements to include the extra time I would need with the examinations as I had to dictate all my answers to a member of the care team. However, they did not get that right and only managed to get me a grand total of ten minutes extra in every hour – not a great help! With my speech difficulties I found this very difficult and, as a result, failed miserably.

I was now going into my third year at Blackpool and Fylde and I knew I would have to work even harder. I took two subjects that year plus an additional subject to keep my interest going. This time, instead of the special needs unit sorting out my exam arrangements, it was done by my course tutor – who had little or no experience of working with people who have disabilities. Fortunately he was able to negotiate a whole day for each of my papers, to include as many breaks as I needed. This time I got good results with an A, B and D.

By this time I had been in full-time education for 13 years and I felt it was time for a change to do something different. So I left college at the age of 20 and started to work as a Disability Adviser at the local YMCA. I quite enjoyed this job and worked with some very nice people. I stayed in that job for about four-and-a-half years then set up on my own as a Disability and Community Care Consultant.

In October 1993 I returned to Blackpool and Fylde college to do a part-time counselling course that I got a lot out of. After eight years out of education it was great to be back.

Looking back to when I was 16, when I still could not read, who would have thought that I could now be a Consultant Trainer. I believe this shows that, with the exception of the 'special' education part of the service, people like me with a disability can achieve within the education system.

CONCLUSION

Without a better societal understanding of the damage done by educational and social separation, there is little prospect that LEAs will follow the example of Newham in East London to progressively abandon segregation as an educational policy for some children. It seems the state education system is incapable of voluntarily initiating human rights-based innovations for children with special needs, and even in a progressive authority like Newham the initiative came from parents. No worthwhile advance in human rights has ever been initiated by the state or its paid servants, and this is no less true of special education policy. The elimination of segregation is being pursued by disabled people and parents of disabled children with little or no support from central and local government or even the voluntary sector.

As Georgiades long ago observed, there are few 'hero innovators' amongst local authority employed professionals since 'schools (and LEAs) eat hero innovators for breakfast'. Any organisation will have its own means of ensuring co-operation from its workforce, and why should the LEA be any exception? That well-intentioned professionals experience considerable frustration in trying to ensure that needs are matched to provision is not in question. Yet there are too many occasions on which insufficient effort is made to resist the systemic pressure to match children to an inflexible range of placement opportunities.

Chapter 5

Service Evaluation in Special Education

SPECIAL EDUCATION AT THE MARGINS

Visible and invisible learning difficulties

'Special' education has, for most people, become synonymous with segregated education, and whilst this is recognised as a caricature by special education professionals, it is hardly one which should surprise us, given the continuing largely negative and devaluing societal attitudes towards disabled people. It is of interest to note in passing that ageism is also endemic, even though 20 per cent of the population are now over 65 and we all aspire to live at least that long and, we hope, very much longer.

If, as is frequently stated, around 20 per cent of children have a special educational need (SEN) at some time during their school lives, one would expect 'special needs' to be construed as less 'special' than is usually the case – if one in five children are struggling, that means around five to six children in every class and therefore special needs must be something with whom everyone is familiar. Furthermore, if familiarity creates understanding, which in turn conditions acceptance, then why should there be a mystery about special needs?

The reality is probably that the overwhelming majority of the SENs experienced by children in mainstream schools are largely invisible because they have no significant physical or behavioural stigmas which would attract negative attention. With such a child, the problem will only become manifest once she has applied herself to her school work. Whereas typical appearance and behaviour serves to mask the large majority of learning difficulties, which only become apparent when the child fails to make adequate progress in her school work. Whereas typical appearance and behaviour may act as an effective mask for some learning difficulties, this will not guarantee a place in the mainstream if, in the view of the teacher, it will set her too far apart from her classmates – or indeed if it is seen by the teacher as creating too great a challenge to her teaching skills.

The question then is: are there two kinds of 'special need' – the type that has no evident stigmas and the type that has? Certainly there is concern in some quarters (Baroness Warnock for one) that the system has gone overboard in trying to meet the needs of the Statemented 2 per cent whilst conveniently ignoring the remaining 18 per cent, some of whom will be experiencing quite serious difficulties and having to face them without the benefit of a Statement. As for the 2 per cent, a further question must be: why is it that visible impairment or behavioural difference retains so much novelty for teachers that they should be so fearful of it?

If for you, the reader, special education is predominantly about meeting the needs of the nine-tenths of special needs children who attend ordinary schools without the protection of a Statement, you should find much of relevance in the remainder of this book. If your main concern is over the plight of children who *will* need a Statement detailing their needs, and who are rejected by the school system through being placed in a segregated setting, you should find this book highly relevant because that is the main model of need addressed.

It is, of course, important to meet the SENs of all children, and any child who has to spend a significant amount of time in an ordinary school with a learning difficulty which is not being addressed is a child who may be emotionally as well as educationally at risk. However, a child who is Statemented (and hence amongst the 20% of those with SENs) is likely to be at far greater risk because of the system's grossly inappropriate response to those needs. Discrimination at the level of a human rights violation against disabled and learning impaired children is widespread, yet apparently largely invisible. So the Statementing process, which is supposed to safeguard and benefit the child, may actually cause harm through its recommendation of a segregated placement.

Segregation may mean a long journey to school

An LEA with over 200 primary and secondary schools may have ten or fewer special schools, and these schools will be dotted around the Authority with children travelling to them from a very wide catchment area. The distance children are likely to have to travel will depend upon the incidence of their disability, so for a child with a moderate learning difficulty (MLD) the journey could be much shorter than for a child with a severe learning difficulty (SLD). A child with a very low incidence disability, such as a deaf and blind child, might even have to travel beyond the authority's boundaries because that LEA has not seen it as an efficient use of its resources to make its own provision. Yet other children are sent away to residential schools, such as those run by Scope and Barnardos, where they remain throughout the year – only returning to their homes during school holidays.

There are degrees of marginalisation for children with SENs, therefore, which are largely determined by the way others see *their* needs and the needs of the *education service* more broadly. We have seen that this spectrum of marginalisation is closely connected with the level of acceptance or rejection felt towards the child on account of his/her level and type of disability.

Having exceptional needs not only means being sent away, it means spending lots of time travelling and special needs school transport services are a significant part of the overall budget of any LEA since there is a duty laid upon authorities to provide free school transport. Such transport will often take up to 45 minutes, and occasionally an hour or more, to reach the school, which means that a significant part of the school day is spent travelling.

WHAT IS 'SPECIAL' EDUCATION?

Later we shall see how being physically separated is a precondition for even worse things happening to a person, and this is as true in education as in any other human service. Once a child is separated (albeit sometimes with the best of intentions) to receive his education, he becomes part of a sub-system within education which is always struggling to understand and meet his needs because it is unclear to all concerned what 'special education' is supposed to be. Such separation not only makes life uncomfortable and inconvenient for the child concerned but also creates problems for the special needs professionals (teachers, care workers, therapists, etc.) who themselves have to be physically separated and hence cut off from their own professional roots. These roots are, of course, the education and health services which provide the major input to segregated schools and units.

Because special schools and separate classes are anomalous within the education system, it is important to understand their role and function as well as their status as educational entities. Special schools, by virtue of their separateness, are perhaps more anomalous than special classes, so we will look at these first.

It is important to understand the situation of special schools to make a judgement both on the way they impact on the lives of their pupils and also on the way in which their work is evaluated and monitored. In what follows two main points will be argued:

1. Special schools are not schools *per se*.

2. To evaluate the work of a special school as though it were just another school is to miss the point of what such places do to further marginalise and disadvantage their pupils.

Are 'special schools' schools at all?

To help prepare the ground for what follows, it will be helpful at this point to engage in a little conceptual analysis to make more explicit the linguistic ground rules people observe when they use such words as 'school' and 'education'. To ask whether a special school is a school might, at first sight, seem as silly as to ask whether an apple is an apple, but it is, in fact, a very different kind of question and one which, on closer analysis, has genuine meaning. The status of an apple is relatively easy to determine in that it has a few key (not core!) characteristics which define its 'appleness': it has a certain shape, texture, flavour, smell and colour which, when taken together, will enable a judgement to be made. There may be quite wide variations in any or all of these characteristics between varieties such as spartan, golden delicious, granny smith or cox, but there is unlikely to be disagreement in a particular case as to whether one or other specimen is or is not an apple. The notion or concept 'apple' is then a relatively simple one, not likely to create much controversy and, on the face of it – the same is true of the concept 'school' but unfortunately things are not quite so straightforward.

It may seem perverse to the point of eccentricity to say that a special school is not a school, yet there are strong grounds for so arguing. Some years ago, I ran a social services Observation and Assessment Centre (O & A Centre) for delinquent and emotionally disturbed teenage boys. Such residential establishments are to be found throughout the UK and provide a temporary 'home' for children whose family circumstances are such that, at a particular stage in their lives, they cannot be adequately cared for or controlled other than in an institutional setting. This particular establishment had three open units and a secure unit which served as a regional facility for boys who were believed to be a danger to themselves or others and were awaiting a court appearance for what was usually quite a serious crime.

The Centre employed a cohort of care staff and also a small team of teachers who provided for the education of the boys in a separate building – a schoolhouse – on the same site. There were five teachers who taught the basics of education to groups of five to eight boys within the age range 12–17 years and, in addition to basic literacy and numeracy skills, they taught history, geography, science, art and craft and so on. All of these boys had missed a great deal of schooling and were years behind the majority of their peers. The education of the boys in the secure unit took place within the lounge of the unit because of the (admittedly high) risk that they might abscond should an opportunity present itself. The question we need to ask about this education building, as well as the lounge of the secure unit, is – are they schools?

WHAT MAKES A SCHOOL?

A school is more than 'a place established for instruction or an institution in which instruction of any kind is given (whether to children or adults). Often with a defining word indicating the special subject taught, such as **dancing, music, riding – school'**. (Oxford English Dictionary 1989). This is because its role is determined, within reasonable bounds, by what is to be taught and by the general expectations of the society or culture in which it functions. Leaving aside for the moment those schools which offer a specialised form of instruction, most societies with more or less universal education organise the basics of general schooling around a few core requirements such that the school should:

- employ trained teachers to teach the children
- be housed in a building with separate classrooms
- probably but not necessarily be local to where the children live; that is, it should serve the community
- organise children into age bandings
- be available on weekdays throughout the year except for school holidays
- teach certain culturally valued skills (reading, writing, arithmetic, etc.).

These common features represent the *facts* of schooling: its *content* and *process*. There are also other aspects we shall deal with later which are more abstract and have to do with the *purposes* of schooling. Broadly speaking, though, this is what we understand schools and education to be. There are, of course, such exceptions as the private (fee-paying) schools in Britain and elsewhere to which children are sent in the belief that they confer privilege and enhanced opportunities of different kinds, but these are very much a minority preference and only around seven per cent of children in Britain attend these schools. Such schools are usually not located where most of their pupils live and may be more likely to have a single-sex intake and be residential, but remain in all other respects just like other schools.

The meaning of schooling is, therefore, culturally defined by the way in which a society chooses to organise things, and on this there is a broad consensus in most developed western industrialised countries.

The question we need now to ask is: what, if any, are the irreducible defining characteristics of a school such that in their absence we would withhold the epithet 'school'?

Clearly the notion of schooling is bound up with the linked notions of 'learning' and 'development' and the whole concept of 'education'. Hirst and Peters (1970) make the point that: '"educating" people suggests a family of processes whose principle of unity is the development of desirable qualities in them' (p.19) and, whilst accepting the impossibility of getting agreement on what these 'desirable qualities' should be, this is nevertheless a useful, if broad, definition of what schools ought to be about. The concept of 'school' should, on the face of it, be less amorphous than that of 'education', and so easier to capture and define. It is not that we should expect to be able to uncover a logically necessary set of conditions for calling an activity 'education' or a place a 'school', but rather that we should be clear about the general parameters that govern our decision-making in marginal cases, so that we can at least say this or that set-up does or does not qualify because some essential ingredient is present or missing. No doubt any place that might be described as a 'school' possesses characteristics which have come to be associated with such places but, as with almost any complex concept, there will be dubious or borderline cases because an insufficient quantity of the necessary conditions are present or are present in a combination which is highly atypical.

Wittgenstein (1953) argued that it is usually impossible to cite the necessary conditions for the use of a word since ordinary language is not static, so it is not possible to pin concepts down. He made this general point by taking the example of 'games'. He claimed there is no one characteristic in terms of which roulette, golf, patience, etc., are all called 'games'. Rather they form a 'family' united 'by a complicated network of similarities overlapping and criss-crossing; sometimes overall similarities, sometimes of detail' – rather like the similarities between the faces of people belonging to the same family. There is, he argued, no one characteristic or group of characteristics which all games possess in order to be called 'games'. We should take this as a warning that we may not always be successful in our search for any set of logically necessary conditions for the use of a word, and this certainly will apply to such words as 'school', 'education', 'learning' and 'development'. Nevertheless, it seems reasonable to at least ask if there are characteristics that all schools *should* possess in order to be called 'schools' since to ask the question will help to clarify our own thoughts on the matter. Whilst this may seem like little more than academic theorising in respect of schools in general, there are, without question, real consequences for children consigned to special 'schools'.

If schools are the means through which society hopes to develop desirable qualities in its young, it is reasonable to ask whether there are any features of schools which are essential prerequisites for this, or, conversely, whether there are features which, were they present, would be likely to work against it.

Difference is not necessarily bad

Before looking more closely at the nature of schooling, it is important to be clear that difference *per se* is not to be construed negatively. Just because a school is different from the majority of others does not mean it must be a bad school or, in the extreme case as is being proposed here, not a school at all. An example would be the afore-mentioned British public (private) school which is organised differently to the typical maintained school in that it does not serve a specific geographical community but rather a 'community of interest'. Children may travel hundreds of miles to such schools and remain in residence for the school year, yet many would argue that the differences involved are strengths rather than weaknesses. Certainly many hold such schools in high esteem and some are oversubscribed. The separate question of whether such schools are fundamentally elitist and socially divisive is an important one in terms of social planning but not one which will be explored here.

Which differences count?

If difference itself is not the issue then we need to look more closely at some of what appear to be the defining features of schools to see which of them seem to confer social value. We have seen that such criteria as being local and serving a local community, whilst being the most widely chosen option, is not necessarily the whole story; we have also seen that the public schools do not meet these criteria yet remain culturally valued institutions. Nor could a case be made for age banding or length of school year since one could easily imagine a school which did not operate in such ways but which would still be seen as a valued school. What is taught is obviously important, although it would be hard to imagine a curriculum which would render an establishment a non-school on curriculum grounds alone – unless it were one which patently made no attempt at the 'development of desirable qualities' in its learners.

Some children were considered ineducable

It might be helpful at this point to look back at the provisions made under the 1944 Education Act (DES 1944) for children who were then described as *educationally subnormal* (ESN) and who previously had been referred to as *mentally defective* but are now described as having SLDs (it is worth paying close attention to the way in which our language for describing these children has become progressively less offensive whilst our determination to keep them separate has remained steadfast).

Under the 1944 Act, such children were deemed ineducable and excluded from education services. The Mental Health Act 1959 allowed parents extra time to appeal against an LEA's decision that their child was incapable of being educated in school, and protest continued to grow until, in April 1971, LEAs were given responsibility under the Handicapped Children Act 1970 'which removed the power of health authorities to provide training for these children, and required the staff and buildings of junior training centres to be transferred to the education service. In this way some 24,000 children in junior training centres and special care units, 8,000 in about 100 hospitals and an uncertain number at home or in private institutions ceased to be treated as 'mentally deficient' and became entitled to special education' (HMSO 1978). These children were then classified as severely educationally sub-normal (ESN-S) and, for the first time, deemed by society to be worthy of receiving an education – albeit still one which was to be separate from other children.

Prior to being deemed educable, these 30,000-plus children spent their time in the health authority-managed junior training centres or hospitals, and the advance to being considered *educable* (as distinct from merely *trainable*) represented something of an endorsement of their essential humanity. This is so because animals are described as 'trainable' but never 'educable' and one of the few applications of the word to children is in the context of toilet *training* in the young infant, which is, of course, a function shared by animals and humans alike. However, the relevant point for our current purpose is that the acceptance of these children into the school system saw many of them remaining in the same buildings, and in the same groupings, but often with different staff standing in front of them. At this stage the curriculum hardly changed and in fact it was not until the advent of the National Curriculum 20 years later that there was seen to be a need for a proper agreed formal curriculum for the special school – even this seemed to many of us like something of an afterthought on the government's part.

The question to be asked then is: did these training centres suddenly become schools, when all that had changed was that a teacher working for a local education authority took charge of the group? If so, the only truly defining characteristic of a school is that teachers should be present. On this thinking, and looking back at the teaching in the O & A Centre for delinquent boys, both the teaching building and the secure unit lounge must be considered to be schools. Yet it is not intuitively obvious that this single criterion should be so defining. Similarly, when a teacher visits a sick child to provide tuition in his home, would we say that for the duration of her visit the home becomes a school? Probably not. Such philosophical speculation might be interesting but does it help us to understand what a school is?

If it is accepted that none of the criteria thus far identified (the building, presence of a teacher, a curriculum, etc.) are uniquely defining of what a school is and that this remains true when the other listed criteria are also taken into account, what is it that makes a place a school? The only other criterion which suggests itself is the presence of children themselves, yet this cannot be sufficient in and of itself since wherever children gathered would automatically become a school. If the presence of children were linked with that of teachers, then again the two O & A Centre situations would qualify – as would that of home teaching. It seems then that none of the obvious content or process candidates, or even a mixture of them, are sufficient in themselves to provide a definition of what a school is, so it is necessary to look elsewhere, towards the *purpose* of schooling. However, before moving on from our consideration of concrete criteria, it might be useful to look at one criterion we have not yet considered – that of the number of children that are necessary before we would describe a place as a school.

Here again it is difficult to be hard and fast but we have one or two reference points. In the very small village school where the numbers may have dropped to as few as half a dozen children, we would not wish to say it was no longer a school. As the numbers drop steadily from around, say, 40 to less than 10, it would be hard to identify a point at which we would no longer call the place a school. Conversely, within special education there are many units for children with specific disabilities such as deafness, blindness or autism which are loosely attached to ordinary schools but which we do not call schools, even if to all intents and purposes they operate entirely autonomously. This, of course, has something to do with the cost and administrative savings involved in not having an additional headteacher and deputy, but this is not the whole story and such arrangements may also have something to do with the way the provision is viewed *vis-à-vis* numbers. This does, therefore, mark a difference in conceptualisation based upon the perceived needs of the learners involved.

The school as a learning community

Perhaps there is something about the social dynamics of schools which serve to define them as such. The idea of the school as a 'learning community' is a more abstract notion than those examined thus far. Hitherto we have dealt with such concrete entities as teachers, children, curriculum, buildings, physical location, etc., and found none of these (whether taken individually or in combination) to be uniquely defining of what a school is.

Introducing the notion of a 'learning community' takes us beyond the realm of the *process* of schooling into a consideration of its *purpose*, and this is where things become a little more difficult. The point to be made is that if, as I have shown, there is nothing in the concrete facts of schools which serve to uniquely define them, we must look elsewhere – which means to those less tangible – although presumably no less real – features which may carry the essential meaning of what a school is.

The idea of a school as a 'learning community' is one which may help us to gain a better understanding of the essence of a school, and here it is useful to look back at one of the dictionary definitions of schools for specific skill development. The examples given were for dancing, music and riding, although the list might have included others, such as drama or art. Here the relevance of the notion of the learning community is helpful, as indeed it would have been in ancient Greece where various schools of philosophy flourished and to which students flocked to learn at the feet of the master. This notion of a school as a learning community in which individuals come together to study a particular subject is not unlike that of the ordinary school for children which, in spite of the broader focus of the teaching, is nevertheless a learning community in the same sense. It is instructive to try and apply this notion of a learning community to the special school, whether in the sense of a specific subject or a more broadly based education? Certainly the special school would see itself as offering a broadly based education but would it be fair to say that this takes place in a learning community in anything like the sense inherent in the earlier examples?

If it is understood that ordinary schools are the places in which a broadly based education is offered to children then what should we make of another version of such places which (1) automatically excluded children who did not have the disability defined as the admission requirement and (2) was the only place on offer for the education of a particular child – such that if education were to be available at all, this would *have to be the place for compulsory atten-dance*?

The importance of relationships

Another feature intrinsic to the notion of a learning community is that of the desirable interactions which take place between the learners and between learners and their teachers. That the special school provides opportunities for personal relationships to develop between teachers and pupils is not in question, but whether the same can be said to be true of relationships between pupils certainly is.

Here it is important to remember that the model of disability used in this book is severe and complex needs.

So what is meant by a 'personal relationship'? A key notion for developing a better understanding of this issue is that of *personal respect*, which means being accorded certain rights – especially of the kind one would wish to have accorded to oneself. It also means being treated in ways which serve to reinforce a sense of self-worth, which for anyone must embrace such things as having one's point of view and needs taken seriously and also having one's aspirations respected.

Personal relationships are so important that they might almost be taken as the *sine qua non* of the learning process, but their ingredients are a little elusive. One key element is the reciprocal knowledge of personal as opposed to public matters, which implies a knowledge of the private life of the other person. For this to develop there needs to be shared experience and mutual disclosure; reciprocity is at the heart of such intimacy. This is, in essence, what we have elsewhere referred to as the 'hidden curriculum', a term much less fashionable than it once was.

Being respected also means being given appropriate opportunities to grow and develop in relationships, and a precondition for such personal growth is the presence of others who are able to facilitate such growth. Children with profound, and perhaps multiple, disabilities are not as well-placed to promote the growth of other children as their typical peers because they do not have some of the essential skill prerequisites for reciprocating, let alone making the running when it comes to relationship-building.

The hidden curriculum

The hidden curriculum may be the desirable core curriculum for the child with complex needs, so helping teachers, psychologists and administrators to understand what the hidden curriculum means is very important if the education of these particular children is to have relevance.

The hidden curriculum is what makes schools the places they are, but its products or outcomes are of no interest to politicians or school inspectors. In addition to the National Curriculum, schooling provides children with the opportunity to learn about relationships and to practice relationship-building. During the course of their school and college lives children will gain a great deal of social knowledge and hone a vast number of essential skills. Such knowledge acquisition and skill development will include:

- making friends – the central role relationship between peers
- conventions of conduct – rules and manners
- sex role conventions

- fair distribution and sharing – the notion of positive justice
- the nature of authority – the central role relationship between child and adult and between adults.

The child can only make sense of society by gaining knowledge of such social relationships as authority, attachment and friendship and of such social transactions as punishment, sharing, kindness and hostility. Through such transactions the child will be able to develop:

- a better sense of self derived from contact with others
- some useful (perhaps essential) skills in getting along with others
- a knowledge of what others of the same or similar age find interesting, important, fun, frightening, boring, etc.
- some skills in doing practical things
- some facts about the world.

It is through those thousand-and-one observations and encounters throughout the course of a single school day that children progressively build a picture of who they themselves are and what makes others tick. Such apparently trivial information about what another child likes to watch on television, what clothes (s)he prefers, where (s)he is going on holiday or what (s)he wants for the future comprise the hidden curriculum which is so important in the lives of children. It is interesting to speculate on how much of this a child in a segregated special school is likely to learn.

Are there different kinds of children?

In the context of schools set up to teach specific *skills* (music, drama, etc.) the idea of a school set up to teach specific *children* is odd to say the least. It is not as though there were even a particular curriculum – such as life skills – any more, although even then it would hardly have fitted with the specialist subject model. Here we are not talking about children with a *specific interest* but children of, what is presumably thought to be, a *specific kind*. But are there different kinds of children?

The answer from the special school sympathiser would of course be that the wrong kind of question is being asked here since it is not being suggested that there are different kinds of *children* but rather that there are children with different kinds of *needs*. It is a subsidiary theme of this book that a distinction needs to be drawn between *fundamental* and *additional* needs and that one of the major misunderstandings in special education arises through the conflation of these two notions. Nevertheless, this confusion has been around for a long time and is not about to disappear since it is rooted in what

Skrtic (1991) has called the 'grounding assumptions' of special education.

It used to be thought that there are indeed different kinds of children – the academic and the practical – and that the way to identify them was to sit them down to do a kind of IQ test called the 11+. This now largely discredited idea is still around and will probably come back into vogue again in years to come in spite of the fact that it is a highly damaging idea because it sells children short. It does this by attempting to reduce the measure of the worth of children to how well they can jump through a somewhat silly little hoop, and this in the interest of maintaining privilege for those who have become accustomed to expect it and who are not prepared to share it around.

If the 11+ test represented a disservice to the majority of ordinary children because it consigned them to a separate school for the 'non-academic/practical', the injustice they suffered (and continue to suffer in some places) pales into insignificance when set against the injustice done to disabled children when they are consigned to a separate school simply because they have an impairment. At least the secondary modern school was seen to be a place fit for most children, even if there was always a more socially valued place for their 'betters'. But what of the child who must spend his school years in a place just for people who have a physical impairment or a learning difficulty?

The children who attend the kind of school we are considering here are, by and large, unable to make the running in relationship-building because they lack the understanding and the social and interpersonal skills which are the prerequisites for such a process. To withdraw such children from their home communities and place them together for their school years in complete isolation from children who do have the requisite skills is hardly a recipe for the development of social skills and relationships.

If, as is being argued here, schools are generally understood to be places where relationship-building is a key ingredient (if not one which is studiously measured) of the learning process, such that a place could hardly be called a school if it could not take place, then some special schools are just not schools. An important part of the explanation of why such places are still claimed to be schools is that they are officially classified and monitored as such by the government. It is the failure of the inspection process to highlight what is missing in such places which makes it so difficult for the rest of us to see the wood for the trees.

EVALUATING THE WORK OF SCHOOLS

The same model for all schools

The approach to monitoring and inspection of special schools is essentially the same as that for mainstream schools and this is one of the reasons why some of the damage special schools do to their pupils' development remains undetected. The standard HMI style of inspection is appropriate for mainstream schools but disastrous for special schools because it is rooted in the assumption that the special school is just another school.

Within any LEA, systems are developed primarily to meet the requirements of its mainstream schools because they represent the means by which the overwhelming majority of pupils are served. Because special schools serve around just two per cent of the school population, it is inevitable that arrangements for them will be tacked on to what happens for the majority. What happens for special schools tends to come as something of an afterthought and this was certainly the case with the implementation of the National Curriculum and Local Financial Management.

There is nothing particularly puzzling or surprising about this in that any organisation will have its bread-and-butter work, the development of which will, quite rightly, occupy most of its thinking because it also demands most of its resources. It will also be the case that an organisation will develop greater expertise in those areas in which it focuses most of its effort, with its more marginal activities remaining less well-developed. This is just what happens with special education.

It is partly because what goes on in special schools is so marginal to the work of the LEA that the way it is evaluated is so irrelevant to the needs of the children concerned, and this marginalisation needs to be better understood in order that a more appropriate form of inspection might be developed.

We have seen that there is a serious question mark over whether what we have hitherto referred to as 'special schools' are in fact schools other than in name. Whatever the view taken on this, it is instructive to look at the way in which the work of special schools is evaluated by those who are supposedly best qualified to do so, that is HMI. This is understood to provide the 'gold standard' for school inspections and, in that sense, a system held in very high esteem by education professionals and the public at large. Developing a clear understanding of the nature and purpose of the HMI inspection is important in that formal inspection is intended to legitimise (or otherwise) the work of the school, and in this sense it serves not only as a standards watchdog but also as a way in which society confers approval on the means determined for the education of its children.

The HMI inspection

Historically, under the general approach to the inspection of schools, the procedure for special schools was precisely the same as for any other school. The only real difference within the system was that which separated the secondary from primary school phases, in which the former involved a more subject-orientated approach and required a larger inspection team. The full inspection was intended to cover 'the whole of the life and work of the school' and the resulting report was to incorporate all of the following elements:

(i) a brief factual introduction describing the nature of the school;

(ii) comment on the premises, equipment and resources, and their effect on the quality of work;

(iii) discussion of how the school is staffed and organised; of the curriculum which is provided and of procedures for record-keeping and assessment;

(iv) the school as a community: such matters as pastoral organisation; behaviour and attendance; extra-curricular activities; and links with parents, other schools and the community at large;

(v) an assessment of standards of work, both generally and in particular subjects and aspects of the curriculum. The degree of detail and the balance between 'general' and 'departmental' assessment will vary according to the type of school and the scale of the inspection; but this is always the most important section of the report; and

(vi) a concluding section. (DES 1986, p.11)

The statutory basis for inspections by Registered Inspectors is now governed by Section 10 of the Education (Schools) Act 1992, which requires that inspection teams report on:

- the quality of education provided by schools
- the educational standards achieved in those schools
- whether the financial resources made available to the schools are managed efficiently
- the spiritual, moral, social and cultural development of pupils at those schools.

It is important to note that this entire framework applies to the inspection of special schools as well as to the inspection of SEN in ordinary schools.

The inspection *Framework* (DFE 1992) requires the following information:

1.1 basic information about the school (type of school, age range of pupils etc.)

1.2 intake of pupils and the area served by the school (nature of pupils and catchment area)

1.3 school data and indicators (number of teachers, pupils, class size, budget etc.)

1.4 record of the evidence base of the inspection (time spent observing lessons, discussion with staff, pupils etc.).

Evaluation criteria must provide evidence of the main findings to include:

2.1 standards, quality, efficiency and ethos: the overall judgement about the school should be based on evaluation of the quality of education provided, the standards of work, the efficiency of management and the effectiveness of the school community in providing for the spiritual, moral, social and cultural development of pupils.

Standards of achievement and quality of learning are also of key importance and should include:

3.1 standards of achievement: what pupils know, understand and can do in curriculum subjects with evidence of test scores on National Curriculum assessments. Also inspectors will observe lessons, discuss matters with staff and pupils, note pupils' work etc.

3.2 quality of learning: progress made in lessons as reflected by gains in knowledge, understanding and skills. Also competence in reading, writing and numeracy etc.

Efficiency too is evaluated:

4.0 the efficiency of the school: how well resources (including money) are used to maximise the school's aims and objectives.

The quality of the school as a community will be judged by:

5.1 behaviour and discipline: how pupils' attitudes and actions affect learning and the overall quality of life of the school.

5.2 Attendance.

5.3 Pupils' spiritual and moral development to be judged by the principles and values for which it stands and the attitudes it fosters.

5.4 Pupils' social and cultural development is to be judged in terms of the relationships in the school and the extent to which pupils show respect for persons and property.

Factors contributing to the findings will include observations on:

6.1 quality of teaching: whether clear goals are set for individuals and groups and how well lessons and activities are planned and presented in terms of whether they engage and motivate pupils.

6.2 assessment, recording and reporting: the extent to which the school's arrangements result in a comprehensive picture of the achievements of individual pupils in relation to the National Curriculum and other objectives.

The quality of the curriculum will be judged by its:

6.3 (i) content, organisation and planning: a judgement of the curriculum in terms of how its content, structure, organisation and implementation contribute to high standards of learning.

(ii) equality of opportunity: how well the school arranges for equality of opportunity.

(iii) provision for pupils with special educational needs: the extent to which pupils with SENs are supported to make the greatest progress possible in the context of national aims for education. How well the school tackles assessment, recording and reporting judged by how good a picture it presents of the achievements of its pupils.

6.4 management and planning: in terms of how the governors and head determine and implement the school's objectives.

6.5 organisation and administration: how efficient and effective is the school's administration and procedures.

In terms of resource management judgements will be of:

6.6 (i) how well teaching and support staff are managed, deployed and developed.

(ii) how effectively the resources for learning are deployed in terms of their effect on the quality of teaching.

(iii) how the school's accommodation effects the quality of work.

6.7 pupil's support and guidance: how well pupils' needs are identified and their progress monitored.

6.8 community links and liaison with other schools: how well parents are informed and served by the school and how well they are supported to contribute to school life. How purposeful are the relations with business and commerce, the community and other relevant agencies.

The standards by which a school will be judged on all of these criteria are that the judgements should be:

- *secure* – rooted in substantial evidence
- *firsthand* – based on direct observation
- *reliable* – consistent with the above evaluation criteria
- *valid* – they reflect the standards actually achieved
- *comprehensive* – they cover all of the above described aspects of the school
- *corporate* – the conclusions reflect the collective inspection team view.

All of this represents a thorough and searching evaluation programme of the work of ordinary schools which, if undertaken by experienced and knowledgeable individuals, ought to produce a useful picture of the life and work of the school within its community. Since the stated purpose of inspection is to 'identify strengths and weaknesses in schools in order that they may improve the quality of education offered and raise the standards achieved by their pupils'(ibid., p.i), there is every reason to suppose that such an inspection programme conducted every four years would serve its stated purpose. The question to be asked here, though, is would such a programme serve the needs of children in special schools in a similar way?

Using our chosen model of a special school (for children with severe and complex learning difficulties) we shall now look at what such an inspection programme would be likely to achieve. In doing so it will be useful to think in terms of the Inspectorate using their

Framework as a rating system which, whilst not being expressed primarily in quantitative terms, nevertheless operates normatively in terms of comparisons being made between schools of a similar kind.

Evaluating the special school

The first thing to note about the HMI approach to inspection is that for a small (less than 51 pupils) special school for children with SLDs the minimum number of inspector days would be nine, which is two more than would be allocated to a junior or infant school of the same size. Regardless of whether this is enough to do the additional work, recognition of the need for additional time for children with complex needs is welcome.

All of what is covered in this *Framework* is unexceptionable in that quality of learning, overall efficiency and the quality of community provided by a school are all clearly important things to measure. Neither is issue taken with any of the listed items in the inspection schedule in that they are all relevant to gaining a picture of the opportunities offered to children. The real problem with this whole approach, as far as the segregated school is concerned, is that it fails to take account of *the kind of place* a special school is, that is to say it does not ask, and is not allowed to ask, the really important questions such as:

- Should *this* child be in *this* school?
- Is the curriculum relevant to *this* child's needs?
- Will attending *this* school promote *this* child's social participation and community acceptance?
- What if any disadvantages attach to the child attending *this* school?
- What are the key issues in *this* child's life?

Certainly the *Framework* for inspection asks the questions that need to be asked about the quality of *teaching* but it pays no attention to the overall opportunities for *learning*, and this focus upon what is offered with so little attention to what it might be possible for the child to take is the real failure of the *Framework* as an inspection blueprint for special schools.

The rating categories of the *Framework* are relevant from 1.0 down to 3.1 but rating 3.2 – *quality of learning* – cannot possibly reflect the true potential of a child when her peer group offers so little of what is necessary to promote learning. Any child, let alone a child with a severe disability, learns a great deal from the models offered by other, perhaps more mature, children, and such stimulation is not available to children with SLDs. In a segregated setting it is not just the absence of role models which creates the disadvantages but also the presence of entirely inappropriate role models within the special school, where grossly inappropriate behaviour may be the order of the day, or, in the case of some profoundly handicapped children, little or no 'behaviour' at all.

One example of important learning-related behaviour is being *on task*, which is crucial if children are to develop good learning habits. The typical ordinary classroom offers many such models but the special school may offer none at all. Indeed it would be surprising if a child in such a school (as the model used in this book) ever saw a classmate on task in this sense.

Rating 5.0, *the quality of the school as a community*, is another which discriminates against the special school child because the special school is, by definition, an artificial community. This is so because it draws children from such a wide catchment area that the odds are stacked heavily against any of the children who attend living in the same community. Even worse, the 'community' of the special school becomes a 'disabled community' which bears no relation to what we understand communities to be.

Rating 5.3, *pupils' spiritual and moral development*, can hardly be measured fairly in a community which is almost by definition adult-determined. Where the dependency of pupils is so great, there is no way that the pupils' spiritual and moral development can be separated from the dominant adult ethos.

Rating 6.3 (ii), *equality of opportunity* (in relation to curriculum access), is the one which should, but probably doesn't, cause inspectors the greatest concern. What does equal opportunities mean in the special school? Does it mean ensuring the children are treated as of equal value to children in other schools in respect of their right to access the curriculum? If so, this is hardly likely to be the case given the limited range of teaching skills and learning opportunities on offer in most SLD schools. If equal opportunities is construed more broadly, there are many questions to be asked about the role of the special school in bringing its pupils into the community.

Rating 6.8, *community links and liaison with other schools*, is another problematic area for the special school in that few develop the kind of mainstream links which could be of lasting benefit to their pupils. In addition, community links tend to be forged in search of financial support in which the pupils are presented as 'objects of charity' rather than as equal partners in a collaborative enterprise as would be the objective of link arrangements with mainstream schools.

There are therefore two broad reasons why the HMI approach to the evaluation of the special school is fatally flawed: (1) limited opportunities for learning because of a reduced curriculum and unsuitable pupil groupings and (2) limited social contacts. Both of these are at the very heart of the educative process as enshrined in the socially valued model of mainstream schooling which the inspection framework was designed to evaluate. Underlying this veritable host of flaws in its inspection framework there remain two key questions inspectors *don't* or *can't* ask because they are so-cial/political questions:

1. Are the right children here?

2. Should there be schools/units like this?

I was myself head of a special school which underwent an inspection some years ago and am familiar with the approach. The inspection lasted a week, with two special needs inspectors present for much of the time and an additional inspector involved for a day to look at the medical and paramedical input from the health authority. The inspection pretty much covered the areas described in the above framework but asked no questions about the appropriateness or otherwise of placements. This was particularly puzzling in that the school was designated as a school for children with severe and complex learning difficulties (which meant they should have, as their primary disability, a severe learning difficulty) yet still retained a small group of children with spastic quadriplegia who were also non-vocal but had 'normal' intelligence. These children were inap-propriately placed by any standards, yet no comment was made about this by the inspectors, nor was it even raised as an issue in their report. At the feedback meeting at the end of the week-long inspection, the inspectors were challenged on their failure to identify anomalies in pupil placements. The reply was that it was not part of the duty of inspectors to ask questions about placements but merely to look at the quality of what children experienced given that they were in the school. It must be a major flaw in the inspection model that the question of whether the child is in the right school cannot be addressed.

The apparently value-free approach to inspection

The statutory basis for school inspections does not contain an expla-nation of its values orientation or ideology because it does not need to. It is simply assumed that the institutions it is designed to evaluate are well-conceived to do their job and hence all that is required thereafter is a means of checking out whether, in the individual case, at a particular time this is so. All this means is that there is an implicit assumption that the *model* to which the school conforms is soundly conceived, so that if it were run efficiently it would inevitably produce what children need and society expects. However, this is to make no comment at all on the curriculum itself (in Britain the *National Curriculum*), which is of course not in the least value-free since it is intended to be a curriculum which will prepare children for the world of work or unemployment beyond school.

Of course the traditional HMI inspection is not really value-free, either could it be, since it is rooted in a set of understandings about what society needs to reproduce itself. As we saw in Chapter 3, in any complex social situation a number of paradigms may exist side-by-side and hence interact in complex and obscure ways. The failure of the state inspection system to make explicit its values and assumptions may be due to the fact that it would be too dangerous to do so, rather than that nobody has thought it important.

The culture of professionalism

If anything, the school curriculum embodies the 'culture of professionalism' (Bledstein 1976) in that in Britain, as in the rest of the industrialised world, social success is defined largely in terms of professional status. To say that the school system, and the means by which it is monitored, is value-free is about as nonsensical a statement as it is possible to make, yet the values it embodies are left to the individual to discern rather than being made explicit either in the curriculum itself or in the organisation of the particular school. Thus it is too with the programme for school evaluation.

That the inspection team approaches its work with no prior doubts as to the human rights status of the pupils served by the school says something about the overall effectiveness of safeguards for children's rights generally. It would, of course, be very unusual for a team to uncover any serious infringements of pupils' rights during the course of an inspection. It is a central thesis of this book that segregated schools themselves represent a serious human rights violation for the children who attend them, though it has to be said that such an idea is wholly alien to the HMI inspection ideology.

Inspectors would be much more likely to encounter poor or indifferent teaching which, though serious for the children concerned, is not what one would understand to be a serious denial of a basic human right. This is not, of course, to ignore those deplorable cases of individual sexual or physical abuse that do occasionally take place in schools due to the actions of a teacher and which will always occur because there simply are not the means to identify such people prior to things going so badly wrong. But, as repeated media reports show, such abuse is far more likely to occur in a segregated setting out of the public view, and hence will involve disabled children. This, it seems, is just another burden created by the need to segregate.

What seems to give the inspector this confidence that things will essentially be in good order is the knowledge that it is a school that is to be inspected and schools are just not the kind of places in which seriously harmful things are done, deliberately or otherwise, to children. In spite of their occasional shortcomings, schools remain valued and respected social institutions, so, in approaching his work, the inspector will entertain largely positive expectations about what he is about to see – and since expectations have a powerful role in shaping perception this sets a very positive tone for what follows.

The problem for the child in the SLD school is that the inspector approaches his evaluation of the school with this same positive mind set. The logic of this is simple:

Premise 1   I am to inspect the work of 'X' SLD school.

Premise 2   'X' is a school much like other schools.

Premise 3   Schools are socially valued institutions where, by and large, good things happen for children.

Conclusion: Therefore this school is almost certainly a place where good things happen for children.

It is this apparent logic which needs to be challenged if children in segregated schools are to achieve a fair deal from the education system. We can call this a basic *category mistake* by the inspector (and, of course, all others concerned) in that the place children with severe disabilities are 'educated' is being characterised as a 'school', and this is a category in which it does not belong and has no right to be, for the reasons outlined above. The same mistake would have been made had the inspector included in this category a junior training centre or a mental handicap hospital – both types of institutions which, until relatively recently, served children with severe disabilities. There never was a temptation to characterise either institution as a school, although it has to be said this was in part because these places were run by the health authority and not education.

Educational 'cleansing'?

As to whether there is an *implicit* understanding that part of the role of the special school is to 'cleanse' the ordinary school of undesirable children – a form of *educational apartheid* – then each individual must make up his or her own mind. It is certainly not encouraging to see the retention of the second qualifying clause on the duty to integrate carried over from the 1981 Act into the 1993 Act, that is that a child should be integrated unless this would be incompatible with *the provision of efficient education for the children with whom he will be educated*. Since this clause is usually only applicable to labelled children, it seems, to say the very least, somewhat discriminatory.

To describe an evaluation approach as 'value-free' in the sense implied here is to say no more than that it is approached as though there were not likely to be a problem – in other words, the way in which the mainstream school is approached. This means there will not be a perceived need to invoke some kind of social welfare ideology to help make sense of what is going on and how to remedy it. A possible need for such an ideology is indicated by the evident devalued social status of people with so-called 'deviant' characteristics and their relegation to the margins of society. The problem is that the school system fails to address the way in which impaired individuals are perceived, assessed and esteemed (or not) by society. This is because it remains unaware that there is a problem.

The need for a moral framework

Because it does not recognise that there is a problem, the HMI school inspection model is an *amoral* framework in that it envisages no need to tackle oppression and disadvantage; were there a greater sense of awareness, it would have to be seen as an *immoral* framework. What children in special schools need now is a *moral* framework, and normalisation theory (as we saw in the last chapter) is an ideology which attempts to make sense of, and reverse, the process of social devaluation amongst vulnerable groups within society. We saw in the previous chapter that there are several well-developed and documented ideologies from which to choose and that choice of an ideology informed by social welfare principles is important. To refresh the memory, we have seen that an ideology is 'that part of a culture which is actively concerned with the establishment and defence of patterns of belief and value' (Fallers 1961) and changing the ideology within a service system, let alone a society, is not likely to be achieved in the short run.

We have also seen that the principle of normalisation is an ideology with significant implications for any human service system. I have proposed (Hall 1992c) that normalisation represents a useful core set of ideas that educationalists might like to draw upon in their formulation of a rationale for the practice of special education. Carson (1995) has shown that, through the application of the principle to the evaluation of segregated settings, much more fruitful insights result than are available through more traditional means.

NORMALISATION – THE BASIS FOR AN ALTERNATIVE EVALUATION FRAMEWORK

In Chapter 3 we looked at the theoretical underpinnings of the principle of normalisation. Now we shall look at the application of the principle in the form of a systematic framework for human service evaluation.

Because normalisation represents an overtly *values-centred* approach to service evaluation, it is likely that those engaged with the more traditional approaches will feel they are being criticised as being immoral or, at least, not concerned with human values. This is not an accusation implicit in the theory. Any approach will have its own values orientation (whether explicit or implicit) and normalisation is very clear that its starting point is an acknowledgement of the dangers inherent in the universal dynamic of social devaluation of vulnerable people.

The PASS framework

Like the HMI inspection framework, PASS (Programme Analysis of Service Systems – Wolfensberger and Glenn 1975) is a highly systematic method for evaluating human services. It is also a *quantitative* approach which enables the user to translate ratings of the 50 separate service dimensions into scores which can be summed to provide an overall statement of the value and likely effectiveness of the service. Although most widely used as tools for training professionals and others in the quantitative evaluation of human services, PASS and PASSING (Programme Analysis of Service Systems' Implementation of Normalisation Goals – Wolfensberger and Thomas 1983) are also service evaluation instruments in their own right, and teams experienced in using them will be asked to undertake evaluations quite independently of any training event. When used as vehicles for training, these instruments do not purport to provide an evaluation of the service because most of those in the team (with the exception of the team and workshop leaders) do not usually have sufficient experience of the instruments.

PASS – preliminary considerations

A PASS evaluation is a highly disciplined affair requiring a number of preliminary site visits to try to ensure that things go well. The organisers will make initial visits to ensure that the service manager and staff understand what is to happen and that those involved in the evaluation exercise are themselves very carefully briefed. In the training context, the service evaluation is most frequently used as part of a four- to five-day highly intensive residential workshop which is designed to teach participants (mostly in small groups of five to eight people) about normalisation/Social Role Valorisation (SRV), and there will usually be two extended visits to the service by the whole team to collect data.

The first visit begins with an initial inquiry interview conducted by the team leader with the head of service; other team members usually remain silent during this session. The initial inquiry is designed to introduce the team members, to find out as much as possible about the service and to get a picture of what the manager of the service understands (s)he is trying to achieve on behalf of those being served.

At this initial visit information is collected on:

- *the people who use the service*: how many, their age, gender, length of stay, how they are described, where they come from and where they move on to

- *how people are grouped*: how they are assessed, cared for etc.

- *how the needs of people served are conceptualised*: what the service says it thinks it does for people, what it would like to achieve, what are its goals and how are they met

- *what the staff are like*: What skills, training, how are they addressed by the people who use the service

- *what model the service operates on*: what are its ideas or guiding principles, how does it decide on programmes, etc.

- *what options are available to clients*: education, work, leisure, place of residence

- *what area the service covers*: how extensive, what other services exist

- *how the service and its parent agency are structured*: who else is served, who makes decisions, who is consulted

- *how well connected the service is*: to sources of information, academic institutions, etc.

- *what, if any, contribution is made to deinstitutionalisation*: who comes from institutions and where do they move on to

- *accessibility*: forms of transport, time taken to get there, physical access

- *funding*: cost per client, financial systems and documentation, income

- *planning process*: who is involved, who sets goals, how related to client progress and who monitors this

- *staff development*: how much is spent and to what end, what form does the training take

- *social participation of clients*: who with, where and in what ways

- *what the needs of the clients are*: are there distinctly different groupings within this service, does the agency cater for other groups and where

- *rights of clients*: do people have rights in accordance with their age

- *what local resources are used*: do clients use generic or specialist facilities/resources.

All of these categories reflect headings which the team will later address in the information collection phase of the investigation. This initial interview may take upwards of two hours, yielding data running to 20 or so pages. The evaluation is therefore thorough. The headings relate to 50 dimensions of the service to be evaluated, of which the following have particular relevance to special needs education.

PASS service ratings

The evaluation framework groups its 50 separate ratings under a few broad headings designed to answer some key questions relating to the needs of the children. These are: where is the school in relation to where the child lives; what are the main needs of the child and how should these be met; is the programme intensive; what opportunities exist for social intercourse; how accessible are useful community facilities; what effect does the school have on the way the child is viewed by others; is the child treated in ways which are appropriate to his age and needs, etc. There are also a number of other ratings which have to do with administration and which will not detain us here.

Physical and social integration

This is concerned with the location of the school or class within both a local area and the broader region, and also how well the school fits into its setting. Its purpose is to identify the levels of opportunity which exist for the pupil to gain access to the school from where he lives and to mix with other children and adults once he is there. It is also concerned with the range of physical resources (shops, libraries, etc.) which exist locally.

This group of ratings is concerned with highlighting practices which restrict the child's opportunity to spend time with valued others. Its emphasis is upon the importance of being able to use mainstream community facilities which offer such opportunities. It is also concerned with identifying any incongruities in the setting of the school, such as a special school placed in a remote rural location. There is also concern with the name of the service, in terms of whether it enhances or detracts from the image of its pupils. Imagery is a very important issue, so there are ratings that look at such things as logos, symbols and wall displays which surround the children to see whether these positively or negatively impact on the way the children are perceived.

Also under this heading are ratings which look at possible different groupings of children, staff and others who have involvement with the school or class to see whether these might in any way have stigmatising consequences.

Age and Culture appropriateness

Whether or not disabled children are treated in age-appropriate ways is clearly an important issue and a number of ratings bear upon this. The external appearance, as well as the internal design, are scrutinised to see whether they reflect the chronological age of the children. Whether the children are *treated* age-appropriately, and whether they are encouraged to act and dress in age-appropriate ways, are also investigated. Here the team will look at the way children are addressed, referred to and described. Included here as well is a consideration of the possessions the children are encouraged to have.

Culture appropriateness tends to be less of an issue with children but it is important to ensure that the classroom looks like a classroom and the school building is also instantly recognisable as such. The pattern of the day, week, month and year should also match that of other schools – this is not always the case with special schools, which certainly tend to have a shorter day than their mainstream counterparts. Rights also come into this and it is important to know whether the school extends the same rights to children as would be the case in an ordinary school.

Development and growth support

Several ratings address the issue of whether children are treated in ways which support their development, and here issues of overprotection in all its forms are relevant. If the service places unnecessary social or physical barriers around children, this may restrict their opportunity to learn. Here also the quality and intensity of the programme of education offered is assessed to see whether it provides an appropriate level of challenge.

Quality of setting

There are also ratings which look at the physical comfort and the overall aesthetic quality of the environment: the quality of the furniture, equipment and fittings; whether there is an absence of noxious smells; whether the temperature is right. All of these are important both in terms of ensuring the child is suitably cared for and stimulated and of the message they send to others about how the children are valued.

Quality of relationships

There are a number of indicators concerned with how children are treated and here the team will look at whether there is an approach based upon *individualisation* or whether the approach is impersonal with a tendency to stereotype. They will look at the ways in which children are addressed and whether their education and care programmes are tailored to the child's own unique needs. It is also important to know how well the staff know the children and what the quality of interactions are between children, and between children and staff.

Summarising the findings

The team will visit the service for quite long periods and each will have a specific brief to collect certain sorts of information relevant to the evaluation programme. Each will also be required to spend some time with one child and to get to know that child a little, to try to gain an impression of what the school feels like from the child's perspective.

When the visits are over, the team come together and, under their leader, share information on the school by going through the 50 ratings in turn, trying to summarise the role of the service in relation to each particular dimension. This is known as the *conciliation process* and requires each member of the team who has any relevant information or observation to contribute to do so. This is how the team begin to build a picture of what the service is like.

Model coherency

At some point the question arises as to whether the service is operating in a way which is compatible with what it is supposed to achieve. Put another way, it is an attempt to answer the question: *do the various elements of the school/class combine to meet the particular needs of the children at this particular time?* Or, more directly: *are the right people working with the right children, who are properly grouped, doing the right things, using the right methods and consistently so?*

There is an important issue here of the *role identity* of the staff, and too many involved in segregated special education services have drifted into a misunderstanding of their task. It is too easy, when the medical model is dominant, to see the task as essentially that of care and therapy, and outsiders do not see the relevance of education to the pupils. In this regard I recall meeting a head of department from a comprehensive school who applied for a special school teaching post. This very pleasant and kindly gentleman spent a morning visiting the school, during the course of which he confided that he felt it was time for a change from the pressures of the busy comprehensive. He went away saying he would think it over before deciding whether to apply. Two days later he called to say how grateful he was for the time I had spent with him but that he would not be pursuing his application as he had '*decided to stay in teaching*'.

PASS and PASSING are extremely thorough programme evaluation instruments which challenge special needs services in a way which the HMI inspection programme fails to do. The difference between the two approaches is essentially that the former is rooted in an ideology as to what a devalued person's life should be like, while the latter works on the assumption that the person's life is fine and that there is only a need to investigate the quality of the education they are receiving. The expectation surrounding the HMI inspection is that things will be more or less in order.

Because of the shortcomings in the HMI evaluative framework, quite a different school evaluation framework is required for special schools, and whilst PASS (Wolfensberger and Glenn 1975) and PASS-ING (Wolfensberger and Thomas 1983) are not instruments designed specifically for the inspection of schools, they have, nevertheless, been used for this purpose. Sam Carson, an educational psychologist, has played a leading role in trying to introduce the principle of normalisation into the special education arena. In 1994 (Carson 1995) he undertook a small-scale evaluation of a group of special schools and units using a shortened version of the PASS-ING instrument. This pilot evaluation involved a team of psychologists, each of whom visited a school making provision for children with special needs. All the children were Statemented and attended schools which, on the integration/segregation spectrum ranged from a separate special school through to an integrated high school. Information was gathered in two main ways: (1) pupil 'shadowing', observation and interview and (2) inquiry with teaching staff.

Evaluation took place on 18 of the 42 PASSING ratings which covered the following issues concerned with pupil image and competency:

1. the likely impact on the way the child is imaged as a consequence of the physical setting of the service, its pupil groupings, its activities and the ways in which children are described and addressed

2. the likely effect on pupil competency development as a function of how and where they are grouped and the relative intensity of the programmes of work provided.

In analysing his findings, Carson used Wolfensberger's notion of the 'culturally valued analogue' – which requires the identification of those arrangements which would be appropriate and valued for *any* child. The procedure here is to look at a valued school and ask *where* (it is located), *with whom* (are the children educated), *by whom* (are they taught), *what* (are they taught) and *how* (such schooling would be organised). The culturally valued analogue provides the standard by which any particular form of education can be judged, in much the same way as the notional '*good and efficient*' school is used as the standard by the school inspection service. The only difference here is that the notion of what is *socially valued* is to the fore.

Part of the evaluation was focused upon providing a snapshot of the school life of an individual child, which was based upon asking the following questions:

- Who is this child?
- What is school like for him?
- What quality of service does he receive?
- What is the likely impact of his school life on his childhood and future?

The criteria against which ratings were made ranged from five (excellent and difficult to imagine improvements) through to one (grossly detrimental/inappropriate). It was found that the most meaningful comparisons were between SEN services which were segregated and those which were integrated. All of the settings were minimally acceptable or better in terms of their proximity to natural community resources, the comfort of the setting and for their efforts in creating life-enriching interactions among pupils, staff and others.

Things were much less satisfactory on image and competency related areas with only the integrated settings scoring consistently at the acceptable level of three or above. Integrated services presented positive imagery within their settings and, in doing so, challenged stigmatising associations. Such settings also provided better accessibility to pupils and their families whilst offering more appropriate pupil groupings.

Other general findings were that:

- with segregated settings there was greater likelihood of negative experiences due to stereotyping images and stigmatising expectations; but these were not entirely absent from integrated settings
- integrated settings offered a greater likelihood of appropriate and positive experiences, relationships and opportunities to learn
- within integrated settings there was more evidence of opportunities for variety and frequency of positive contacts, interactions and relationships
- within segregated settings there was less evidence of meaningful and productive programmes (this in direct contradiction of the assumption that 'special', that is segregated – means greater focus on purposeful and structured learning).

Elsewhere Carson (1992) makes the point that it is puzzling that educational services have not taken on board the principle of normalisation, as has been the case in other services for people with disabilities and mental health problems, since 'people working in education have long been in the forefront of thinking about the importance of integration, the intensity of programming, the relevance of activities and the curriculum, early intervention and many other aspects in keeping with this principle'.

CONCLUSION

Evaluation of the work of segregated special schools and special needs classes within the mainstream is all part and parcel of the evaluation programme for schools generally, but with a few minor adjustments to take account of the wider range of professionals involved and the more specialised programmes they implement. This approach is inappropriate for a child with SENs in direct proportion to the severity of the child's disability and/or learning difficulty, that is the more disabled the child, the less relevant the evaluation framework. The irrelevance of the HMI inspection is rooted in its failure to acknowledge the predicament of disabled children (and disabled people generally) within the broader society. In rejecting such children, the education service is itself merely compounding the low social value placed upon them by society.

There are alternative evaluation instruments (e.g. PASS and PASS-ING) which can be adapted to provide a much more relevant and searching assessment of the work of a special school or class. Such instruments are able to provide a very different account of the value of what takes place in segregated settings because they are overtly values-centred.

Chapter 6

Securing an Inclusive Placement

BEING INCLUDED – A RIGHT NOT A PRIVILEGE

It will be hard work all the way

This chapter is for parents, their allies and any professional who wants to take a principled stand over a basic human rights violation – the compulsory segregation of a child against his or her parent's wishes.

If what is recommended here seems unduly bureaucratic and time-consuming, then so be it. Please take my word for it that your valuable time and effort expended putting in place the following safeguards will prove to be not only worthwhile but necessary, if you really want your child to be included. Take it from me, County Hall will be bureaucratic and unless you try to match them you will surely lose.

Your starting point is that British law enshrines the right of your child to be integrated, although it is important to understand this is very much a qualified right. Indeed the law is so mealy-mouthed on this issue that it has proved no real obstacle to an LEA pursuing a systematic policy of compulsory segregation for those children it chooses to educate separately. In spite of this you can still point to the legal duty of your LEA to educate your child in the mainstream school of your choice. You will find more information on this in Chapters 2 and 4.

I first addressed the issue of systemic resistance to mainstreaming, from the perspective of what the parent needs to know, in an article with the same title as this chapter (Hall 1993). I tried to clarify the steps which need to be taken by a parent to secure an inclusive placement and, in so doing, outlined some of the common obstacles – both attitudinal and systemic – that are likely to be encountered if you as a parent are determined to see your child fully included. What follows is intended as a more detailed guide through the minefield that will be encountered.

The professionals are against it

The debate over integration all too frequently becomes bogged down through a simple failure by the parties to agree their terms of reference. Endless discussion of the pros and cons of integration can take place before one side discovers that the other is talking in terms of the *feasibility* of integration *now*, while the other has all along assumed that the discussion was addressing the matter on an *in principle* basis assuming that conditions were favourable. Such discussions frequently kick off with the sceptical party saying 'I believe in integration but...'. It is important at the outset to clear the decks of all such misunderstandings and to try and use language which is clearly defined or, in that horrible term, operationalised.

In what follows it should be assumed that feasibility is *not* in doubt and the child *could* attend her local school if others could be persuaded of the desirability of her doing so. This means that the necessary conditions are met, that is the LEA, school and parents agree and the school is accessible or could be made so, the professional staff say they can teach/care for the child and any additional therapeutic input could be made available (this is a highly unlikely scenario but please suspend your disbelief for the purpose of the argument). So, there are no obstacles and the child could attend the school. But let us not forget, the model of need we are using in this book is that of a severely or profoundly handicapped child. Let us then assume that the child is blind and has a severe learning difficulty, is non-ambulant and doubly incontinent. The debate now is not whether the child *could* attend the school but whether she *should*.

Having cleared away the confusion as to which particular question is being asked, we now find that most professionals would still say that the child should *not* attend her neighbourhood school. This is the fundamental reality parents need to understand about the integration issue – that most of the people the parents need to help try and make it work will vote against it when the chips are down, and this notwithstanding the fact that most of them will still maintain they are pro-integration.

There is no evidence that integration works

This is the argument of last resort for the beleaguered professional (frequently the psychologist) whose initial position has been undermined by judicious quizzing. The reply can only be that there is equally no research evidence worthy of the name which shows that segregation works and, in fact, plenty of evidence that it causes great damage. You will need to point out that segregation just evolved without any attempt whatsoever to measure its efficacy, so why defend it other than that it happens to be the *status quo* and many professionals are comfortable with it. The 'is ness' of the *status quo* (whatever that might be) is safe and comfortable and there is no pressing necessity that it should actually work. Professionals are people like all others and change implies risk and requires effort.

What parents need to know

The following advice is essentially for parents and their supporters (this might also include a sympathetic professional) and represents a strategy for securing an inclusive placement for a child who has not yet commenced schooling or is in a segregated placement such as a special school, a resourced school or a special class in an ordinary school.

It should be said at the outset that of all the provisions parents might choose to pursue for their child, an inclusive (i.e. fully integrated) placement is probably the most difficult to achieve where an LEA has set its face against it. In taking on the LEA, it is important to be well-informed, determined, organised and impatient (yes impatient!), but also calm and resolute. You should also appear to be in possession of the facts and know your rights from the outset; you should keep meticulous records of everything that is written or said, you should not allow the LEA's own timetable for dealing with your concerns to dictate the course of events (for it may be extremely slow) and you should at all times retain control of your emotions if you possibly can so that you cannot readily be labelled as a disturbed, irrational or unrealistic parent. That you will be labelled something or other is not in question – you will just have to live with that – but try not to give them any excuse to use these particular labels. Since the documentation you have is the only tangible record of your dealings with the authority, it is important to ensure it is comprehensive and well-organised.

Record keeping

It is a good idea to keep your records in a large ring binder with sections for different types of information. You may eventually end up with more than one of these. Your documentation will include: letters, notes from telephone conversations (timed and dated and with the name of the person who phoned), professional reports, draft Statements, etc. You should keep copies of everything you send and every letter you receive should be dated by you when it was received and kept safely.

When you have attended a meeting, you will need to take a minute of what is said and send a copy to the relevant parties. This applies also to any relevant informal conversation you may have with a professional in passing, and any telephone conversation. Make a note of any concerns you may have – even if you do not at the time intend to send them to anyone, they will act as your own *aide memoire.* If the school or any professional agrees to do something, insist they put it in writing. In all correspondence state a date by which you expect to have a reply.

Meetings, meetings, meetings

If you have not hitherto been a 'meeting person' then you will surely become one before you are finished. It is important to remember that the people you are up against are highly experienced at meetings and will run rings around you unless you watch out. You will find yourself becoming involved in a variety of different types of meetings.

Support groups meetings

If you create a support group then try to ensure that your meetings have structure and a few necessary ground rules. Some people will say that too much organisation and structure leads to the same problems experienced by the LEA and other agencies which eventually render themselves helpless because of the bureaucratic web they weave. The answer to this is simple: if you are casual and leave things to chance then you will fail because to win you will have to be highly efficient and well-informed. It is not sensible to leave matters to chance. Try to have a regular chairperson and make sure it is someone who can stand back from a debate whilst facilitating contributions from others. You will also need a secretary to take a minute of what is discussed and agreed; members should have copies of these minutes sent to them as soon as possible after the meeting.

Your support group is separate from any other help you may organise and must be accountable to you as a family. You may have an offer of direct action from a member of such a group, but do give this careful consideration as you need to be confident that their actions do not backfire. The offer of heroic intervention may be well-intentioned but it might meet more of the needs of the activist than of your child and family.

It is only worth having people in your support group if they are prepared to *work* because passengers with soothing words will not solve your problem. It also goes without saying that confidentiality will be crucial.

Meetings with the School/LEA

Go into any such meeting as though you truly believe you are the valued customer whose child's needs are the only important item on the agenda. Never go alone. Take your child to the meeting so that people can meet her but ensure that you have someone with you who can take her out if she is not able to sit through the whole meeting or, if for some other reason, you feel she should not remain in the room. In such a circumstance you will, of course, need another person to remain with you in the meeting.

Your child's needs are what counts

Ensuring that the meeting addresses your child's and your family's needs does not mean acting in an off-hand and arrogant manner, but rather that you try to create a climate in which it is understood who is to be served and whose needs are at issue. Maintaining a calm and polite manner in the face of what you may hear will not be easy but it would be a tactical blunder for you to lose your temper and express your feelings in a hostile and aggressive way. Some of the people you will be dealing with are expert labellers and you do not need to be labelled. However, do not be afraid to interrupt if you feel an important point is being missed or if you feel someone has failed to understand something.

In general you should set meeting dates that are convenient to you and your family and not just accept those convenient for the LEA or school. Always remember that everyone else present at these meetings is being paid to attend and also to travel to the meeting. You and your supporter/advocate will be the only ones not being taken care of in this way. Remember also that the professionals are being paid to do a job which involves meeting your child's real needs. If there are people at the meeting you were not expecting, then ask who they are and what their role is. If you feel strongly that they have no place there, then politely ask that they leave.

The focus must be your child not the budget

If documents are handed out at the meeting, do not respond to them immediately but say you will need time to read and reflect upon them before commenting. It is also useful to have a photo album depicting your child's accomplishments and interests because some of the people at the meeting may not have met your child and some of those who have will, in general, have had little or no regular contact with the children they will make decisions about. Good photographs will make the child more immediate and real, and hopefully aid understanding.

The focus of the meeting should be the needs of your child and not the resourcing problems of the school or the authority. Administrators these days pay obsessive attention to budgets and the 'bottom line', and will try to persuade you that they simply cannot afford what you want. *Do not get drawn into such a discussion.* Gently and persistently bring the meeting back to *your child's needs* by saying that you are not unsympathetic about their budgetary difficulties but that this is not your concern or responsibility.

Prepare well

Before agreeing to attend a meeting *they* have called, find out what the purpose is, and be clear in your own mind that such a meeting would be likely to carry things forward. Prior to the meeting, prepare a list of the questions you wish to ask and the points you would like to make and try to make sure all are dealt with before the meeting ends. Always take someone to minute the meeting for you and, if the other side are having a minute taken, agree to exchange these. Do not agree that only their side make a minute because minutes can be highly subjective. Beware of hidden agendas by trying to think at every turn what it is they might be after, even when the words they use seem to suggest it is your child's needs they are trying to serve.

Take along any written material you wish to share but try to make this succinct, otherwise it will not be read. Should you feel the need to be confrontational, try to ensure this is part of a planned strategy and not just the expression of anger and frustration. At the end of the meeting *do not agree* to anything, and certainly *do not sign* anything you are at all unsure of – ask for time to think about it. Always speak last of all, repeating your case simply and directly.

When you have received the minute from the other side, and this will be quite some time after the meeting, review the minute you have taken in conjunction with that from the school/LEA (you will probably have to chase theirs but send yours as soon as you can and this will oblige them to reciprocate) and make a checklist of points you have made and others that still need to be made. In doing this, ask yourself frankly whether you got what you wanted, and if not, why not. Review what further actions are to be taken and highlight the agreed dates for these to be achieved.

Getting support

Even if you are the most capable and knowledgeable person around, it is advisable to have someone who can act as a friend or advocate in your dealings with the authority. Just such a person is referred to in the Code of Practice (Section 4.70) which came into effect with the 1993 Education Act and was given the title *Named Person*. Just who this might be and what skills they might possess is discussed in greater depth in Chapter 8.

There are any number of reasons to have someone supporting you as a friend/advocate but the most important is that you should be able to talk everything through with someone whose judgement you respect and who you know you can trust implicitly. If you have a friend who knows your own and your child's needs well, you may need to look no further. If though, at a later stage, you should need to pursue an appeal to the Special Needs Tribunal (SNT), then you will need advice of a different kind so should look to a person who has knowledge of special needs education and the law.

Opening shots – be organised

Whether your child is about to start school or is already in a segregated provision, the following is applicable. You have decided that you want your child to attend her local school and, having thought matters through, you cannot see any insurmountable obstacle to her being able to function there. Whether your approach is to the school or to the authority, you should be absolutely clear *what* you want and *why* that will be better for her than that which a segregated place could provide. Here you should try to cover the following points:

HER *FUNDAMENTAL* DEVELOPMENTAL NEEDS

- to be with her neighbourhood peers because those are the only ones she can realistically expect to cultivate friendships with
- for appropriate role models, so that she can learn typical (normative) behaviour
- to be known by others, so they will know how to approach and help her
- to attend a school which is valued by those who share her community, so that she is not negatively imaged because of the place she receives her education.

HER *ADDITIONAL* NEEDS

- for certain items of personal equipment (e.g. standing frame, personal computer, toilet seat)
- for a personal support worker to help her with her care needs and education
- for paramedical input such as speech, physio or occupational therapy.

For each of these things you should have a clear idea of how they can be provided in the local school. You should be prepared to deal with objections from therapists about the need to travel or that they will not have the space to work, etc. Professionals will always find reasons why something or other is impossible, because, if at all possible, they like to offer their services on terms congenial and familiar to themselves. Expect a smoke-screen of problems and have your arguments ready.

WHAT YOU WANT FOR HER DURING HER SCHOOL YEARS AND IN LATER LIFE (YOUR VISION STATEMENT)

It is important that you are very clear about the life you want your child to live: the experiences she needs, the influences she should come under, the relationships she should form. This is important because you can show that a segregated education would make no worthwhile contribution towards such a future and in fact will work against it.

Having a clear idea of what your child needs and what you want for her will put you several steps in advance of the professionals you deal with since they will almost certainly not have been motivated to give such thorough consideration to these key issues. They will not have adequately considered these things because they are largely working within the medical model framework, which is not conducive to the development of such a broad-based and longer-term needs analysis.

PREPARE A VALUE-FOR-MONEY RATIONALE

Although you do not have to justify the cost-effectiveness of an alternative placement for your child – since the law is clear that services should be needs rather than resource led – it might help your case to point to a saving that a local school placement would make for the authority, for example if your child lives quite close to the school she might not need to use the special needs transport service, which could involve a major cost saving.

If the authority point to the increased cost of your child attending her local school, you might wish to raise the *value-for-money* argument. This is that the absolute cost of a service is only one dimension on which it should be judged and that the least expensive is not necessarily the best value. If you are genuinely persuaded that the option you are proposing is more expensive than the one they are recommending, you might wish to explain that an ineffective or positively damaging educational experience is not just *money* wasted but part of a *life* wasted.

If there is an issue about making expensive adaptations to the school then point to the fact that any such improvements would benefit future children and adults who would then be able to access its buildings. This re-frames the cost issue so that it can no longer be argued that it is simply not cost-effective to spend such an amount on a single child. The important point here is that a decision to include your child helps the authority to develop its facilities and expertise and so represents a positive step in longer-term service development.

DESCRIBE WHAT YOUR CHILD CAN GIVE TO THE SCHOOL

That your child will be an asset to her local school should not be in doubt. Her presence there will serve to show that the school is one which truly wishes to serve *every* member of its community and this is a badge of merit for any school; a school which operates such a policy brings honour to its staff and governors and reassurance to members of the local community.

Your child's presence in the school sends a message to other children that 'in our school and community everyone belongs and is valued for *who* they are and not *what* they can do'. The message implicit in this is that 'nobody has been "sent away" so we do not have to worry about that happening to any of us since that sort of thing just does not happen here'.

Just because your child has an impairment (or even several impairments), she does not have to be disabled. Being disabled is often about not being given the opportunity to get involved just *because* you have an impairment. When other children see how impairments can be partially or completely overcome through the provision of supports, they come to understand how to help others and how important that help is. When children learn these things they become more competent and useful members of society, and your child can help them to become that.

GIVE EVIDENCE FROM FRIENDS AND NEIGHBOURS

If parents of other children in the school you want your child to attend are supportive of your cause, you might get one or two to write a letter to that effect. At a later stage, if the resistance is strong, you might raise a petition to show that you have public opinion behind you.

SHOW THEM THAT YOU KNOW WHAT *YOU* MEAN BY INTEGRATION

The professional workers and administrators will have a confused idea of what they understand integration to be, so it might be as well for you to ask them to tell you what they understand by the term. While they are doing this, you should stop them periodically to check that you understand what they are getting at. Either during their explanation or later, you might wish to make a few notes on what they said. You should then explain what *you* understand integration to mean in terms of *full inclusion*. You might like to refer them to somebody who is working in this way with a child who has similar needs to those of your own child. Thoroughly familiarise yourself with the arguments developed in Chapter 4.

BE PREPARED TO DEAL WITH *THEIR* PROBLEMS OVER INTEGRATION

With a group of people, some of whom know about schools, brainstorm all the reasons the authority might come up with as they try to resist integrating your child. They frequently argue that she will:

- be bullied or ridiculed
- feel overwhelmed by the size and level of activity
- feel her handicap all the more acutely being with such able children
- be at risk in the playground in all that rough and tumble
- not be able to work in the small group situation the psychologist says she really needs
- have too much distraction in a class of 30+
- feel ashamed because she will be bottom of the class in everything and hence will feel a failure
- miss her handicapped friends in the special school
- not understand what the teacher is talking about
- not make friends.

Also, in respect of the services she needs, she will:

- not be able to have her physiotherapy (speech therapy, etc.) because the therapists do not come to this school
- not have the benefit of a special needs teacher because none of the ordinary school staff have had such training
- not be able to get around the school because we have no lifts/ramps
- not be able to come out on school trips because we cannot transport her in her wheelchair as you say she needs to travel
- be a fire risk (the spontaneously combustible disabled child).

As far as the other children are concerned, she will:

- disturb them with all those strange noises she makes
- not be welcomed by some of the parents because they will feel their children are not getting the attention they need because your child will need so much
- make the other children feel responsible for her
- never be able to go to the comprehensive that do not take children with her needs
- clutter up the classroom with all her equipment.

Some professionals have nurtured a highly-developed faculty for imagining what might go wrong if a disabled child were to enter an ordinary classroom. This is part of what Marsha Forest has called the 'Yes but' syndrome – if asked whether a child should be integrated, the stock response is *yes* (in principle) *but...*

DO NOT LET THEM CREATE UNNECESSARY DELAY

You should take the initiative in determining the time limit for decisions and actions. Do not allow open-ended arrangements where people have no time limit placed on their actions. Most professionals are busy people and there will always be a number of pressing issues competing for their attention.

RESIST ANY ATTEMPT TO GET YOU TO COMPROMISE

You are not being unreasonable in asking for precisely what you believe your child needs. If they tell you that it is not fair to expect to get everything your child needs then point to the fact that you are only asking for what every other parent wants for their child as of right – a place in their local school.

RESIST ANY ATTEMPT BY THE PROFESSIONALS TO CAST YOU IN THE ROLE OF EXPERT

They may try to do this in the hope of later showing that you are in fact *not* an expert and hence that your views are not worthy of consideration. Present yourself as an informed layman and point to the views of some people with experience of integrating children with similar needs to your own child. Make it clear you believe there are few, if any, experts on educational integration because, in Britain at least, there is precious little integration of such children taking place.

Building a support group-types of support

In addition to the aforementioned *Named Person* who will provide the moral support you will inevitably need, it is also important to reach out to others so that both you and your adversaries know you have a network of sympathisers who may be mobilised should the need arise. The core membership of such a support group should ideally consist of other parents who have, or would like to have, their child included. There might already be an informal group of such individuals providing support for one another in your area, in which case you could simply ask to join. If not, you might consider starting up your own group.

Parents of disabled children usually derive the greatest support from one another because they know from personal experience what it means to have to battle with a resisting system of professionals who, with the best will in the world, can rarely relate to their life circumstances. However, in such an important struggle it is essential to recruit allies wherever they may be found, and individuals in all sorts of positions will have something to offer – even if this is not the much-needed empathy.

General support

It is important to have support from sympathetic neighbours, friends and acquaintances, although it might not be reasonable to expect that such individuals will be able to offer a particular type of expertise. Just to know that others are aware of your struggle and are with you in spirit is comforting, even though you might at times feel that your privacy is being undermined by the fact that so many others know about the struggle you are having.

Elected members of the local authority council and your MP might also be willing to support you, and certainly your local councillor should be approached. If your child is already at school, you might try to get the support of a member of the governing body of that school (perhaps unlikely) and you should certainly approach governors at the school you want your child to attend. However, you should do this only after having spoken with the headteacher in an attempt to bring him or her on side. If there is no support from this quarter, and you still wish to pursue a place, then by all means approach the governors.

The school you wish your child to attend

Ask the LEA (or get another parent to ask) for a copy of the mainstream school's *mission statement* or school plan – all schools should have some sort of policy document for new parents and for inspection purposes. The 1993 Education Act requires every school to formulate a policy on special needs so something should be available. If things start going wrong, you might be able to use comments from such a document in support of your case for integration – such documents have a tendency to make high-sounding general commitments to policies, which it is good (ideologically sound) to be seen to be endorsing. It would not be surprising if such a document contained a statement in support of integration.

Try to get a clear idea of the layout of the school, with particular reference to any areas where there might be obstacles to your child getting access. Try to work out where a ramp or lift might be sited and then seek advice on the feasibility of having the necessary alterations made – you might even be able to get someone to do rough costings. Such information will be invaluable if things move on to the stage where the LEA themselves commission such costings, as they sometimes produce figures which are surprisingly high.

In discussions over such costs you may be told that it would just not be cost effective to have such alterations made for just your child as this would not represent an *efficient use of resources* (one of the qualifications of the duty to integrate in the 1993 Act). Your response here should be as outlined above: that this is entirely the wrong analysis. The cost should be related to both the present and *future* access needs of all children, as well as any disabled adults who might wish to work at or visit the school. Taking this into account changes the whole frame of reference and puts any necessary current expenditure in the context of the need to pursue an *equal opportunities policy* for all citizens.

Professionals

If you can find allies amongst the paid professionals within the statutory or voluntary services, it would greatly help your cause. You should, however, not expect too much from such individuals because their first duty is to their employer. Those employed by the LEA, the health authority (or NHS Trust), the social services department and such major voluntary organisations as Scope (previously the Spastic Society) and Barnardos work to set policies within structures which limit their freedom to act and speak on behalf of families. They may sound like potential advocates but beware!

Generally speaking however, professionals from the voluntary organisations will be less constrained than those from the statutory agencies, but even here they have to consider their relationship with these agencies because they need to work with them and co-operate to develop new services.

Put bluntly, many such professionals would face a *conflict of interest* were they to come down unequivocally and wholeheartedly on your side because it could mean they were then challenging the policy of their employing authority. Such a sensitive issue as integration would almost certainly mean they were placing themselves in such a position. This issue is discussed in greater depth in Chapter 8.

Legal advice

It is likely that you will need legal advice should the authority finally refuse to accede to your request. Many balk at seeking such advice because they may see it as a major escalation of the conflict and there is, of course, the not inconsequential matter of cost. If it should have to come to this, you should not feel guilty because the LEA will themselves not think twice before seeking advice from the legal department of the authority. The only difference is that they can have such advice at the snap of a finger at public expense while you will have to dig deep into your own pocket unless you qualify for the sometimes limited financial support that may be provided through Green Form Legal Aid.

We are just beginning to see the extent to which LEAs are prepared to go in their determination to resist meeting certain needs because some are now using public money to pay lawyers (in some cases QCs) to argue their case at Tribunal hearings. This is extremely expensive – around £2000 per day – and may be seen by some as a little unfair because the parent must face them across the table with perhaps only a friend for support.

If you decide to see a solicitor, you should seek prior advice because there are very few solicitors who specialise in Special Educational Needs (SENs) law. You will not want to be used so that an inexperienced solicitor can gain experience at your expense. You may wish to seek the advice of the Independent Panel for Special Educational Advice (IPSEA) or the Children's Legal Centre on this. (See Appendix 1, p.64).

Voluntary advocacy

There are very few true advocacy projects for parents in need of such specialist advice, although IPSEA is a national organisation which will offer highly professional help. It has great expertise in special education law and a total commitment to supporting parents. It has been a source of free second opinions, through its panel of professional experts, for some years and has recently launched a free representation service for parents having to appeal to the SEN Tribunal.

Beware of local so-called *Parent Partnership* schemes which are run by or with the authority, because their independence may be questionable given the source of their funding and the way in which they are managed.

Support from the media

You may wish to draw your local newspaper, radio or television into the struggle to publicise the injustice that is being done to you and your child. You will not wish to do this until it looks as though the LEA is not going to agree that your child should be integrated. Should you decide to take this step, it is important you know they will not understand the issues and that, left to their own devices, they will certainly describe your child in demeaning and patronising language. Accepting this, you might still decide to go ahead – there is nothing like strong media support to pressure the LEA into climbing down.

The angle much of the media would like to take is not necessarily one you will find at all palatable but it might be worth your while to cultivate a particular journalist and spend some time going over

the issues; you might even want to give this individual some educational reading material in the hope that something might stick. In
the end though, they will be wanting to milk a 'human interest' story
and that will be the constraining factor.

Beware of assessment/labelling

Insist on being present at every assessment and examination, even
if things have to be arranged so that your child is not aware of your
presence. Write to the school and to the LEA making it clear in
advance that you must be informed of any proposed assessment.
You might also want to take along your *Named Person* so that you
can prompt one another and compare notes on what took place for
later use.

The means by which your child has (or may) been excluded from
her local school is the label which describes her condition(s). Labels
do matter! A whole variety of conditions may contribute to a child's
special needs and these conditions usually result in a variety of
professionally attached labels. Attachment of the label is the first
task of the relevant professional and this has a positive aspect in that
it is important (in the present system) to attract the necessary resources. However, the down side of the label is that it may also attract
prejudice, fear, misunderstanding and segregation.

It is important that you keep a close watch on professionals – on
the way they go about the assessment and what they say in their
reports following assessment – because herein will lie many of your
later problems when the decision is to be made about a placement.
There is little you can do about the headteacher or psychologist who
does not believe in integration, but you may be able to persuade
them to amend some of their more unhelpful comments. If they
refuse to amend their report by removing what you see as the more
negative aspects, you should write to their employing authority to
ask that this be done – it is just possible that their line manager will
accede to such a request.

Psychological/educational assessment

Testing is a minefield and very much the province of the educational
psychologist (EP), although schools do some as well. You may well
need an independent psychological report if you find that the LEA
psychologist has used test results and observations as an argument
against your child being integrated. For children with severe disabilities, educational and psychological assessment is sometimes
not an option and here the psychologist will pick up what she needs
to know by questioning others and observing the child. In such a
situation it will not be possible to use test results to support a
segregated placement, but other arguments will be deployed.

It is important to be clear that there is *no test which can tell you whether a child should or should not be integrated*. Testing should not be used for placement decisions, but rather to identify the child's needs *wherever she is finally* placed. Such decisions stem from the subjective individual beliefs of professionals who work within structures which have well-established ways of responding to perceived needs. (This is code for saying they are inflexible and bureaucratic).

Always speak with the person who is doing the assessment and ask for an explanation of anything you do not understand. Try to formulate a view on *where they are coming from* (i.e. what their core values, assumptions and beliefs are) in what they are saying.

Independent professional advice

Seek independent professional advice (see Chapter 8), either through IPSEA (which means you will not have to pay) or by contacting someone yourself. The British Psychological Society have a list of chartered psychologists, some of whom work entirely independently so are free to give *unconstrained advice*. There are also private therapists (speech, physio and occupational) who will undertake assessments. Many parents will not be able to pay the £150 – £600 which such an independent assessment might cost, and if more than one report is required then things become impossible. However, a family on income support, or possibly another state benefit, may apply for Green Form Legal Aid – which will cover an initial (hour-long) consultation with a solicitor and one, or possibly two, reports.

It is essential that before you commission anyone to do an independent assessment (including an IPSEA panel member), you satisfy yourself that they are pro-integration. Members of the IPSEA panel come in all shades on this issue and it is not a pre-condition for panel membership that they support integration. A report that is only half-hearted on this matter will be of no help should you have to face a Tribunal. Also, if you are seeking an alternative therapy report, you should make absolutely sure that it will contain specific and *quantified* recommendations otherwise it may turn out to be money wasted.

Offer your own assessments

Without, of course, claiming any scientific validity for them, you may wish to offer your own report on your child's accomplishments and needs. When it comes to the Statementing process you will be asked to contribute your *Parental Advice*, so keeping records on your child's development will serve to make this task a little easier. Professionals will always, but always, patronise you by saying that *you* are the *real expert on your child*, yet when it comes to all the major decisions about her schooling, completely ignore your 'expert' opinion.

Do remember though that neither you nor they are experts on integration because such people do not exist in Britain, due to the fact that proper integration for the children in question is so rare. What you do know, however, is what *you* want for *your* child, and, because you know her better than any other living person, this should bolster you in remaining confident in your dealings with professionals, who as yet hardly know her at all. Remember, the EP may only meet your child once or twice before delivering her, not entirely inconsequential, verdict on what kind of school life your child should have to experience/endure.

Knowing about the statutory services

Because the needs model of this book is a child who will require the protection of a Statement, it is more likely that agencies in addition to education will be involved, and these will have to be consulted over the drawing up of the Statement in any case. It might be wise to get somebody to collect some of the following information for you, because too much digging around on your part may make the school unnecessarily anxious and it will also alert the LEA to your possible future intent. On this latter point, it is usually wise to keep your powder dry for as long as possible so that you do not alert the other side; they will certainly not make you privy to their every thought and action, and you will be surprised at some of the things they will be prepared to do.

In all of this it is important not to have expectations which are too high, nor to get into blaming individual officers or professionals as though they were evil people. It is essentially the *system* which is hostile to your own and your child's needs. Many of those who find themselves in the firing line having to give you the bad news will certainly not enjoy the task, and may even themselves feel that what is being done is unjust, yet still see themselves as powerless because 'this is the way things are'. This is not to say that all such individuals remain entirely blameless because every professional must retain some responsibility for the actions of the organisation which employs him/her. In the extreme, they could choose to leave – and this occasionally happens.

The Local Education Authority (LEA)

You should try to find out as much as you can about your LEA. A starting point might be to get a copy of the management structure tree (organisational chart) which shows lines of accountability; you need to know clearly where the buck stops. At some point you may find that your 'case' has become sufficiently worrying to the LEA that those more junior in the hierarchy are no longer dealing with the matter and you have to relate directly with somebody more senior, such as an assistant director or the principal psychologist. When this happens, it is code for several things: that you are beginning to be seen as a thorn in their side, that what you are understood to be wanting is either against LEA policy or might create a precedent, and/or that what you are asking is being viewed as prohibitively expensive.

You should certainly try to get a copy of any policy statement on integration and statistics on where children are placed. There may be a variety of arrangements and you may well unearth examples in which the LEA have already agreed to another parental request similar to your own. Getting in touch with the parent concerned would also be a good idea.

Details of all the special needs provisions within the LEA should also be helpful – this will include the range of placement options (special schools, units, classes, etc.) available. Also ask for the number (you will not need or get personal details as these are confidential) of children supported on an individual basis in mainstream classrooms and the type of support given. Here you will need to know the level of support (how much time) and the salary scale of the person(s) appointed (qualified or unqualified rate). You should also try to find out what arrangements have been made for paramedical support.

Get to know the LEA culture

Learning about the culture of the LEA and its protocol is also important, otherwise you will be constantly wrong-footed in your actions and this can be frustrating and ultimately damaging to one's credibility. Never forget, it is *their* court you are playing in and they make the rules and act as umpire. It will probably not have occurred to them that you pay their salaries and that, as a 'valued customer', they should really be striving to meet *your* needs. This is the paradox of local government and the statutory services generally and it has to do with your not actually directly hiring and firing them.

As well as knowing as much as possible about the structure and workings of the LEA, it is important to know about its procedures – particularly in respect of the Statementing process and the linked appeals process. Here it will be important to have some knowledge of the 1993 Act and its Code of Practice to ensure that the LEA is operating within the requirements of the law (for further advice see Chapters 2, 7 and 8 of this book).

The Health Authority

If your child needs resources managed by the health authority, it is important to remember that you are dealing with a completely separate organisation with its own culture and ways of doing things. It certainly has duties under the 1993 Act (see Chapter 2) but, in most respects, simply responds to approaches made by the LEA for such key provisions as speech, physio- and occupational therapy, bioengineering (specialist seating), hearing and sight specialists. Also, for the children who are the main focus of this book, it provides the necessary medical advice through its clinical medical officers (school doctors) and consultants.

Whilst the Health Authority have the responsibility for making these various provisions, it is only the LEA who have the legal duty to ensure that education-related needs are met (by writing them into Section 3 of the Statement) and the health authority have no such direct legally binding duty to an individual child in the same way. This means that if there is an issue about therapy, it has to be dealt with through the LEA – *if it is an educational need.*

The Social Services Department

The part played by social services is usually relatively minor compared to that of the education and health authorities in relation to the Statementing process, although it might be highly significant in other areas of the child's and the family's lives.

Background issues

Although you are dealing with an education authority over the *education* of your child, do not for one moment believe that a decision to send her to a segregated setting is an educational decision – it is a political decision. It will, of course, be presented as an educational decision and, depending upon the level of consciousness of the person concerned, it may in some degree be believed to be an educational decision, but this is not the case.

Knowledge that this is the case will make things much easier for you and your supporters because it will relieve you of the temptation to feel that you are being difficult or unreasonable. It will be helpful if you spend a little time (if in fact you have any time after all this) examining your own feelings about what is happening to you as a family. This is just the kind of thing to share with your *Named Person.*

Don't be afraid to trust your instincts, because your commitment to having your child included will not have been an easy one and nobody will know better than you what you are risking. The fact that you know this, and still want it, means that you are probably right in believing it would be the best thing for your child. There will, of course, be times when you will feel like throwing in the towel and this is when you will really need to take some of the pressure off and look after yourself until you are feeling strong again. However bad it gets, try to persevere, because you may well win.

Make sure that many people know about your struggle – you will find that most will be supportive; the more who know about it the more chance there is that somebody, somewhere, will be able to offer help just when it is needed.

Should you win, that is just the time *not* to relax. The very same pressures that created the resistance in the first place will still be around and your best assumption is that you will have merely subdued them for the time being. Getting your child into her local school is only the first hurdle – a very important hurdle – but just the first. You should intensify your efforts to ensure that any problems that may arise are dealt with, and also that the longer-term planning begins to happen. Your child's first mainstream teacher is just one of a succession of people who will have to meet the challenge of teaching her and, although school policies exist, many headteachers are not strong enough to ensure that all teachers follow them. Then there is preparation for the secondary phase if your child enters at primary level.

Keep the pressure on

You might wish to organise letter writing to key people in the authority. Ideally, such letters should come from people in your community. Along with a possible petition, it is important that the LEA receives a constant stream of letters and you might wish to put together a format to guide others as to what to write. This will be easier once a lot of people know your story. You might also ask voluntary organisations to support your case; such groups as the Downs Syndrome Association have a strong commitment to integration. You could also try Scope if your child has cerebral palsy. You will be able to get further information from the Centre for Studies on Inclusive Education (CSIE) and, although the people who run it are journalists and not educationalists, they will be happy to put you in touch with people who know about education integration.

Chapter 7

The Politics of Statementing

OF COURSE IT'S POLITICAL

We have already seen that the problems arising out of the Statementing process are legion and frequently result in a bitter and protracted dispute between parent and LEA. The conflict which arises is usually, but by no means inevitably, linked to issues of resourcing, and the LEAs feel they have no alternative but to fight off the myriad demands being made upon their finite and dwindling budgets.

If, as someone once said, 'politics is the art of the possible', then LEAs up and down the country have shown parents that, for them, Statementing too is the art of the possible. That the lives of vulnerable children should become politicised in this way is understandably a source of anger and frustration to parents, yet we should not be surprised that local authorities who face rate-capping unless they remain within budget should feel the need to play politics on the matter of resource conservation.

What is a 'special educational need' (SEN)?

There is a fundamental problem in the management of resources for children who experience a greater than usual difficulty in learning what schools require them to learn. This difficulty is compounded by the lack of an adequate definition of what is to count as a SEN. The 1993 Education Act (Section 156) offers no more help on this than did its predecessor the 1981 Education Act, for it says: 'a child has 'special educational needs' if he has a learning difficulty which calls for special educational provision to be made for him'. All that this is essentially saying is that a child has a SEN if he has a learning difficulty and vice versa, and this is a circular definition. Hence if he has a learning difficulty he has special needs and if he has special needs he has a learning difficulty.

By way of clarification, the Act goes on to say that he has such a learning difficulty if:

(a) he has a significantly greater difficulty in learning than the majority of children of his age;

(b) he has a disability which either prevents or hinders him from making use of educational facilities of a kind generally provided for children of his age in schools within the area of the local education authority; or

(c) he is under the age of five years and is, or would be if special educational provision were not made for him, likely to fall within paragraph (a) or (b) when over that age.

Things are helped along a little by the qualifying clauses (a) and (b) in that the former makes the definition normative, that is it relates the degree of difficulty to that which is typical for the population, and the latter helps by extending this notion to a difficulty in using provisions typically available. However, this clarification essentially rests upon the somewhat fuzzy notion of what the 'typical' school is able to provide in terms of the attitudes and skills of staff and the physical resources they have available. This, as we have seen, is highly variable.

This attempt at an essentially normative definition of what is to count as a SEN is also one which is rooted within a particular time and culture. This is so because reliance upon what the typical school is able to cope with will inevitably vary over time and hopefully increase as schools become more tolerant of difference. Indeed, such tolerance has begun to increase during recent years.

A further limitation on this notion of a learning difficulty is that it is defined solely in relation to what schools expect of children. Many great men and women had previously been written off by their schools yet managed to achieve things their teachers could only dream of.

This lack of a coherent definition of SEN is compounded by the lack of a clear understanding of the respective responsibilities of the school and the LEA (Audit Commission/HMI 1992), and this is hardly surprising when schools themselves vary so greatly in their ability to cope. The Act also makes it clear that a child should not be regarded as having a learning difficulty solely because the language of the home is not that of the school.

The purpose of a Statement

Statementing is that complex process by which a child is assessed so that his needs can be ascertained, documented and linked to a set of appropriate provisions. It is a process which needs to be much better understood by parents and one which many would say has fallen into disrepute because of the widespread disregard of the law by LEAs.

The main reason for having a Statement is to ensure that a child's needs are met when the school itself does not have the necessary resources, since the existence of the Statement places the legal obligation firmly upon the LEA. Yet this is not the only reason why a parent should require a Statement to be drawn up, for even if a particular school does have the necessary resources to meet the child's needs today, that situation might not continue and without the protection of the Statement, any loss of capacity by the school would leave the child unprotected.

Circular 2/75 brought in a more educational approach to assessment through the introduction of what were known as the 'SE forms'. SE (Special Education) forms 1–4 replaced the earlier HP forms. SE 1 was completed by a teacher, SE 2 by a medical officer, SE 3 by an educational psychologist (EP) and SE 4 (the summary) by an EP, education officer or adviser. Under these earlier systems, no formal attempt was made to elicit the views of the parents or the child.

The present Statementing process was introduced as part of the 1981 Act in response to a recommendation in the Warnock report that certain children would need the special help they require protected. These children were to be those seen as having severe and complex learning difficulties. The children who were to receive this protection were not more clearly defined, nor was there a very clear idea as to what proportion of those with special needs would require such protection.

In September 1989, the then Department for Education and Science (DES) issued guidance on procedures for Assessments and Statements in its *Circular 22/89*. This was done by way of a review of the workings of the relevant sections of the 1981 Act. This Circular emphasised a more positive approach to looking at SENs by recommending that there should be a focus on *needs* rather than *disabilities*, so prior to the 1993 Act there had been a gradual improvement of the system for identifying and recording the needs of that small group of children who would require the protection of a Statement.

The Warnock report (HMSO 1978, p.40) estimated that somewhere in the region of 20 per cent of all school children would have some sort of SEN at some time during their schooling. Now we know 10 per cent of these children, that is 2 per cent of the total school population, would have a need sufficiently severe to warrant the protection of a Statement (Audit Commission/HMI 1992a).

The idea that some children needed the protection of a legal document detailing their specific SENs and that the provisions necessary to meet those needs would be provided with a Statement to protect those needs, was an important and very welcome innovation. The fact that this system was not respected by LEAs should not detract from its significance. It is also important to understand what has gone wrong with Statementing, so that parents can now begin to deal more effectively with the shortcomings in the way the system is administered.

A further remaining difficulty which surrounds the Statementing process is the lack of criteria for determining the kind of *special* or, more appropriately, *additional* need, which should attract the protection of a Statement. However, given the unique individuality of every child's particular difficulty, it is probably unreasonable to expect that things will ever become quite so clear cut. Nevertheless, it is agreed that a child with a severe learning difficulty (SLD), or a complex set of interacting difficulties, will always qualify and the numbers, according to government statistics (Audit Commission/HMI 1992), vary between LEAs in the range 0.8 per cent – 3.3 per cent, say roughly 2 per cent nationally. This does, though, represent an enormous degree of discretion on the part of the individual LEA in deciding whether a child's needs warrant the protection of a Statement.

Once again it is hardly surprising that we find such inconsistencies in practice between LEAs, which were not found to be correlated with differences in ability between LEAs or their schools in being able to cope with special needs problems (HMI/Audit Commission 1992). In fact, they found that schools which LEAs with low levels of Statementing were no better at meeting special needs than schools within LEAs with high levels of Statementing. Neither was there a correlation between level of social deprivation and the number of Statements to explain what, in one case, was a four-fold difference. The report could only conclude that 'the likelihood of a child getting a Statement depends more on the LEA's interpretation of the 1981 Act than it does on the proportion of pupils with SENs in the LEA' (p.14).

So we find that special needs education is dogged both by imprecise analysis and language and also confusion as to what should count as a SEN requiring the protection of a Statement. The differences in standards between LEAs is also matched by lack of agreement between different officers within an LEA, which can lead to individuals construing their duties idiosyncratically. In my view 'politicking' is clearly going on here, and I have evidence from parents up and down the country which suggests that the Statementing process has indeed become *the art of the possible*, leading all too frequently to the thought 'what might we possibly be able to get away with as far as this child is concerned?'

Assessment prior to Statementing

It is important to have an understanding of the process by which a Statement is produced in order to have a clearer grasp of what can, and very likely will, go wrong for many children who are in need of its protection.

Prior to the LEA deciding to undertake an assessment of a child's assumed SENs there will (in most cases) already have been a quite long process of investigation by the school as to why the child is experiencing difficulty in learning. This will obviously not have been the case where a child has not yet started school or where the child has a severe physical, sensory or learning difficulty such that there is unlikely to be any doubt that a Statement will be required.

For a child already in school, identification will occur within the cycle of teaching and assessment which the school has in place for all its children. This process should take account of the very different aptitudes, abilities and interests of the children, and a child experiencing difficulties which do not seem to respond to the normal measures available to the school should become the focus of additional attention and investigation.

The 1993 Act introduced additional safeguards to ensure that such children would not be neglected, placing as it did specific duties upon the governing body and the school management. These are described in the Code of Practice which accompanies the Act and to which the LEA must have regard (Section 157). Being required to have *regard* to the Code of Practice does not make it binding in law, nor does it mean it must be applied as a rigid set of rules. However, it was introduced to try and create greater uniformity and consistency across England and Wales and to progressively remove some of the absurd disparities which had existed under the 1981 Act. An LEA which can be shown to have acted with a clear disregard of the Code will not be expected to receive the sympathy of the SEN Tribunal should a parent pursue an appeal.

Every school is required to produce an explicit policy on the provision it will make for children with SENs (Code 2.10). This requires the school, as part of its statutory duty to provide:

1. basic information about the school's SEN provision;
2. information about its policy for identification and assessment of pupils; and
3. information about the school's staffing policy and links with other bodies.

In every school there must also be an SEN co-ordinator.

Early identification and assessment is stressed as crucial, and the Code suggests a five-stage model – stages 1–3 of which are school-based. The school will retain responsibility for stages 1 and 2 with the LEA becoming involved from stage 3 onwards. Matters only move beyond stage 3 if there is likely to be the need for a formal assessment. It is envisaged that the majority of children will not move beyond the first three stages.

The elaboration of this five-stage model should not be taken to imply that a child must proceed through each stage in a mechanical fashion in order to reach the point at which an assessment is necessary. The majority of children will have non-complex difficulties and so will not pass through all of the three school-based stages of assessment and provision. Clearly, a child with a severe learning difficulty (SLD) or disability will, at the earliest stage, be seen as requiring assessment and the protection of a Statement. It is important that the school-based stages should *not* be seen as steps on the way towards a statutory assessment which will usually not be necessary.

PROCESS OF STATUTORY ASSESSMENT

Since the model of need used in this book is that of a child with, what in the jargon is likely to be called, a 'severe and complex disability', and because every such child will require the protection of a Statement, we shall now turn to the procedures for this.

Once the decision has been made that the child probably has needs which will require the protection of a Statement, formal procedures come into play. This is the point at which a parent *will* need some expert advice as well as the informal support of a *Named Person* or friend. Guidance on this is provided in Chapters 6 and 8.

The legislation dealing with the criteria for making a Statement is covered in Sections 167 and 168 of the 1993 Education Act. Section 167 deals with carrying out an assessment. The decision to assess is made by the LEA, and this might have come about by way of a referral made by the school or a request from the parent. Where the school refers, it will give its reasons along with any information it will have collected during the course of its own investigations. Where the parent is the source, the LEA must comply with the request – unless an assessment has already been undertaken within the previous six months or it considers such an assessment unnecessary (Sections 172–173). A parent may appeal a refusal (Sections 172 or 173).

Having received a parental request, the LEA must investigate the cause of the parental concern and this will involve informing the child's headteacher. The LEA is also required to inform the parent of the part they will be required to play in the assessment and to seek information from other agencies who are required by law to provide advice (essentially health and social services).

A decision on whether to initiate a full assessment should be made within six weeks of the request being received. If a request for an assessment is turned down, this can be appealed by the parent

(Sections 172 and 173). LEAs also have a duty to react consistently to parental requests for assessment and also to operate in an open and consistent manner.

Having decided an assessment is necessary, the LEA must send a formal notification to the parent explaining the procedures to be followed and details of a *Named Officer* for future contact. The procedure for conducting a Statutory Assessment is described in the Code of Practice (Chapter 3), under Sections 165 and 167 of the Education Act 1993 and the Education (SEN) Regulations 1994. Statutory assessment is the focus of stage 4 of the five-stage model for assessment. The assessment must be completed within the allocated ten-week time limit and advice must be sought from the parent, the school, the LEA psychologist, social services and health authority (NHS Trust).

This list represents just the basic advice the LEA should seek. They may also take advice from any other source they consider appropriate. If any such advice has been obtained within the preceding 12 months, the LEA do not need to seek new advice. The advice should be drafted so as to highlight:

- the educational, psychological, medical and other features of the child's case which appear to be relevant to his current or likely future educational needs.

- how these features could affect the child's educational needs; and

- the special educational provision and the non-educational provision that is necessary given the specific features identified.

(SEN Regulations 6 (5)).

Time limits for the assessment

The length of time LEAs have generally taken to complete an assessment (up to 3 years in the extreme) was a major difficulty under the 1981 Act. This has been addressed in the 1993 Act through the imposition of statutory time-limits. The total time taken from request to final Statement should not exceed 26 weeks, with the following limits for the various stages of the process:

- decision on whether or not to proceed with an assessment, 6 weeks

- making the assessment, 10 weeks

- drafting the proposed Statement, 2 weeks

- finalising the Statement, 8 weeks

(SEN Regulations 1994).

Criteria for deciding to make a Statement

The LEA have the sole responsibility for deciding whether or not to issue and maintain a Statement. They must also collect all the relevant information (advice) which will serve to determine the content of the Statement. The Code of Practice (Chapter 4) outlines the criteria for deciding to draw up a Statement. This follows on from the aforementioned school-based assessment procedures 1–3. It is reasonable to assume that once an assessment has commenced, a Statement will result.

One problem with the way in which the Code is written is that it deals only with the theoretical situation with respect to the provisions likely to be available in a mainstream school, and not whether in a particular case such provisions are actually present. So when an LEA is planning to issue a Statement, it has a duty to ascertain whether the provisions it will contain are *in fact* available in the school in question. It is also important to be aware that the LEA cannot avoid making a Statement simply because it has delegated funds to a school for the kind of purpose required by the child's particular needs. If the child's needs are sufficiently great, the LEA should issue a Statement irrespective of the school's present ability to meet them. The issue here is about providing *protection* for the child.

The Statement

The Statement itself is in six parts (or sections):

Section 1.	**Basic biographical information** on the child: Name, address, date of birth, etc.
Section 2.	**A detailed description of the child's SENs**, in terms of the child's learning difficulties which call for special educational provision.
Section 3.	**The Objectives** the special educational provision should aim to meet and **the educational provisions** necessary to meet the needs and objectives, also **the monitoring arrangements** to keep a check on progress.
Section 4.	**The placement** (name of the school).

Section 5.   **The Non-educational needs** (therapy, transport, etc., where it is a non-educational need).

Section 6.   **Non-educational provisions** (therapy, transport, etc., where it is a non-educational need).

What parents and advocates need to know about Statements

LEAs sometimes try not to issue a Statement, to avoid committing themselves to additional expenditure. For the same reason, they issue Statements which fail to specify certain provisions which they would rather not have to pay for. Where they do issue a Statement it may well contain descriptions of needs and provisions which do not fairly or adequately reflect the needs of the child. This may be done in two main ways: First, the LEA might not identify a need that a child has – such as for specialist teaching, physiotherapy, intensive classroom support or whatever. This would be a simple *act of omission* on their part which, if not challenged, would mean that an important need might not be met. Second, to *apparently* acknowledge a need but describe the necessary provisions in such a way as to fail to guarantee that the necessary resources will be provided to meet it. The following are just a few examples of how this might be done in practice.

These political manoeuvres on the part of the LEA are outlined in Figure 7.1, which traces the process of deception perpetrated upon a parent because the LEA do not wish to commit themselves to making provisions they feel they cannot afford.

The entirely inadequate Statement

With the new requirements under the 1993 Act it should be much easier to challenge an authority which produces a Statement which is patently deficient in its specifications of needs and provisions. Under the 1981 Act an authority might have been able to get away with the most perfunctory comments under each heading, such as:

Needs (Section 2): 'To be educated as a child with severe and complex learning difficulties'.

Provisions (Section 3): 'Special education in X special school.'

Not only are such general statements entirely unhelpful but the placement (which should have been in Section 4) is masquerading as a provision. It is still not unusual for special needs professionals to conflate needs and placements in this way and it tends to be

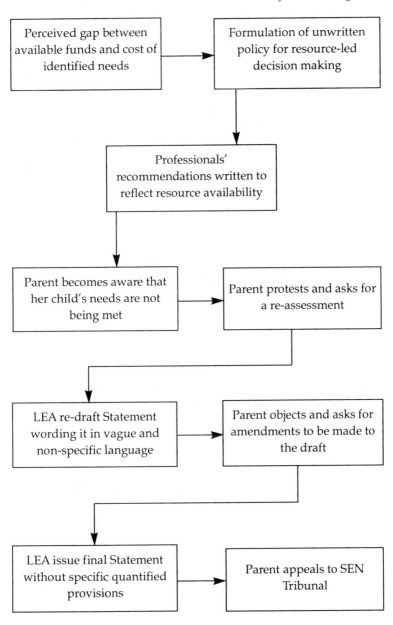

Figure 7.1 The politics of Statementing

expressed in the form 'this child has a SLD so *needs* a special school/small group teaching environment'.

Sometimes in such Statements all of the child's therapy needs were consigned to Section 5 (which was for non-educational provision), which meant there was no recognition of their educational relevance when they were, in fact, crucial to the child's education. Since these were not included in Section 3 as provisions, there was no duty placed upon the LEA to provide them, and if the Health Authority chose not to, then they would not be obliged to.

The above is an extreme example of what might have been found – although many more would have had a few more needs and provisions identified, but in very general language which would commit the LEA to no more than the most minimal provisions.

The apparently adequate Statement

More difficult to deal with is the Statement which seems to promise everything but which can be used to deliver virtually nothing. Such a Statement is immediately recognisable in that it has reams of information in the relevant sections which, on closer analysis, says little or nothing about the resources to be made available. An example is the following:

> **Needs** (Section 2): 'She needs to develop her communication skills and especially her ability to use and understand "yes" and "no" verbally or non-verbally...'

> **Provisions** (Section 3): 'Engage her in structured exercises and experiences designed *in conjunction with a speech therapist*'

This looks fine on the surface, but neither here (in Section 3), nor elsewhere in the Statement, is there a defined amount of speech therapist time specified to work on this important developmental area. The term 'designed in conjunction with' certainly suggests the involvement of a speech therapist but this may only be in the capacity of a consultant offering advice and not necessarily working 'hands on' with the child.

The term 'to be monitored by' is another which is frequently used as a device for implying that a particular specialist will be working with the child, but in practice may never become involved on a one-to-one clinical basis.

Some children with severe disabilities need one-to-one support in the classroom and elsewhere or else their education is largely meaningless. Such children are typically educated in special schools although there is no reason why they should not be in the mainstream. Education for such children may become a farce because of the lack of relevance or intensity in what they are offered, and much of their day may be spent waiting for attention. I have spent time observing children in classes in segregated schools, and it is not unusual for 50 per cent – 60 per cent of the child's school day to be spent waiting for the next activity or for someone to do something for him. For such a child, the comment in Section 3, which relates to her individual attention needs, may be something like: 'to receive support in an environment with a high staff-pupil ratio which will enable her to have frequent individual attention'. This sounds fine but the reality may well be as described earlier.

Before accepting a Statement for her child, a parent should be clear as to what provisions are actually being made. It is important that the parent is clear about this so that they will be able to take the necessary action over what is not being provided.

Government guidelines on staffing

Government guidelines on staffing levels for children with special needs tend to influence LEA formula funding in what is known as the authority's Local Management of Schools – Special Needs LMS(S) policy. There have been two such Government Circulars during recent years: Circular 4/73 and Circular 11/90. Circular 4/73 dealt only with teacher-pupil ratios – which was not particularly helpful for children who would be attending certain special schools – while Circular 11/90 provided broad guidelines for both teaching and non-teaching staff.

Helpful though many LEAs find Circular 11/90 to be as guidance for framing their own staffing policies, it is stressed by the Government that it should not be treated as a blueprint. Indeed it offers guidance based upon broad impairment categories, with little or no reference to the implications arising out of the location of a child's education. Also its discrete categories are not treated as summative, so the needs of children with multiple impairments are not comprehensively addressed.

Needs and Provisions must be matched

In writing the Statement, the law is clear that the LEA must serve a copy of the proposed Statement within two weeks of the date on which the assessment was completed (Regulation 14(1)), and this Statement should be in the form described above with all of the advice obtained appended to the Statement document.

The Statement should be drafted in language the parent is likely to be able to understand and be clear and unambiguous with as little technical jargon as possible. Section 2 of the Statement should describe all the child's learning difficulties – the needs – and include a general description of the child's functioning. The needs listed should be drawn from the advice received, and where there is conflicting advice the LEA must give its reasons for having accepted one view at the expense of another, or at least explain how it resolved the conflict.

Section 3 of the Statement should first set out the main developmental and educational objectives then go on to list the provisions to meet the identified needs. *For every identified need there must be a linked provision.* Some of these provisions will be made by the school and others by the authority centrally and it should be made clear who will do what.

The need to quantify

As to the way in which provisions are to be specified, the Code (4.30) says:

> The provision set out in this sub-section should normally be specific, detailed and quantified (in terms, for example, of hours of ancillary or specialist teaching support) although there will be cases where some flexibility should be retained in order to meet the changing special educational needs of the child concerned.

It should always be insisted that the following be quantified:

- the level of individual classroom non-teaching support (X hours per day/week)
- the amount of speech, physio and occupational therapy (minutes per session and sessions per week)
- the amount of specialist teacher time (minutes per session and sessions per week).

Qualified must mean qualified

It is also important that the non-teaching classroom support should be spelled out as *qualified, experienced* and *trained*, when that is required. This might need to be described as a person on the NNEB (Nursery Nurse) pay scale – even if that particular qualification is not essential or relevant (as in the case of children over about eight years of age) – for this will at least provide sufficient funding to get someone suitable. With therapy time this may come in a variety of forms, which may need to include:

1. hands-on 'treatment' by the qualified therapist;

2. group work orchestrated by the therapist who directs the work of others who are not qualified therapists;

3. work undertaken by a therapist's aid or assistant, who will not be professionally qualified but has received intensive training; and

4. work carried out by a teacher or classroom assistant (or even a volunteer) following some instruction from the therapist.

Each of these ways of working may, in the Statement, masquerade as 'therapy', but clearly it is wrong to present them all as such. If it is only acceptable to say a child is being taught if there is a qualified teacher in front of the class, then it hardly seems right to claim a child is receiving therapy when a non-therapist is delivering the programme. There is also the other issue that if more and more of the work of the teacher and assistant involves delivering what the therapist would have been doing were she available, then the rest of the child's educational programme will become watered down.

This is not to say that there is no room at all for the therapist to engage in 'cascade teaching', that is the giving away of skills approach, for clearly all professionals in this field of work must do so and that is what is meant by multi-professional or inter-disciplinary working. However, because of claimed resource difficulties, this is fast becoming the dominant style for some speech, physio and occupational therapists and children are losing out. It is also becoming more prevalent amongst some specialist teachers for sensorily impaired children. An additional longer-term problem for these professional groups is the likely effect of this style of working, which will inevitably lead to a dilution of their clinical skills because of their low level of 'hands on' practice.

Clearly the child's educational programme *must* be informed by the professional knowledge of a range of disciplines and this will require cross-discipline/agency working practices. The best practice has long reflected an understanding of this. However, parents should be alert to the subtle changes in working practice which may occur when resources are under pressure.

Such are some of the political issues around special needs education. We shall now turn to some examples of the practice which may result when politics are to the fore.

CASE STUDY

The following is a case study of a child of 12 years called Andrew, who was described as having 'severe and complex learning difficulties' and who was attending a day special school in the UK. This case study is offered to demonstrate the improvements it is possible to bring about in an LEA's approach to Statementing by offering constructive advice and support.

Biographical information

Andrew has severe spastic quadriplegia and secondary microcephaly. He has little spontaneous movement and is hypertonic with uncontrollable spasms. His abilities depend very much on his level of physical well-being and state of alertness. He has a severe visual impairment but on a good day seems to be able to focus quite quickly upon people and track them by moving his head. He can also sometimes focus on objects.

Andrew seems to rely mostly on his hearing and enjoys music and the company of others. He uses certain sounds and movements which can be interpreted by those who know him well and he can take turns in a 'conversational' manner. He has difficulty ingesting food and often experiences breathing difficulties. Andrew is doubly incontinent.

Where he is able, Andrew contributes positively to his education. Andrew's fundamental needs are: to experience the loving care of others in his home life, at school and within the wider community, and to grow and learn in community with others so as to be able to take his place in society. These needs translate into the following requirements for his education.

His physical well-being

Andrew needs to:

- be able to travel to and from school in a stress-free way
- be positioned safely and comfortably with his present deformities well-supported while preventing the occurrence of further deformity and contractures
- change position frequently throughout the day to relieve pressure and poor circulation and to improve breathing
- develop good breathing patterns and maintain clear lungs
- maximise relaxed muscle tone
- ingest food more comfortably and efficiently
- remain comfortable despite double incontinence.

His motor skills

Andrew needs to:

- improve his lying abilities, his sitting ability and his joint movements
- develop and maximise all voluntary movements to enable him to:

    (i) explore and interact with his environment; and

(ii) to develop voluntary directed movement so as to be able to operate with an alternative means of communication.

His communication

Andrew needs to:

- be able to communicate his feelings and needs
- improve his expressive sounds
- develop means of expressing choice and preference.

His perceptual and cognitive skills

Andrew needs to:

- perceive the world more accurately in order to better understand and act upon it.

In the mid 1980s the LEA issued the following Statement for this child, who was born in 1982 (see Figure 7.2). The Statement was unsigned and undated. An amendment was made towards the end of 1987 when he was moved to another special school. The amendment applied only to Section 4 of the Statement and named the new school which he had already been attending for two years.

Need (section 2)	*Provision (section 3)*
1. Andrew suffers from severe spasticity affecting all four limbs and shows severe developmental delay	i. Special school for children with severe learning difficulties
2. He needs a curriculum geared to the needs of children with very severe learning difficulties	
Appropriate school (section 4)	*Non-educational provision (section 5)*
In section 4 his earlier special school was named	Transport/Physiotherapy

Source: Hall 1995

Figure 7.2 Andrew's original Statement

The only other information contained in this Statement was the basic biographical data on the first page. The appendices were as follows:

a. A cyclostyled 'Medical Report' from the heath authority which contained the following information:

    vision: non-assessable

    hearing: non-assessable

    speech and language: none

    motor function: severe spasticity affecting all four limbs.

    general health: grand mal epilepsy, recurrent upper respiratory and chest infections. Developmental progress is markedly delayed.

b. The 'Psychological Advice from the LEA, which read as follows:

    Andrew is a little boy who suffers from severe spasticity affecting all four limbs. He has been receiving Home Intervention since... Andrew's development is very delayed and it has been impossible to accurately assess his degree of vision or hearing, although it is reported that he turns towards his mother's voice. Andrew needs a placement that can offer stimulation together with physiotherapy and care.

c. The Portage Home Teacher also submitted a four-paragraph report covering half a side of A4 which essentially listed the things Andrew could *not* do.

Such was the Statement for one little boy with a number of pressing needs. When the parents began asking why a number of their child's needs were not being met, they received no satisfactory answer from the LEA. The school was also concerned that none of its own internal review recommendations had resulted in an amendment to the Statement. When the school pointed out to the LEA that it had not been undertaking its duty to review Statements annually, it was told that this was a misunderstanding on the school's part and that the school's own internal reviews were in fact the LEA's annual reviews. The fact that no psychologist or officer had been present at any of these over the years was the reason given why none of the recommendations had been acted upon. The school had routinely invited the LEA to send a representative but none had appeared.

Need	*Provision (shortcomings)*
For one-to-one support in his learning and care programmes throughout the school day	(i) No mention of additional staffing resources for the school, which was funded to provide for its pupils on an adult/pupil ratio of 1–2. This would mean around 50–60% of his school day being spent waiting for attention. There is reference to the need for *'flexible staffing levels* to meet his needs at any particular time, e.g. to support his joints when he is moved and positioned.'
Intensive specialist physiotherapy input for his physical care needs	(i) 'That his environment be organised and adapted to give access to his wheelchair together with specific activities, *designed in conjunction with a physiotherapist and/or occupational therapist...'* Also to 'integrate his physiotherapy programme into the processes of his general care and education...'
Specialist speech therapy input for his communication needs with an exploration of an alternative means of communication	(i) Here the commitment is to 'involve him in activities, designed *in conjunction with* a speech therapist, that will develop his ability to communicate with others'. Also to 'involve him in specific exercises designed *in conjunction with* the speech therapist...'

Source: John Hall 1995

Figure 7.3 Shortcomings in Andrew's first draft Statement following re-assessment

The parents were advised by the school that their child had a number of needs which required very specific staffing provisions, namely: one-to-one support at all times, daily physiotherapy by a physiotherapist and daily speech therapy by a speech therapist. There were also many other specific recommendations relating to items of equipment, etc. The parents sought a re-assessment of their child's needs and this was granted, and, although the Statement which eventually materialised contained much more information, there was little by way of additional resources. The strategy adopted by the LEA was to provide a very full and wordy document in which each section of the Statement was replete with descriptions of need and provision but which, in almost every particular, was vague and non-committal, such that the parent would not be able to pin down a particular level of input.

In fact, the recommendations the parents put forward on the basis of the advice they had received were completely ignored. Figure 7.3 is a summary of the key resource areas in which the draft Statement was deficient.

It will be apparent from the above that as the assessment and Statementing process was conducted, the politics of Statementing were very much to the fore. No mention was made of additional personal support staffing and although the need for physiotherapy was acknowledged, this was seen largely as something delivered by non-therapist personnel on an 'integrated' basis. Also the speech therapy reference implied no commitment of therapist time. It is clear from the form of words used that the LEA were unwilling to make a commitment to specific levels of support and therapy input, thereby leaving the situation as uncertain as it was under the previous Statement.

The parents sought independent assessments from an EP and a physiotherapist who both agreed with the position of the parents and the school and recommended constant individual one-to-one support (a personal assistant), five hours per week physiotherapy and two hours per week speech therapy.

The parents rejected the final draft of the Statement and, with the support of an advocate, instituted an appeal to the SEN Tribunal. The appeal was on the basis that the Statement failed to describe the child's needs with sufficient specificity, reflect the recommendations in the advice, link sections 2 and 3 of the Statement and quantify professional input.

The appeal was upheld by the Tribunal on every count and it made the following order:

1. A requirement for physiotherapy and speech therapy provision, being one hour per day of physiotherapy individually with Andrew and his support worker and two hours per week of speech therapy individually with Andrew and his support worker.

2. The provision of a support worker of not less than NNEB qualification on a full-time basis to form part of the multi-disciplinary team delivering the provision set out in section 3.

3. An amendment to section 5 to state that because of Andrew's profound disability, physiotherapy and speech therapy form part of his special educational provision and the provision of

speech and physiotherapy specified in section 3 will be requested from the health authority.

This had been a long and frustrating struggle for the parents and they needed support over a number of aspects of the appeal, most notably:

1. A clarification of what the law requires of an LEA in the drafting of Statements of SEN.

2. Support in focusing on the central issues.

3. Explanation of the procedure for rejecting a Statement and asking for a re-assessment.

4. Advice on how to seek alternative expert independent professional advice to challenge that adduced by the LEA.

5. Representation at the Tribunal hearing, which in this case was undertaken on an expenses only basis by a trainee barrister.

The parents concerned were extremely able, yet still needed specialist advice and support because the issues are very complex. It was also important that this support came from a source which was entirely independent of the local authority.

CONCLUSION

LEAs, by and large, do the best they can to meet the SENs of children within the limitations of their understanding of those needs and the budget available. The SEN policy of the LEA is determined by elected politicians and paid officers and overseen by central government to ensure that it falls within the law and its regulations. Since all the major educational decisions are made by politicians in central and local government, SEN policy and implementation is a political matter – hence the Statementing process too is political.

LEA officers are pulled in a number of directions through having to meet the competing, and often conflicting, demands of parents, local councillors, professionals and central government – not a scenario for peace and tranquility – and, in order to displease as few people as possible, make decisions which, on reflection, they would perhaps rather not have had to make. One such decision is to issue instructions to their paid professional staff not to make recommendations which carry resourcing implications they cannot afford. This, then is the heart of the politics of Statementing and it is as much an issue within the health authority as the LEA.

Chapter 8

Advocacy Support for Children with Special Needs

THE ROOT OF THE PROBLEM – INADEQUATE LEGISLATION AND POOR SERVICES

Better use can be made of current legislation

It is now abundantly clear that the 1981 Education Act failed to bring about a just allocation of resources to children with special educational needs (SENs) because systems put in place by that Act proved too easy to ignore by LEAs. Also, whilst it is accepted that the 1993 Education Act is an attempt to remedy some of these shortcomings, there is little optimism amongst those campaigning on a human rights platform that it will be able to effect more than marginal improvements for many of the most vulnerable children in the school system.

Nevertheless, in spite of weak legislation, much can still be done to improve opportunities and resourcing for individual pupils by using the existing, although still sadly much under-utilised, regulations. It is, however, extremely difficult for parents to do this without support because of the complex procedures and bureaucratic technicalities which have to be negotiated. Nevertheless, although with well-informed and intensive support, much can be achieved and an advocacy service is one way of supporting parents to achieve what their children need.

The complacent view of service development

It might seem surprising to some professionals that a book about special education should devote a whole chapter to advocacy support. Certainly many of my previous colleagues genuinely saw themselves as advocates for the children they served. Many would honestly admit that they did not have the freedom they would ideally have liked to function in an advocacy capacity, but they were able to express a view and such views were often taken into account.

Those who will be surprised to find so much space devoted to this topic will, in all likelihood, be working as a paid professional in one or other of the statutory services. Such an individual may also hold the view that, although things are not entirely satisfactory in the way services are provided, needs are identified and met in a more or less satisfactory way and that where improvements are still necessary, these will be effected in due course.

That the overwhelming majority of service professionals subscribe to something like this view cannot be in doubt. Also, the holding of such a view is marked by an attachment to the idea that because things are immeasurably better than they were a generation or so ago, and we now have a modern and much more enlightened body of practice which only needs to be further refined and tweaked into shape, all will be well.

This way of viewing the service one is paid to deliver is one feature of practice which does not change over time. At whatever point in the history of service development one arbitrarily chooses to scrutinise public and professional attitudes, the picture is precisely the same: 'we are almost there, just a little more of this and a little less of that and all will be well for those we serve'. We have seen that this belief is sustained by a failure to question the prevailing societal and professional ideology – which confirms that our service model, and the various practices to which it gives rise, are really in pretty good shape.

Day by day things get better and better

It is an inescapable characteristic of human nature, and not just professional attitudes, that our own age is morally more enlightened and humane than the one which immediately preceded it, and that, in turn, was better than its predecessor. Indeed the tendency is always to cast one's gaze back over preceding centuries and see the human journey as one marked as much by moral as technical evolution. Such reflection is, sadly, mere self-deception, and whilst self-deception may, in many of its guises, be quite harmless, this is certainly not the case where the quality of the lives of vulnerable children are at stake.

Because professionals themselves remain largely complacent about the problems of special needs education, to that extent they cannot become part of the solution. The solution, if there is one, lies with the parents, their allies and government. Let me offer just one example of the way in which professionals have betrayed parents.

The professional as reluctant and unwitting traitor

In the small publication referred to earlier, *Integration – Problems and Possibilities for Change* (AEP 1989) the Association of Educational

Psychologists (AEP) published the results of a working party on integration involving five of its own members who introduced their report in the following way:

> No matter how 'integrationist' we may appear we would like to make two qualifications:
>
> (a) At present and possibly for some time into the future, there will be some groups of children for whom attendance at a mainstream school could only, at best, be 'locational' integration, and even this could only be achieved by a massive injection of human and material resources.
>
> (b) We recognise and commend the good practice which occurs in many special schools and in examining ways of enhancing the normalisation process we have drawn heavily on such exemplary practice.

This conclusion by the AEP goes directly against the tide of public opinion as well as against the spirit of legislation, both of which say that children should have a *right* to be integrated. It also conveniently ignores the damaging consequences of segregated education over the last century or so. To choose to heap praise on 'many special schools' for their 'exemplary practice' is utterly at odds with what we know to be the generality of practice; worse still, such a statement can only be taken as an endorsement of the principle of segregation since, if the practice is *exemplary*, on that account alone it is hard to see how the practice of segregation itself is to be faulted.

Of all the professional groups that ought to know about the damaging effects of segregation in the lives of children with SENs, educational psychologists (EPs) should know better than most that children deserve better. Yet for reasons best known to themselves, these gate-keepers to the world of segregation come down in its defence. Maybe they like the sense of power they hold or maybe they are just afraid to alienate their teacher colleagues or upset their employer, neither body seemingly champing at the bit for change. I have discussed this in a recent article on school-based advocacy (Hall 1994) in which I characterise the dilemma of the EP as one having more to do with the basic economics of everyday life than with any grand theorising about the needs of children (see Figures 8.1 and 8.2).

Perhaps a more charitable explanation of this resistance to change is more appropriate. It may well be the case that the LEA psychologists, like all professional groups, are caught up in a system which just will not allow them the freedom to act as they would like.

95% of LEA psychologists have a mortgage to pay

Source: Hall 1994

Figure 8.1 The psychologist

100% of education managers know
that 95% of LEA psychologists have mortgages to pay

Source: Hall 1994

Figure 8.2 The psychologist and his manager

Given the continued denial of such basics rights, it is surprising that so little advocacy work has developed within special needs education – although this is beginning to change with the new Tribunal Appeal system which, as we have seen, became operative under the 1993 Act in September 1994.

The lost opportunity for partnership

The idea of parent-professional partnership, which was supposed to arise out of arrangements made by the 1981 Act, has not been widely embraced by professionals, and up and down the country parents are doing battle to try and force from the LEA the provisions their children should have been given as of right. Sometimes this has resulted from the failure of an LEA to provide a mainstream placement, but there are many other issues over which parents feel aggrieved. These include: the lack of an appropriate educational programme, the shortage or complete absence of speech, physio or occupational therapy, insufficient specialist teacher input, sub-standard home-to-school transport or the failure to provide essential items of equipment.

It is the author's view that that there will always be a needs-resource gap of some kind is not the issue; the issue is that professionals are now too often required to tell parents their children do not need provisions the parents know are essential, and that fundamental untruth is at the root of much bitterness and anger on the part of parents. It is one thing to diagnose a need and then apologise that there are insufficient resources to meet it, but quite another to pretend that that need does not exist.

Resource-led rather than needs-led recommendations

The core problem then, has to do with the LEA writing Statements which reflect the *provision* available rather than the evident *needs* of the child. This means quite simply that the LEA has a certain range of services into which the child has must be placed, rather than making a response having taken a careful look at the child's specific individual needs and, in a flexible manner, adapting the service to accommodate the child. Too often the Statement of special need is reduced to a tool for making a placement, rather than as a vehicle for describing needs and their necessary provisions. The fundamental dishonesty of this approach may not be evident to many of those involved because they have accepted the premise that because the pot is always limited, what is available needs to be shared around – not in accordance with need but in accordance with some formula which will do the trick on a utilitarian basis (the least misery principle).

But there is of course no need to accept this premise at all since just as the pot is never big enough so there are always other pots to be raided, which becomes evident when one notices that an LEA, having said it has absolutely no more money to meet a need, suddenly comes up with the necessary when the Tribunal directs it to, or when they are determined to win a Tribunal and opt to spend up to £4000 to hire the services of a QC to represent them.

So, one would ask two things of LEAs and their special needs professionals:

1. Don't allow yourself to be manipulated to collude with policies which obscure a child's real needs.

2. Exert more pressure within the system to make good things happen for children who are vulnerable and need your help.

The compromised professional

No parent is going to blame a professional who, having honestly said what their child needs, then has to admit that there is no money to pay for it. But this presumes also that that professional has shown himself willing to speak up on behalf of the child within his service and, in some degree, to act as advocate on the child's behalf. This does not mean that he creates such havoc that his job is put at risk, but merely that he has honestly done what he can to bend the system to the shape the child needs it to be. There is sadly too little of this happening and professionals are more and more putting their own career interest before that of the child.

This interest divide between professionals and those they are paid to serve is increasing as our lives become more and more 'managed'. What some (McKnight 1987) have come to see as the 'over-professionalisation' of our lives is destroying our ability to think and act for ourselves and, equally importantly, undermining our ability to offer help to one another. It is as though the only ones who are capable of helping are those with a professional qualification. Yet, while this is happening, a gulf is opening up between helper and helped and the helper's primary loyalty is increasingly to his professional peers and his employer.

This situation cannot go on indefinitely without a consumer backlash, and that is what we saw from parents who were unhappy with the workings of the 1981 Act. It is important to note that the parents saw the problems in special education much more clearly than the professionals, most of whom were content to muddle by or at least keep their heads down. It required strong parental protest to bring about the process which led to the 1993 Act. In the end though, it comes down to a simple consideration of what is right and wrong.

But things are no better in Nobshire

But things *were* certainly much worse years ago, and many involved at the provision end of things find comfort in reflecting upon this in a way which is difficult for the consumer to understand. In these times of *moral relativism* it is even easier to take refuge in such historical comparisons, for we are now persuaded that there is no absolute right or wrong in human affairs since all that really counts is the individual's personal beliefs in the matter.

When criticised for their own shortcomings in service provision, LEAs typically take comfort in reflecting upon the fact that some other authorities they know are providing a yet worse service – 'if you think things are bad here you should live in Nobshire!'. This is another form of moral relativism which reflects the low expectations of those charged with providing services. Such an attitude betrays the indifference of those concerned to rise to the challenge of providing the very highest quality service to children, which can only be one based upon *excellence*. Many parents would reply that they are not even asking for excellence, *relevance* would be a big step forward.

Tom Peters, the American management guru, tells a story about a large and influential company which was known to be selling shoddy products. When challenged on this, the director replied: 'if you think our products are bad you should see those of X, our competitor, their's are even worse'. Peters, with his customary hyperbole, envisions a marketing manager rallying his sales force to get out there at 7am in the morning with the message 'buy our widgets, they're no worse than anyone else's'.

Coincidentally, an education officer said the self-same thing to me in the context of a discussion about the quality of Statements the authority were producing. He said they were no worse than those of surrounding authorities so what was my basis for complaint. The fact that others are doing worse is certainly interesting and worthy of discussion but it should never lead to complacency and low expectations, either in industry or in education. Our duty on behalf of vulnerable children is to aim for the stars and then closely analyse the reasons why we are falling short.

In education, as in industry, low standards based on low expectation can never be a basis for service planning since it can lead only to further deterioration and ultimate failure. Education authorities have a duty to provide the very best services they can, based upon what they understand children to need. This duty can never be reduced to level where a parent is told her child must remain segregated because this authority is no better or worse than its neighbours at providing for children in the mainstream. The only issue, as far as the law is concerned, is whether the child's needs have been properly identified and linked to the provisions necessary to meet those needs.

In commerce and industry there is a growing awareness of the importance of customer satisfaction and the need for quality control. Not so in education – in spite of vigorous, although largely misplaced, efforts by the present government to raise standards. Furthermore, this lack of awareness is more evident in the special school sector than elsewhere within the education service. As has been argued earlier, this shortcoming is rooted in a failure to provide a coherent rationale for special schooling, while placing reliance upon an inspection model devised for ordinary (real) schools, which fails to identify bad practice.

The critical view of special education

The critical view of special education is still very much the minority view and comes in a variety of forms. Most such criticism still comes from non-professionals, that is parents on behalf of their children, students and ex-students who have themselves been subjected to poor or discriminatory practice. There is a small but growing body of individuals who describe themselves as 'special school survivors', amongst whom my friend, Martin Yates (whose story was told earlier), has very definite views on segregated education. Martin attended a segregated school and an FE college and has written forcefully about his experiences in both settings (Yates 1994).

The central criticism levelled at the generality of special needs services is that they segregate when they should integrate and that they offer a second rate education to children who cannot easily compensate in later life for the disadvantages that such a practice inevitably creates.

Organisations of disabled people have been actively campaigning for a number of years on this issue and are, of course, the most powerful voice in the debate – since it is they who have been at the receiving end of the injustice of a school system which denies them a place in the educational mainstream.

The team at the Open University have presented a consistently pro-integration agenda for many years (Booth and Potts 1983) and Joe Whittaker (of the Bolton Institute), a leading British advocate for inclusive education, has carried out some excellent research on segregation in FE colleges. In terms of sharp end practice, Newham Council in East London have done more to end segregation in their education service than any other LEA in Britain and, as far as I am aware, remain the only authority to issue a policy statement aimed at the eventual elimination of all forms of segregated provision.

We have already seen that the government report *Caught in the Act* (HMI/Audit Commission 1992) also provided a damning indictment of special education, citing 'serious deficiencies in the way in which children with special needs are identified and provided for'. It said these deficiencies are caused by three key problems:

- lack of clarity both about what constitutes SENs and about the respective responsibilities of the school and LEA
- lack of clear accountability by schools and LEAs for the progress made by pupils and lack of accountability by schools to the LEA for the resources they receive
- lack of incentives for LEAs to implement the 1981 Act.

It is one thing for parents to complain, and they have for many years now, but quite another for such staid bodies as HMI and the Audit Commission to produce such strong criticism. As the report makes clear, we are not just looking at the need for a few adjustments here and there in terms of the LEA's approach to special needs schooling, we are talking about a root and branch overhaul of a system that has become inefficient and self-serving and, in some respects, actually damaging.

Section 3 of the 1993 Act was an attempt to put right many of the shortcomings of the 1981 Act and some have found grounds for believing that it may achieve something of what is required. However, the Act fails to go to the heart of the problems which beset special education and which are rooted in fundamentally devaluing attitudes and practices which are most clearly exemplified in the continued strength of the special school sector.

With legislation placing a clear duty on LEAs to integrate for nearly a decade, one might be forgiven for being surprised by the fact that in 1992 the proportion of children sent to special schools in England increased from 1.47 per cent in 1991 to 1.49 per cent. This may seem only a minor rise but it might turn out to be a reflection of the new duties placed upon schools by recent legislation, but it is hardly reflective of a serious response on the part of LEAs to act upon their statutory duty to integrate.

If children are to have even less chance of being integrated, in the future what are we to conclude about the real meaning of legislation which is supposed in essence to be integrationist? It is clear that our legislation is failing to keep pace with parental expectations that their children should be included in the mainstream and that their SENs should be met without constant carping about resource limitations. Since LEAs seem unable to deliver on these two key requirements, and because these are seen as basic rights which parents will never stop demanding, there is a need to ensure that their voice is heard more clearly. One way of supporting this is through organised advocacy support.

SPECIAL EDUCATION ADVOCACY SUPPORT

I have spoken with parents in various parts of Britain and the picture is pretty much the same wherever you go. The problem is complex but not necessarily intractable. It has to do with ill-informed, and sometimes unhelpful, attitudes on the part of many professionals and administrators. It also has to do with services being *existing provision led* rather than *needs led*. This means quite simply that instead of professionals looking at a child in terms of what their assessed needs require, they look first at the provision they already have and try to slot the child in irrespective of the child's particular needs. This practice is now very widespread and creates enormous distress to parents because it can lead to inappropriate, and possibly damaging, social and educational experiences for children.

Why professionals make bad recommendations

Professionals may make the wrong recommendations for a child for one or more of a number of reasons. One obvious possibility is that they may not actually be very good at their job, so may not understand what is most important in the lives of the children and families they are paid to serve. Alternatively, they may know what is best but be afraid to say so because they know it will be frowned upon by their colleagues. This is frequently the case where an EP knows in her heart that a child would get along better in his local school but where the policy within the authority is to segregate; this might be on the grounds of cost but more likely on the basis that 'this is the way we have always served such children here'.

Whatever the reason(s) for making bad decisions, the professional structure is extremely powerful in enforcing them and all too frequently a parent will be faced with a united front by the various individual professionals and their administrators. Whether the blame for bad decision-making can be located with the individual or the system as a whole is often very difficult to ascertain, and for the family who are at the receiving end of such a decision, the only important question to ask is: *what can we do to seek redress?*

Appealing the decision

LEAs have procedures by which parents can register their disagreement with an administrative decision, and where the child is the subject of a Statement of his SENs this can be quite a lengthy process (these procedures have been outlined in some detail in Chapter 2 so need not detain us here). LEAs will always provide parents with their own policy on this and the 1993 Act (Section 3 of which replaces the 81 Act) provides the legal framework binding upon all authorities. The Advisory Centre for Education (ACE) publish an excellent Special Education Handbook which explains the law governing what LEAs can and cannot do. Sadly, many parents believe that LEAs are prepared to blatantly ignore, or even knowingly break, the law – even when a child has a Statement describing her needs.

The Named Person

The 1993 Education Act, which came into force on 1 September 1994, contained the notion of a 'Named Person' who will provide advice and information to the parent in connection with their child's SENs. The Act placed a duty upon LEAs to identify such a person when they issue the final draft of the Statement. The Named Person should not be confused with the Named Officer, who is the LEA employee who will act as the point of contact with the authority over all matters connected with the Statement and who has a duty to ensure certain information is made available.

The concept of the Named Person is briefly outlined in the Code of Practice (Sections 4.70–4.73) where it says the role is that of someone who 'can give the parents advice and information about their child's special educational needs'. Although, as has been said, it is the responsibility of the LEA to identify such a person when a Statement is made, a parent may choose to have such a person to help them prior to this. The Code goes on to say that 'the Named Person should be someone whom the parents can trust. He or she should be capable of giving parents accurate information and sound advice. LEAs may wish to consult local voluntary organisations, parents' groups and relevant professionals in order to identify individuals who are willing to act as Named Persons.' According to the Code, such people should preferably be independent of the LEA and perhaps someone who works in a parent partnership scheme. If the parent chooses not to have a Named Person, then that is entirely their choice.

This new requirement has created something close to panic amongst many voluntary sector workers who, during the past year or so, have been trying to fathom the implications of taking on such an apparently onerous role. A number of conferences were hurriedly arranged by the voluntary sector during the early part of 1995 in an attempt to share perceptions on the best way to establish a co-ordinated approach to this new challenge. Discussion focused upon a number of key issues:

- should there be a register?
- should the LEA or an independent organisation or group take the lead role in providing a register of Named Persons?
- how should the register be compiled?
- how would names be canvassed?
- what, if any, checks should be made on candidates?

- what kind of training should they have and who might/should provide it?
- should people be paid for more than their out-of-pocket expenses? If so, where would the money come from?
- what are the priority skills and areas of knowledge for a Named Person?
- would service professionals make credible Named Persons or might they experience too much conflict of interest?
- what level or type of supervision would the Named Person require?
- should the Named Person be expected to advise and support the parents up to and through a Tribunal appeal?
- should the Named Person take out personal indemnity insurance in case a parent sues them for mishandling their case?
- at what point in the assessment process should the person be identified?

These and many other questions remain to be resolved, and as yet there is no clear indication as to how a system for ensuring that Named Person support for parents will be provided.

Looked at from the parent's viewpoint, it would be reasonable to ask just what it is they need as they do battle with a resisting LEA. One parent offered the following as his and his wife's personal needs at such a time: reassurance, support, a listening ear, explanations and an articulate voice to speak on their behalf. Having offered this list, he concluded that the role should be that of befriender/advocate. The important elements of the befriender were seen to be such qualities as the ability to identify with, and relate to, the family. Also, someone to rely on and trust. Such a person should have common interests and understandings relevant to the situation the parents find themselves in. It was also seen that such a person should be available locally. In addition, the individual should conform to the norms of the local community in which (s)he and the parents both live so that their views would be respected.

As for the advocacy element of the role, the person should have a knowledge of the system linked to the ability to explain it in language the parent understands. Such a person should have contacts and knowledge and command respect through being an opinion leader. They should also have links with, and access to, the wider community. This description is very much that of the notional effective leader.

This parent felt that the best place to look for such an individual would be within the community of the school itself, amongst other parents. The role envisaged would be more that of a well-informed friend than quasi-professional.

It seems then that this is potentially an extremely demanding role and one which may well be interpreted very differently by parents and professionals. This particular parent's emphasis on a local respected befriender with the abilities both to listen and speak articulately on the parents' behalf is clearly important, yet given the complexity of both the legislation and the system, a number of further requirements spring to mind. These would include:

- knowledge of legislation and the Code of Practice
- knowledge of special needs
- knowledge of local provision
- knowledge of independent specialist professionals: psychologists, therapists lawyers, etc.
- knowledge of local government
- good interpersonal and communication skills
- ability to manage conflict.

A piece of research carried out by Mencap during the Autumn of 1994 to elicit LEA views on the role of the Named Person asked how they would identify individuals for such a role. Specifically, would the role be that of adviser, advocate, befriender or as a professional? This piece of research showed that 25 per cent were still considering the matter, 90 per cent saw the person as befriender, 70 per cent as adviser and 60 per cent as advocate, while only 20 per cent saw the role as that of professional. This reflects an encouraging grasp on the part of LEAs of the need for independence although there is probably still insufficient understanding of the need for advocacy.

In the ongoing discussion of the role of the Named Person, there is also a great deal of uncertainty over the way any formal organisation of any Named Person service should be structured; whether it should be co-ordinated by the LEA or whether a local, or even national, voluntary organisation should take on the task.

The need for independent advocacy support

Advocacy for children with SENs is less well established than advocacy for adults with learning or physical disabilities. In particular, there is still insufficient recognition of the need for advocacy over educational issues. This may seem a very perverse statement given the number of major voluntary organisations which have served children for so long – Barnardos, Scope, The Children's Society, Mencap (adults and children), Downs Syndrome Association, etc. – and also the host of smaller disability-specific support groups which grow by the year. Yet things are not quite what they seem.

Most of the major charities were indeed true advocacy organisations when they began because they came about largely through parental anger and frustration to draw attention to societal injustice towards their children. They were, unfortunately, victims of their own success. As they grew, they began to provide services – schools, homes, etc. – which were initially models of better services which the statutory sector was intended to mimic, and in this they achieved undoubted success. However, those which became the most successful have gradually lost their way as they have evolved to become remote and highly bureaucratic major service providers with greater and greater interest in protecting and extending their own personal empires. Some are now sadly locked into growth for the sake of it, and to the enhancement of personal careers at the expense of those they claim to serve.

Such a state of affairs is not only incompatible with carrying out an advocacy role but requires that those who must continue to use their outdated services themselves need advocacy support to protect them from their erstwhile benefactors.

There is something of the inevitable about this process of what we might call the *conservatisation of protest* in British society, which no doubt has something to do with our constitutional inability to shake off the past. The system seems nearly always to be able to draw the sting of protest by rewarding its potentially most effective critics with gongs.

So, our impetus towards advocacy needs to be continually reviewed through a spirit of renewed anger over perceived injustice. If the lesson we must learn from the successful voluntary organisation is that it forgot what had originally made it angry, then we need to ensure that such anger is frequently revisited. This book is written in anger on behalf of those children who could least afford to be failed by the very services that were supposed to be their salvation.

History is replete with all manner of injustices to individuals and minority groups – amongst whom people with physical and learning disabilities have been to the forefront. However, they have not been alone and similar injustices have befallen those experiencing a mental illness or people who are just very poor or perhaps belong to an ethnic minority group. More and more, the elderly are suffering injustice in a materialistic world obsessed with youth, beauty, wealth and power. Some of these groups have attracted advocacy support or have had the wherewithal to become self-advocates.

It is assumed that the natural and most effective advocate for a child is his or her parent, and that is usually the case. Sometimes though, the system is so resistant to what the parent is asking for, and so complex, that without technical support there is no way in which the parent can be a match for it. At that point there needs to be an equaliser.

So what is advocacy?

Advocacy is standing up for a person or a group of people when they have an important interest or right which is being threatened. Such advocacy may take a number of forms, such as speaking up, writing letters or taking some form of direct action. All of these supportive actions are aimed at righting a wrong and this may involve protecting a right that an individual presently has which is under threat. Alternatively, it might be aimed at achieving something desirable for a person to whom it has hitherto been denied.

Advocacy is essentially about seeking a *remedy* (the word 'remedy' is used here in the sense of a form of legal redress) for a person who is relatively powerless when they face an individual, organisation or system which has much greater power than they themselves have. The provision of support in such circumstances is simply an attempt to equalise matters so that those in power are helped to see more clearly and respond more appropriately to the needs of the person over whom they exercise power.

Advocacy is most likely to be needed by those members of society who have the least power and these individuals and groups have tended to be those upon whom society has placed a low value and who, because of this, have historically been treated unjustly.

Advocacy is most likely to be provided most effectively where there is no *conflict of interest*, and this means also that it is unlikely to be provided by a professional who would be compromised because of his/her perceived primary duty to their employer or to fellow professionals.

The actions of advocates

Advocacy requires the advocate to take an action of some kind: to speak, write or even physically intervene. Such actions might be on behalf of a single individual or a group or class of such individuals who are experiencing a common threat.

Because advocacy involves confronting an individual or an organisation which is powerful, the advocate will have to be vigorous and emphatic in the way he or she speaks and acts. It is also likely to be the case that other more low-key approaches have been tried and found wanting, so a stronger approach needs to be adopted.

The dangers of advocacy

In principle it is generally true that advocacy places both the advocate and the advocatee at potential risk, since by definition the actions taken to remedy the injustice will be directed towards a powerful individual or organisation which holds sufficient power to place the rights of the advocatee(s) in jeopardy. In certain extreme circumstances the advocate may place him/her self in physical danger when, for example, there is the need to physically intervene to prevent physical abuse to the advocatee. In a totalitarian regime such advocacy could result in death for either or both parties. Advocacy on behalf of vulnerable individuals in a democratic society will, of course, not result in any such dire consequences for the advocate. However, where the advocate is a paid professional within a service, and is seen to be openly challenging the policies of that service, there is the possibility of the individual's continued employment being placed in jeopardy. There have been several highly publicised cases over recent years involving local and health authorities in which the 'disloyal' employee has paid for his advocacy with his job.

Limitations on advocacy

Advocacy by a human service professional on behalf of an individual or group of clients whose rights are placed at risk within the human service system is, of course, a much less dangerous business, but may yet incur significant penalties such as the loss of respect from colleagues or the loss of employment. It is these pressures which make it virtually impossible for most professionals to engage in advocacy because they are very quickly faced with a clear conflict of interest. When the stark choice is between losing credibility, or even employment, or keeping quiet, then the choice most likely to be made by the professional is the latter.

An additional danger for the advocate in these litigious times may come from the advocatee, who may be unhappy with the advice and support they have been given and blame the advocate for their having failed to achieve the remedy they sought. Because of this danger it is advisable for the advocate to take out professional indemnity insurance to protect herself against such a contingency. In reality, such a precaution is unlikely to be sought where a friend takes on the role of advocate, but where advocacy is provided from an organisational base, such a policy will have been taken out to cover all workers and volunteers.

Avoiding conflict of interest

Effective advocacy is most likely to be provided where there is no conflict of interest, and as has been said, this means that it is unlikely to be provided by a professional who would be compromised because of their perceived duty to their employer or to their fellow professionals.

Because the provision of effective advocacy requires minimal conflict of interest, it is most likely to be provided for children with special needs by an individual or agency which is completely separate from the authority with whom the parent is in conflict. Only complete independence of the agency against which redress is being sought will negate the likelihood of a conflict of interest.

Special needs advocacy

A number of allegedly independent Parent-Professional Partnership schemes set up with GEST funding in England remain deeply contaminated by conflict of interest. In many such schemes an LEA-employed psychologist or teacher will provide a parent counselling service (possibly from a local voluntary organisation base) and it is simply not possible for that individual to provide truly independent advice.

The Special Needs Advisory Project (SNAP) in Wales is similarly placed in that a number of its local offices are wholly, or at least in part, funded by the statutory services whilst the organisation nationally receives a grant from the Welsh Office. In view of this, it is hardly surprising that SNAP does not see itself as able to support parents through the Tribunal process.

Staff within schools are also unlikely to be able to provide advocacy support because of their own personal conflict of interest. As employees of the school or LEA, most individuals are persuaded that their first duty is to the organisation and not to the individual pupil. So, advocates will have to be independent of the education service and have no other loyalties that might get in the way of their acting in an emphatic manner on behalf of their client.

Natural candidates for this advocacy role are parents of children who have special needs. Such parents will, in all likelihood, have experienced their own difficulties in having their child's needs met properly, although they may not have sufficient time to devote to providing the necessary support.

GIVING THE RIGHT SUPPORT

The Statementing process, which is described in Chapter 7, raises all manner of problems for parents, and those who are prepared to support them, to achieve what they feel their children need. Statements both within and between LEAs vary enormously and one occasionally comes across a specimen which one would have been proud to write oneself; overwhelmingly, this is not the case. The advocate should have a good understanding of the tricks LEAs play over the Statementing process, otherwise, they will be caught off guard.

The politics of statementing

To recap briefly on the purpose of the Statement, it is a document intended to ensure that a child's needs are properly identified and that the provisions necessary to meet those needs are also clearly spelled out. Sections 2 and 3 of the Statement respectively deal with these matters. The Statement must identify *all* of a child's educational and non-educational needs and, where these are included in sections 2 and 3, their provision is legally binding upon the LEA which has drawn up the Statement.

The challenge for an LEA which feels it cannot afford a certain form of provision is to write the Statement in such a way that it *looks* as though the provision will be made without actually committing itself to it. This involves the cunning use of language, of which the following are just a few common examples. All of the children described in the following examples would be described as 'profoundly and multiply handicapped'.

The typical Statement (for a child with complex needs) may contain a fair amount of apparently promising verbiage but, on closer analysis, little by way of firm resource commitment. Professionals in the LEA and the health authority have become the masters of linguistic inference and evasion to protect their resource-led services. The trick is to make the parent believe you are making human resource provisions when you are doing nothing of the sort.

SPEECH THERAPY

Jane

Actual need: For an intensive language development programme because the child has no useful speech. This will require a detailed investigation of the child's difficulties and regular intensive speech therapy.

Stated provision: Jane will have a language development programme designed in conjunction with and monitored by a speech therapist.

What actually transpired here was that Jane never actually saw the speech therapist following an initial assessment, but the therapist called into the school to discuss the progress of about ten children once every six weeks.

Peter

Actual need: For investigation into the reasons why he has not developed speech, and the development of an alternative means of communication. Intensive daily treatment by the speech therapist and a

	communication programme to be continued at school and in the home.
Stated provision:	Peter will be involved in activities and experiences designed in conjunction with a speech therapist.

The actual level of input from the therapist was an initial assessment of his need followed by a monthly monitoring of his progress on visits to the school. This 'monitoring' took the form of brief chats with school-based staff.

PHYSIOTHERAPY

Angela

Actual need:	For an intensive daily physiotherapy programme to help Angela gain head and trunk control. This will require a daily session of not less than 40 minutes with the therapist.
Stated provision:	Angela requires daily activities designed after consultation with a physiotherapist.

Here the child saw the therapist once or twice a term and the rest of the time the actual 'physiotherapy' was carried out by an unqualified classroom assistant.

Kate

Actual need:	Kate needs intensive one-to-one physiotherapy at least three times a week.
Stated provision:	Access will be arranged to a physiotherapist for a weekly group session and individual sessions as required.

Here the situation was that Kate never actually saw the therapist individually on a regular basis following the initial assessment. However, the therapist ran weekly group sessions in which unqualified staff carried out 'treatments' under the direction of the physiotherapist.

Brian

Actual need:	For intensive daily hands-on physiotherapy to avoid further deformities and contractures and to relieve pressure and

poor circulation and keep lungs clear.
Need is for intensive one-to-one treatment
for one hour daily.

Stated provision: Integrate Brian's physiotherapy programme
into the general care programme.

What actually happened was that Brian received little or no hands-on treatment from a qualified physiotherapist, although a nursery nurse carried out a daily programme for about 20 minutes. The physiotherapist had 'trained' the assistant to do the work.

Tammy

Actual need: Tammy has the need for constant one-to-one support for all activities throughout the school day because without this nothing can be achieved.

Stated provision: Flexible staffing levels to meet her needs at any particular time.

In reality, Tammy spent between 50–60 per cent of her day waiting for somebody to do something for or with her because she had no means of communication and no voluntary movement and was totally blind. Without a dedicated support worker, much of her day was wasted just waiting.

In the above examples the actual need was determined through an independent professional assessment.

Language games

It will be apparent from the above that two things are happening: professionals are not quantifying the amount of help the child needs and provisions are being expressed in a vague and indefinite way. In such circumstances it is easy for the LEA to *appear*, to the inexperienced parent, to be making provisions – which may never materialise. It is only by gaining a clear and unambiguous *quantification* of the amount of any professional input that the parent can both know what her child needs, and also be in a position to seek redress should it not be forthcoming.

These 'language games' are routinely played by Statementing officers, psychologists, teachers and therapists, and all with the same intent – to protect their employer from acknowledging the real resource implications of a child's needs. The only way to combat this is for the parent to ask the authority to describe the child's needs precisely, and, if they refuse to do so, seek independent expert advice which does just that.

Because most parents are trusting in their early encounters with such professionals, they are easily duped into believing that the necessary provisions will be made for their child. However, when this trust eventually evaporates, the parent is left feeling angry and frustrated, with their trust in professionals severely undermined.

Sometimes the parent is simply told that their child does not need therapy sessions, specialist teaching or individual support in the classroom and here the situation is clearer and less frustrating because there has been no attempt at duplicity and the family can then decide whether they wish to pursue an appeal. More often than not there is an attempt on the part of the LEA to imply a certain provision will be made without any intention on their part that it should be.

APPEALING THE STATEMENT WITH ADVOCACY SUPPORT

Given the likely extent of professional duplicity where resources are concerned, it is important that the parents understand the challenge they face. The LEA will inevitably dig in and continue to resist spelling out what the child needs, so an appeal to the Special Needs Tribunal (SNT) is probably inevitable. Here there will almost certainly be the need for specialist advocacy support and the task for the advocate is to:

- understand what it is the parents want for their child
- make sense of what has already happened between the parents and the LEA and the school
- advise parents on:

  (a) their rights under the law;

  (b) how LEAs typically behave in such circumstances;

  (c) their child's needs (if parents are clearly making a mistake); and

  (d) tactics in pursuing their cause.

- join with the parents as supportive advocates in further negotiations with the LEA/other agency
- help parents understand when no further concessions are to be forthcoming from the agency and at that point to ask for their final decision to be put in writing
- help parents to begin preparation of the case for Tribunal appeal
- commence the appeal procedure

- seek legal support/legal aid
- acquire any necessary independent professional advice.

In most complex cases independent professional advice will be essential because the LEA and Health Trust professionals will have submitted recommendations which are means rather than needs led.

Commissioning the independent expert

The parent and her advocate (Named Person) will need to be very careful in their selection of an independent professional expert, to satisfy themselves that the individual concerned will experience no conflict of interest in making their recommendations. The following are some indicators of potential difficulty:

- the professional works full or part-time for another (perhaps a neighbouring authority)
- the person knows relevant local professionals
- the person seems to be wary of quantifying the professional time a child needs.

It is usually much more promising if the person approached has retired from or at least has no links with, the relevant statutory services.

Before commissioning such a professional it is essential that the Named Person and the parent come to a clear understanding with him or her about the key issues which are frequently, although not exclusively, resources and that there will be no obstacle to them making clear and strong recommendations which they would also be prepared to support at a Tribunal hearing. This means that they should be prepared to say that a child needs constant one-to-one support, if that is what they believe following assessment, or that he needs an hour a day physiotherapy or whatever.

The expert advice should be written in clear unambiguous language with details of the relevant test results and observational data which underpin the recommendations. Also, because the Tribunal will need to weigh such advice against that provided by the LEA, it is important that the professional qualifications and standing of the independent expert at least match up to those of the LEA expert witness.

Speed is of the essence in acquiring independent expert advice and matters should be put in hand immediately the LEA have issued the final Statement. The appeal system leaves parents somewhat at a disadvantage *vis-à-vis* the LEA in this matter in that the latter will already have their advice to hand prior to issuing the final Statement. Parents will not wish to spend money on independent advice prior to receiving the final Statement because there would still be some hope that the LEA might relent.

It can take a good deal of time to arrange reports and here it is important that the family are being supported by an individual or organisation with experience in these matters. The Independent Panel for Special Educational Advice (IPSEA) have their own panel members throughout Britain and the Dyfatty Advocacy Project (DAP) are in contact with a number of experts they could call upon.

It would also be advisable to let the independent professional know that they may be required to attend the hearing as a witness and that this might mean their not receiving the full cost of a day's work but just the token amount paid by the Tribunal to a witness.

There are a number of independent psychologists, speech therapists, physiotherapists, etc., and some work in group practices or as associates. One such group with an excellent reputation in Wales is *Class Consultants* which is based in Abergavenny but offers a service throughout Wales. The group offers a broad-based service, but their main area of expertise in the current context is the assessment and support (through teaching, counselling and Tribunal and legal representation) of children with SENs and their parents. As well as educational psychologists and teachers, the group can call upon the service of counsellors and therapists. They also have a consultant solicitor who is an expert in the education law.

Paying for the advice

IPSEA panel members will give their services free of charge and only their out-of-pocket expenses will need to be covered. Where advice from an EP or a therapist is required, the fee could be anything from £150 – £600. This will cover the cost of the assessment and for providing the written report but may not cover expenses and will certainly not pay for attendance at the Tribunal. In some cases parents may need two or three such reports.

For many parents, having to pay such large sums makes it impossible for them to even think of getting independent advice and they would have to go into the Tribunal process with no concrete evidence with which to challenge that presented by the LEA. Although Legal Aid is not available under the 1993 Act, there is the possibility that a family on income support and receiving Green Form Legal Aid support of up to £600 (in some cases a good deal more) could thereby meet the cost of a brief consultation with a solicitor and a report or (possibly) two.

Grounds for Appeal

Although this has already been covered in Chapter 2, it is as well to repeat here the grounds on which a parent may appeal a decision of their LEA. Parents have a right to appeal against the decision of their LEA if:

1. *The LEA refuse their request that an assessment be made.*
   Possible outcomes: the Tribunal could dismiss the appeal or order the LEA to make an assessment.

2. *The LEA refuse to re-assess their child who already has a Statement*
   Possible outcomes: the Tribunal could dismiss the appeal or order the LEA to re-assess.

3. *The LEA refuse to draw up a Statement*
   Possible outcomes: the Tribunal could dismiss the appeal or order the LEA to draw up and maintain a Statement. Alternatively, it could ask the LEA to reconsider its decision.

4. *They are unhappy with the way the LEA have laid out the needs and provisions, or if the LEA have refused to amend the Statement*
   Possible outcomes: the Tribunal could dismiss the appeal or order the LEA to amend the Statement in terms of needs and/or provisions. It could also order the LEA to cease to maintain the Statement.

5. *The LEA refuse their request not to change the name of the school on the Statement*
   Possible outcomes: the Tribunal could dismiss the appeal or order the LEA to name the parental preferred school in the Statement.

6. *The LEA decision to refuse to maintain the Statement*
   Possible outcomes: the Tribunal could dismiss the appeal or order the LEA to continue to maintain the Statement.

Making the appeal

As has already been said, parents would not be advised to embark upon the appeal process without expert advice and support. This is not to say they could not do so, and possibly even win, but rather that there are so many potential pitfalls that the odds are stacked heavily against them, in spite of the fact that the Tribunal make every effort to be parent-friendly.

At the time of writing (summer 1995), it is much too early to make a generalisation about any policy implications arising out of the pattern of decision-making in the Tribunal system. The Tribunal was established under the 1993 Act and came into existence on 1 September 1994.

THE DYFATTY ADVOCACY PROJECT (DAP)

Its beginnings

Early in 1993, Paul Burrows and Negeb Dahan, both parent governors of Dyfatty school in Swansea (a school for children said to have severe and complex learning difficulties), began talking with other parents of children attending the school about their aspirations for their children. Paul and his wife Marion had been engaged in their own personal struggle to have their daughter, Beverley, transferred to her local Primary school. They had been trying for three years to get their LEA to understand that Beverley could not possibly grow and develop properly in a segregated school and that the part-time arrangement they had for her to attend her local school should be extended so that she could leave the 'special' school and be educated full-time in her local school alongside the children in her home neighbourhood.

Through informal contact with other parents, Paul and Negeb knew they too were experiencing their own problems so both decided to offer their services on a voluntary basis to the school's PTA – the Dyfatty Home-School Association – as parent advocates. This offer was gratefully accepted.

Ken Rowley was the chairman of governors of the school, having spent a highly successful career manufacturing cars with Ford of Britain. As a recently retired senior engineering manager, Ken was steeped in management, production and business methodology, and brought to the school a management approach which is rarely found in such an educational setting. Ken's philosophy was simple and highly effective: 'these children have many needs which must be identified and described by the relevant experts then linked to a specification of just how those needs are to be met'. Ken claimed no expertise in the field of special education and was always prepared to be advised by the 'experts', but what he did know from a lifetime in production engineering was that the *specification* is everything, for without it there is no basis for action. Having himself seen some of the Statements, he concluded that, since the needs had not been formally identified, there was no basis on which to provide an appropriate education and the first step must be a new needs assessment for every child.

The succeeding six months proved extremely interesting as Paul, who was now established in his own office in the school, listened to parents talking about their children and what they wanted for them – both during their school years and in later life. These early discussions tended to revolve around concerns parents had about such basic things as the level of staffing in the school and additional health authority provisions like speech and physiotherapy. There was also concern about school transport because the LEA were in the throes of a 'rationalisation programme' aimed at reducing costs and parents were worried that this would threaten the individual arrangements made for their children.

Dyfatty school was recognised as providing a relatively good service to its pupils and this had been acknowledged following an HMI inspection in 1989, however, the long-standing problem over Statements meant they were in urgent need of re-drafting so that they reflected the needs the children were known to have. As a school for 'children with severe and complex learning difficulties', these needs were, in every case, very extensive and, although well-documented in twice-yearly educational reports, were not reflected in the children's Statements. Over a period of 9 years these reports had been sent to the LEA and the other professional service agencies, but in not a single case had this resulted in an amendment to a Statement; clearly the annual review system was not working.

Paul was soon in a position to provide a summary picture of the existing Statements for governors and their view was that all of the children were in need of urgent re-assessment, following which a new Statement would be drafted which would hopefully include a comprehensive account of the child's needs linked to a description of the provisions necessary to meet those needs.

With Paul's help, each parent wrote to the Director of Education asking that their child be re-assessed and citing the relevant Sections of the 1981 Education Act. The LEA agreed to do so and the re-assessment process began. At this time it was becoming apparent that the work involved in supporting parents was much greater than had been anticipated because of the legal and local government organisational complexities governing special needs education.

Paul's work had been based upon the intensive casework model – somewhat similar to that provided by IPSEA – which takes a great deal of advocate time. As a parent governor, he was well placed to acquaint the governing body with his concerns over the dangers inherent in any undue delay and they agreed that the work needed to be given the highest priority and that an advocacy project should be formally established.

During the Autumn of 1993 the Home-School Association, which is responsible for the school's fund-raising and social activities, undertook to seek funding to establish a parental advocacy organisation and by December they had been offered a year's funding.

The Dyfatty Advocacy Project (DAP) formally commenced its work in January 1994 with Paul as a salaried full-time project worker and leader of the Project and Rita Fred, a qualified and experienced legal adviser, working in a similar capacity on a part-time basis. The initial grant was for £20,000 and a further £6000 was allocated from the school fund.

By September 1995 nearly all of the children had new draft Statements and virtually all were in the process of being appealed because the parents were unhappy with the descriptions of needs and provisions. Three had reached the Special Needs Tribunal (SNT) which, in two cases, found in favour of the parents, while the third was dismissed.

How the project operates

Funding was provided for the project on the understanding that the service would be available to any parent within West Glamorgan. This was a condition the school fully understood and approved because there was a recognition of the fact that parents of children with special needs generally need support, not just those who have children in a special school.

The Project was housed in two rooms within the Ken Rowley Resource Centre, which is an extension to the school donated by the school's chairman of governors. The project was able to make use of the school's training facilities, kitchen, etc., and its offices were in some ways ideally located because the school has a number of facilities which are available to children and their families throughout the County. In particular, the hydrotherapy pool and the toy library attract many children and their parents and it was convenient for them to call into the Project whilst visiting to use these facilities.

Referral to the Project can be from a number of sources: parental self-referral, social worker, teacher, health visitor, psychologist, etc. Parents will ring or call into the school or perhaps ask that a project worker visit their home. Sometimes the referral is of a very young child who has not even started playgroup or nursery, but more likely it will be a child who is in the school system and has a Statement or is in the process of being Statemented.

The initial meeting

Having made contact, the parent will be offered an initial meeting to discuss their concerns. At this meeting the parents (both parents are encouraged to be present) are given an opportunity to talk about their concerns and to describe what they want for their child, both in school and in his or her life generally. This is often a difficult thing for parents to discuss – especially when their child is still quite young and they may still be coming to terms with their child's disability and the adjustments this will require of them and the whole family.

This initial meeting may not produce anything like a clear picture of the issues which are of concern to the family, although parents have frequently remarked that they found it helpful to have this opportunity to talk about their worries even though they were still far from clear what it was they wanted for their child.

Sometimes, at the initial meeting, it is possible to clearly identify the concerns the parents have and for many this will be over provisions they feel their child should have which, for one reason or another, are not being made either by the LEA or the health authority. The next step is for the project worker to explain to the parents their rights under the law, as well as any possible remedy they might have should it not be possible to reach agreement.

Follow-up work

In a small number of cases, and having become clear about their legal rights and the procedures to be followed, the family will choose to continue without further support from the Project. More likely though, there will be further contact involving a number of meetings with LEA officers before matters are resolved satisfactorily, although for some there will be no such resolution and parents will be supported in an appeal to the SNT.

Experience to date suggests that special needs legislation is poorly understood by most parents; indeed it seems to be a source of puzzlement to many special needs professionals, so perhaps this is not so surprising. Many parents will accept the offer of support in drafting letters and attendance at meetings with the school and the LEA and this is seen as an important part of the role of the advocate since there is a power differential between the parent and those managing services which can be intimidating for some families.

Where there is a dispute over whether the child needs a certain provision – speech therapy, physiotherapy, a personal support worker – then it might be necessary to organise an independent professional assessment. The advice contained in a report based upon such an assessment will be used in support of the parent's case when it goes to appeal. Such advice may be available free of charge through IPSEA or it might have to be paid for by the parent, the Project or through the Green Form Legal Aid system, although in the latter case the parent will need to be on income support or a similar state benefit to qualify and the financial support is usually quite limited. Such expert advice may prove extremely costly and a typical assessment and detailed report will usually be in the region of £300. The real problem here is that the parent may need two or three reports to combat a similar number of reports provided by the LEA and this means that this limited form of legal aid will not meet the full cost, so prioritisation has to take place.

In addition to securing independent professional advice, it is sometimes necessary to arrange representation at the Tribunal hearing. Such representation may be undertaken by a project worker or an independent solicitor or barrister – this in spite of the fact that the

Tribunal hearing is intended to be relatively non-legalistic and informal so as not to intimidate parents. Where the LEA employ a barrister or QC to represent them, it would be unwise for a parent to attend the hearing without expert legal support. However, the view has been put that an LEA which attempts to out-gun parents in this way will not find favour with the Tribunal panel and may actually damage their chances of winning. These are still early days and only time will tell whether this is in fact the case.

Preparing for the Tribunal

It is with the greatest reluctance that most parents take the step of initiating an appeal to the SNT and most only do so once they are convinced their authority is not going to make the provisions they feel their child needs. This reluctance seems to be rooted in the (perhaps mistaken) perception of the Tribunal as a quasi-court of law and also their understandable concern at having to take such action against a local authority which is there to provide services their child needs.

Parents need to understand the role of the Tribunal and the way it operates, which is not nearly as formal and forbidding as they fear and which has been put in place to resolve inevitable disagreements between parents and local authorities. That the parent should feel guilty about having to take such a step says something about the way they may have experienced certain officers and professionals and it is not uncommon for parents to report having been told that, in asking for a certain provision for their child, they are threatening provision for other children because there is only so much resource to go round.

The process of preparation for the Tribunal hearing takes place only after the authority have issued the final draft of the Statement (there are, of course, other grounds for appeal – such as where there is a refusal to issue a Statement) and between then and the hearing itself there is an exchange of information and evidence between the parent and the authority through the intermediary of the Tribunal. At any point during this process either party may withdraw, so the process itself may be viewed as offering the possibility of conciliation even though this is not overtly part of the Tribunal's role.

Since the role of the Tribunal is to exercise the jurisdiction conferred upon it by the relevant sections of the 1993 Act, it does of course have legal powers, yet it attempts to exercise these powers in as informal a manner as is compatible with the need to follow procedures for hearing evidence and for maintaining the dignity of the proceedings. There are two key features of the Tribunal on which parents generally need a good deal of support: (1) the collation and presentation of evidence and (2) representation.

Evidence and its presentation

Parents are frequently confused as to what the real grounds of difference are between themselves and their authority. This is partly because of the professional language barrier, which means that both sides are expressing themselves in ways which are failing to effectively communicate meaning. Sometimes the essence of the disagreement is buried quite deeply within the letters and reports which may, over the months and years, grow to fill a couple of large ring binders. Given this volume of paperwork, and the inevitable frustrations that build up on both sides, it is perhaps not surprising that either side might lose sight of what it is they understand the child needs.

This lack of clarity about objectives *must* be resolved before the parent is supported through the appeal process, otherwise it will just not be possible for their representative to present their case in a coherent manner; likewise, the authority must be clear about the nature of the disagreement in relation to their own perception of the child's needs.

The evidence the parent needs to adduce must bear directly upon the source of their disagreement with what is contained in the draft Statement: if the Statement says the child needs only 'termly monitoring by a speech therapist' and the parent believes he needs daily or weekly individual therapy, then the evidence they must produce for the Tribunal must support what they are asking for, otherwise they may lose. Their independent report should, of course, be provided by a therapist with the kind of qualifications and experience which will impress the Tribunal panel. She will need to be able to convince the panel that she knows what she is saying, that is that what is being provided is indeed expert advice.

The LEA should not be allowed to get away with the excuse that it has not made a particular provision because its own policy does not allow it to do so. Such a statement could be construed as fettering their discretion and it has a clear duty to address individual pupil needs independently of its own policy guidelines.

Present needs are what count

Following a direction of the Tribunal President to members of the Tribunal (15 March 1995), it was made clear that the role of the Tribunal is to decide as best it can 'what is the appropriate decision at the date of the Tribunal hearing' and the decision 'should not be a judgement of the correctness of the LEA's decision *when it was taken*'. This means that it is the duty of the Tribunal to judge as best they can what is in the child's best interest *on the day of the hearing*, and not simply whether the LEA had been correct in their judgement *when they issued the final Statement*. This is a crucial distinction and one which bears directly upon the nature of the evidence that both parties need to present. Getting to the core of the issues is a challenge for all three parties (LEA, parent and panel) in the hearing and there is no guarantee that, even with good countervailing evidence, either side will necessarily win.

Presentation of the evidence is probably too important and technical an issue (even allowing for a sympathetic panel) to be left to the parent or an inexperienced advocate, which is why some LEAs are turning to their own or hired lawyers and why parents need to be similarly represented, but parents do not have the resources available to the authority which are, of course, paid out of the public purse. This represents a serious disadvantage to parents and explains why IPSEA have set up their Free Representation Service (FRS), which uses lay individuals who have been given training to take on this role.

Initiatives like the Dyfatty Advocacy Project (DAP) support parents through what tends to be a complex and stressful process of negotiation to have their child's needs addressed in the way they *feel* is necessary if (s)he is to obtain optimal benefit from their school years. In the process of negotiation with the LEA this is initially a debate over *needs*, but the parent is likely also to construe this as a disagreement as to their own and their child's *rights*. DAP operates as advocate for the child/parent at this difficult interface.

The main national special needs advocacy organisation is IPSEA, with which DAP had strong links from the outset. IPSEA provided constant advice and training support to the project – without which it would not have achieved its level of success in supporting parents through the appeal process.

Postscript: the end of the project

After the initial injection of funding support, considerable efforts were expended by the staff and management committee to ensure that continuity of financing of the project would be achieved. Unfortunately this proved extremely difficult and in January 1996 the project was facing a bleak future. That summer Paul Burrows left helping and Rita Fred continued alone, the growing number of parents in need of support. For many months Rita continued this work without salary until in December 1996 the project finally closed. Working from home Rita continued to help a small number of parents who had been receiving support from the for a considerable period of time.

Small voluntary parent support projects like DAP tend to have to live a hand to mouth existence with the larger more establishment-friendly voluntary organisations attracting the bulk of available funding. This was indeed the case with DAP who had to compete with the Welsh-based Special Needs Advisory (SNAP) which tended to corner available funding. SNAP is essentially an information and advice-giving organisation which, because it is funded by the Welsh Office and local authorities as well as the more traditional charitable sources, is not able to engage in full-blown advocacy support.

Rita Fred continued to work as an advocate for parents long after her somewhat meagre salary ran out. She did so because she identified with the plight of the children and parents she represented. Because she chose to immerse herself in her work she frequently saw at first hand the pain families have to endure when they have a child whose life is blighted dy an inadequate or inappropriate Statement of their special educational needs. Rita responded to the pain of her clients in a way that special needs professionals, for whatever reason, rarely do.

IPSEA AS AN ORGANISATION

IPSEA was established in 1983 and is a registered charity providing:

- free advice on LEAs' duty in law to provide for children with SENs

- free second professional opinions for parents who disagree with an LEA's assessment of their child's SENs. (These are provided by IPSEA's panel of volunteers, who are qualified and experienced professionals in the field of special education, e.g. teachers, EPs, speech therapists, physiotherapists, etc.)

- a Free Representation Service at the SNT for parents who want to appeal against an LEA's decision. (This service is provided by volunteers who have undergone specialist training for the role of parent representative).

Since 1983, IPSEA has grown into a national network with 140 volunteers across England, Wales and Scotland and is recognised as 'one of the leading advocacy groups in the UK'. (*Times Educational Supplement* 25.2.94).

IPSEA occupies a unique position within the voluntary sector serving the families of children with SENs. It is a source of legal advice and practical support for families in their dealings with their LEA and it is actively involved in lobbying for improved legislation. In fact, IPSEA were at the forefront during the passage of the 1993 Bill in arguing for improvements to the Bill and its Code of Practice. This aspect of its work is seen as crucial because the provision of independent advice through its network of volunteers would never be enough in itself to bring about the desired changes.

IPSEA's approach to lobbying over the Bill is described in an article by their administrator John Wright (Potts *et al.* 1995). When the government's White Paper setting out the proposed changes in the law on special education (later included as Part 3 of the 1993 Act) was issued in July 1992, IPSEA circulated photocopies of these proposals to about 130 of its parents asking for comments and suggestions on what else needed to be changed. From the responses received, a formal response to the White Paper was prepared. This not only provided a response to the proposed changes but included an additional 18 areas for the government to think about. Later IPSEA published and circulated an expanded version of its response to the White Paper entitled *Putting right the 1981 Education Act*, which included a total of 22 points arising out of its own casework. At the same time, IPSEA encouraged parents and concerned professionals to write to their MPs.

IPSEA next set about drafting 20 specific amendments to the Bill, and briefings for MPs, and these too were circulated to parents. When the first draft of the 1993 Education Act appeared at the end of October 1992, IPSEA was able to identify three of its clauses: (1) the responsibilities of 'new' LEAs to meet children's needs when families move area; (2) a parental right to request a formal assessment; and (3) a fixed procedure for reviewing Statements. In 1994 they were able to identify a further eight from their original set of proposals.

That a number of other organisations in the field were also arguing for some of these amendments should not detract from the fact that IPSEA, in collaboration with other special needs organisations, was influential in improving the Bill and hence bringing about better legislation.

In collaboration with other organisations, IPSEA also supported amendments aimed at strengthening the right to mainstream integration, but these were rejected by the government at the Commons Committee Stage.

IPSEA provided assistance to over 1,000 parents of children with SENs during 1994, and both the needs of the children and their parents' difficulties with the LEA were immensely varied. However, it is IPSEA's involvement in casework which makes it absolutely indispensable because its advice is completely independent with no conflict of interest to inhibit the integrity of the organisation.

Parents initially make contact with IPSEA by telephone or letter and at that point may receive the advice they are seeking and need no further help. Many, though, will need more intensive help and this might be achieved through correspondence and the involvement of a member of the Independent Panel of volunteers, all of whom, as has been said, are qualified and experienced professionals. If it is clear that the parent needs a second opinion to challenge that of the LEA professional, a member of the IPSEA staff will contact a panel member and link them with the family. The panel member will meet with the parents and discuss their concerns and, if (s)he feels able to help, will undertake his or her own assessment and provide a report. IPSEA's volunteers act completely independently of the LEA and their reports are the sole property of the parent.

IPSEA's Free Representation Service

In response to changes brought about by the 1993 Education Act, IPSEA introduced its Free Representation Service (FRS). This was in response to what it saw as the most significant change in the Act, that is the establishment of an Independent Tribunal to hear parents' appeals against LEA judgements on children's needs. The earlier two-tier system of appeals (LEA-arranged committee then Secretary of State) was agreed to have been unsatisfactory and the Tribunal was welcomed as a likely improvement. The Act gave parents substantially increased grounds for appeal against decisions made by their LEAs. The aim of the FRS is to ensure that no parent who needs advice, help or representation goes unsupported to the Tribunal. However, IPSEA recognised that parents would need a special kind of help if they were to be able to make best use of the Tribunal procedure and that the key area of support would be a knowledge of the law. So IPSEA set out to recruit, train and thereafter support a network of advocates who could provide:

- initial advice and practical support with the preparation of a case, including advice on whether a second opinion from one of IPSEA's volunteers (or elsewhere) would be of value and whether a case requires the support of a solicitor

- support at hearings, including direct representation when necessary

- advice following hearings when the outcome goes against parents.

The recruitment and training commenced early in 1995 with the objective of having 50 advocates in the field available to parents nationally. The core training involved attendance at a two-day workshop which covered the law on special education and the procedures for the SNT. During the workshop participants were required to analyse cases and present their key features. Following assessment, successful participants were certificated and included in the personal liability insurance cover maintained by IPSEA.

PROGRESS OF THE SPECIAL NEEDS TRIBUNAL

The SNT began operating on 1 September 1994 and the following is a brief summary of its work to 31 August 1995.

Trevor Aldridge QC, President of the Tribunal, has hitherto (August 1995) released a couple of digests in the form of progress reports and a full report of the Tribunal's work during its first year (Special

Educational Needs Tribunal: Annual Report 1994/95). The President said the first year's work of is bound to be atypical because of the way its duties came into force.

Over its first year of operation, 1170 appeals had been registered (170 in 1994 and 1000 in 1995). Of these, 245 appeals had been withdrawn by parents and a further 7 were struck out as they did not fall within the Tribunal's jurisdiction. As at 31 August 1995, 246 cases had been heard at Tribunal. More than a quarter (28%) of appeals were against the contents of a Statement, with slightly fewer (21%) against a refusal to assess and 21 per cent against a refusal to make a Statement. The only other significant category of appeal was against the school named in the Statement (18%). Forty per cent of appeals were by parents of children with a specific learning difficulty (literacy), with a much smaller proportion coming from parents of children with moderate learning difficulties (9%) and severe learning difficulties (6%). The decisions of some LEAs were challenged on appeal more frequently than others with the numbers (per 10,000 of the school population) being in the range 0 – 9.9 per cent. The average time for disposal of cases was five months. During this first year, 15 per cent of the parents appealing to the Tribunal were represented by lawyers and a further 23 per cent had other representatives. This meant that two-thirds of parents were not represented and, given the complexity of the issues in many cases, this must be a cause for concern. It was less common for LEAs to send along a legally qualified representative, leaving this role to a psychologist or educational officer.

The President of the Tribunal expressed surprise that he was asked to issue a number of summonses to ensure the attendance of prospective witnesses. He said: 'I have been surprised that there has been a number of such requests. In the spirit of parent partnership engendered by the Code of Practice I had thought that those most closely concerned with the child in question would have no hesitation in coming forward to offer their help'. Given the vast experience of the President, this comment might be a little tongue-in-cheek for it is unlikely he will not be aware of the difficult position special needs professionals find themselves in if they are seen by their employer as being too supportive of their clients, particularly over resourcing issues. I have myself had to be summonsed to appear on more than one occasion.

Of the 242 appeals disposed of during its first year, the SNT upheld 112 (46%) and dismissed 85 (35%). Twenty-seven (11%) were upheld or dismissed in part and 11 (5%) were remitted to the LEA for reconsideration. Two hundred and forty-five (21%) of the appeals lodged during the year were withdrawn.

The average time taken for a case to be disposed of (by hearing or withdrawal) was five months. The President issued the following breakdown of type of appeal for the first 1120 registered appeals:

Type of Appeal	%
Against refusal to assess	21
Against refusal to make a Statement	21
Against contents of Statement	28
Against refusal to re-assess	2
Against refusal to change name of school	2
Against decision to cease to maintain Statement	7
Against school named in Statement	18
Against failure to name a school in Statement	1

Nature of SEN	%
Autism	3
Emotional and Behavioural Difficulties	6
Epilepsy	1
Hearing Impaired	4
Moderate Learning Difficulties	9
Physically Handicapped	5
Severe Learning Difficulties	6
Specific Learning Difficulties (Dyslexia)	40
Speech and Language Difficulties	9
Visually Impaired	1
Other	16

(SEN Tribunal, 1995, p.6–7)

An earlier digest suggested that some 60 per cent of Tribunal decisions had gone in favour of the parents.

SEN TRIBUNAL – THE PROFESSIONAL UNDER FURTHER PRESSURE

I have on more than one occasion in this book referred to the conflict of interest that professionals experience when required to make recommendations they feel will not be welcomed by their employing authority. This is a reality which I understand from personal experience and the following two quotes from reports that appeared in the Times Educational Supplement during 1996 confirms my own experience:

'MPs hear of teachers being bullied' – Nicholas Pyke

> *Some teachers are bullied into not appearing before the special educational needs tribunal, the Commons select committee on education weretold last week, writes Nicholas Pyke*

(TES 1996a)

The committee which is conducting a small investigation of special needs, heard from John Wright, a special needs lobbyist, that teachers who may provide vital evidence for a child are put under pressure. 'They are having some pretty nasty things said to them.' said Joh Wright of the Independent Panel for Special Educational Advice. 'The authority is saying don't attend.'

Adrian Faupel, fro the Association of Educational Psychologists, told the committee that the tribunal system could hurt disadvantaged children because they have no one to act on their behalf. There has been no appeal to the tribunal from children in local authority care, he said the committee was told by all its special education witnesses that SEN co-ordinators need more time to do their job properly.

'Special needs staff "face intimidation" ' – Nicholas Pyke (TES 1996a)

Some local authorities are trying to prevent teachers attending tribunal hearings for parents who have appealed for better special educational needs services for their children, according to a new report by a leading advice and lobby group

The report, by the Independent Panel for Special Educational Advice (IPSEA), which has represented parents at 60 hearings of the special needs tribunal set up by the 1993 Education Act to allow dissatisfied parents to challenge local education auhtorities' assessments of their children's needs, is based on a survey of 42 of the families it has helped.

The survey found that only three cases in which local authority employees attended tribunal hearings "quite willingly". Twelve families felt obliged to issue summonses to compel staff to attend.

"In the majority of cases parents issued the summonses to protect their witnesses, because they were sensitive to the position of the professionals involved," says the report. Teachers are unwilling to attend sessions of the special needs tribunal because they are fearful of their job prospects, and some local authorities are intimidating staff, hoping to prevent them supporting children who have appealed.

"There were several examples of a summons being used in a straightforward way to force a reluctant witness to attend," the report says. "In two of the cases reviewed, however, a summons was issued in response to a more sinister set of circumstances."

One parent told IPSEA: "We called the special needs co-ordinator in our child's school and put her on oath. She had been threatened by the LEA who said he job was at stake and told her she wouldn't find a job anywhere else." In some cases, says the report, concern for the people involved had actually prevented parents calling the witnesses they wanted. "We were going to ask the child's teacher but she diclined after presssure from the LEA," said one parent.

Trevor Aldridge QC, president of the tribunal, said in his annual report "It turns out that in some cases local education authorities are reluctant that any of their employees, and this will particularly apply to teachers, should give evidence 'for' the parents and 'against' the authority. This takes a confrontational view of the appeal to the tribunal which seems unfortunate."

EXPLORING THE LIMITS TO ADVOCACY

Clearly it is hazardous for special needs professionals working within the service system to identify too closely with those they are paid to serve. Just over two years ago I wrote a brief article about school-based advocacy (Hall 1994) and there I described some extraordinary events which occurred on 22nd and 23rd July 1994.

Joe Whittaker is a senior lecturer at the Bolton Institute of Higher Education and John Kenworthy is a consultant clinical psychologist. Both had for some years been deeply involved in the movement to bring about an inclusive school system in the United Kingdom. Their commitment lead them to become advocates on behalf of two children – Nicky Crane and Zak Lewis – who were being denied the opportunity to attend a mainstream school by an education authority which took the view that they could only be educated in a special school.

Having seen the pain and frustration experienced by the families of these two children for several years as they battled for proper schooling for their children and having themselves been involved in a number of fruitless meetings with the families and LEA, John and Joe finally decided that the LEA would never change their position unless there was greater public pressure. They decide to confront the officers of the authority personally as advocates on behalf of the children and their parents. This proved impossible as they were simply denied access to the Director of Education and other senior officers. In frustration they decided to stage a 'sit-in' at the council offices in Preston. Their unauthorised occupation lasted two days and resulted in Joe having to be hospitalised. Later, both were placed in police cells before being hauled before the magistrates. This, possibly the first piece of direct action by professionals on behalf of families who did not want their children to be compulsorily segregated, was the subject of a good deal of media coverage, but it did not result in a change of heart on the part of the LEA concerned.

It might be that we have not seen the end of such direct action which, when it is pursued by otherwise mild and reasonable individuals, should give pause to those service system managers and professionals who enforce compusory segregation upon vulnerable children.

There was clearly a major difference of perception on the part of the protagonists over the needs and the perceived best interest of these children. The LEA was simply doing what it has always done with children it perceives as having 'severe and complex learning difficulties' – that is to separate them away in a school with other children seen to have the same needs where there are staff who are trained to meet their needs. The parents and their circle of supporters saw such a placement as likely to damage their child's development. Clearly this difference (at least in part) comes down to a mismatch over the perception of 'need'. This gulf between parents and professionals is widening and it seems likely that in the years ahead we shall see further direct action against the continuing policy amongst nearly all LEAs to compulsorily segregate children.

CONCLUSION

There is a clear need for parents of children with SENs to have access to advocacy support should their dealings with their LEA not result in their child's needs being honestly acknowledged. With the provisions of the 1993 Act, and in particular the right to appeal to an Independent Tribunal, parents will need expert advice and support in the preparation of their case.

Hitherto many Parent Partnership schemes have not demonstrated their independence from the local authorities in which they are located, so may not be able to provide advice and support which is not tainted by a conflict of interest. In such circumstances, parents will need to seek the support of truly independent projects such as IPSEA and DAP.

Some Useful Organisations

INDEPENDENT PROFESSIONAL ADVICE

Class Consultants,
The Old Mill,
Mardy Park,
Abergavenny,
Gwent NP7 6HT
Phone: (01873) 858717 (9am – 5pm)
Fax: (01873) 858717 + 855130 (24 hour)

Class Consultants is an independent support service for children, parents, teachers, students and schools. The services of Class Consultants are provided, broadly, through assessment of children, the counselling of parents and by delivery of in-service courses for teachers. The inspection of special needs provision in schools is offered.

VOLUNTARY ORGANISATIONS – GENERAL

Advisory Centre for Education (ACE),
Unit 1B, Aberdeen Studios,
22–24, Highbury Grove,
London N5 2EA
Phone: 0171 354 8321
(Advice line: 2–5pm weekdays)

ACE is an independent national education advice centre for parents. It is run by expert staff under the direction of a Council and is financed by funds raised from grants and charitable donations and from sales of ACE publications.

Centre for Studies on Inclusive Education (CSIE),
1, Redland Close,
Elm Lane,
Redland,
Bristol, BS6 6UE
Phone: (0117) 923 8450
Fax: (0117) 923 8460

CSIE is an independent educational charity which gives information and advice about inclusive education and related issues. It produces and sells booklets on good practice and publishes regular analyses on LEA trends in special school placements.

Children's Rights Development Unit,
235, Shaftesbury Avenue,
London WC2H 8EL
Phone: 0171 240 4449

The UK Government ratified, and thereby agreed to implement, the United Nations Convention on the Rights of the Child in December 1991. The Unit was set up as an independent organisation to monitor the Convention in the UK.

DIAL UK,
Park Lodge,
St. Catherine's Hospital,
Tickhill Road,
Doncaster
S. Yorkshire DN4 8QN
Phone: (01302) 310123
Fax: (01302) 310404

DIAL UK is a National Organisation for the DIAL network of Disability Advice Centres. Contact DIAL UK for details of local disability Advice Centres.

Dyfatty Advocacy Project (DAP),
c/o Ysgol Crug-Las,
Croft Street,
Swansea SA1 1QA
Phone/Fax: (01792) 653305

The Project provides professional advice and advocacy support to the families of children with SENs who are likely to require a Statement. The support offered is entirely independent and available to children who live in South Wales. This project was forced to close through lack of funding in Autumn 1996.

Free Representation Service,
Contact: Kevin Barett
31, Lightwoods Road,
Bearwood,
West Midlands BG7 5AY
Phone: (0121) 420 3007
Fax: (01212) 420 3195

Greater London Association of Disabled People (GLAD),
336, Brixton Road,
London SW9 7AA
Phone: 0171 274 0107
Fax: 0171 274 7840

GLAD works with a London-wide network of borough-based disability associations. It is a capital-wide forum for disability issues and works with National and regional voluntary organisations to help shape the latest developments in London.

ICAN,
Contact Fraser Mackay,
Charity Administrator,
Barbican Citygate,
1–3, Dufferin Street,
London EC1Y 8NA
Phone: 0171 374 4422
Fax: 0171 374 2762

ICAN is a National charity for children with SENs.

In Touch,
Contact Mrs Ann Worthington MBE.
10, Norman Road,
Sale, Cheshire M33 3DF
Phone: (0161) 905 2440

In Touch is a registered charity which provides information and contacts for children with special needs.

Independent Panel for Special Educational Advice (IPSEA),
Contact: John Wright, Administrator,
22, Warren Hill Road,
Woodbridge,
Suffolk 1P12 4DU
Phone/Fax: (01394) 382814

IPSEA provides independent advice for parents of children with SENs. It also provides a Free Representation Service for parents who wish to appeal to the Independent Tribunal for SENs.

MIND (National Association for Mental Health),
Granta House,
15–19, Broadway,
Stratford,
London E15 4BQ
Phone: 0181–522 1728 (Information Line)
Phone: 0181 519 2122
Fax: 0181 522 1725

MIND is the leading mental health charity in England and Wales. Working for a better life for people suffering from mental distress, MIND campaigns for the right to lead an active and valued life in the community and is an influential voice on mental health issues.

National Association of Toy and Leisure Libraries,
68, Churchway,
London NW1 1LT
Phone: 0171 387 9592
Fax: 0171 383 2714

Toy Libraries loan carefully chosen good quality toys to families with young children. Some provide specially adapted toys and equipment for children with special needs. It also offers a befriending, supportive service to parents and other carers. Leisure libraries provide equipment for young adults with special needs.

National Library for the Handicapped Child,

Contact: Desmond L Spier (Librarian)
Reach Resource Centre,
Wellington House,
Wellington Road,
Wokingham, Berks RG40 2AG
Phone: (01734) 891101 (Voice and Minicom)
Fax: (01734) 790989

The Centre provides a resource and information centre for those who work with children whose disability, illness or learning problem affects their reading, language or communication. The Centre contains both printed books and books on sound tape and video, plus micro-electronic equipment and software. The collections are for reference only.

National Portage Association,

Contact: Brenda Paul (Administrator),
127, Monks Dale,
Yeovil,
Somerset BA21 3JE
Phone/Fax: (01935) 71641

Portage is a home visiting educational service for pre-school children who have special needs. It assesses the needs of young children with learning difficulties, including physical disabilities and, in partnership with parents, builds on the abilities the child already has, teaching skills the child has yet to master. The Portage team of home visitors offers a carefully structured but flexible system to help parents become effective teachers of their own children.

PHysically Disabled and ABle-Bodied (PHAB),

Contact: Peter Gooch (Chief executive)
12–14, London Road,
Croydon CR0 2TA
Phone: 0181 667 9443
Fax: 0181 681 1399

Phab is an organisation that helps to integrate people with and without physical disabilities through a network of some 350 clubs in England. Clubs in Scotland, Northern Ireland and Wales are covered by a different organisation.

Pre-School Learning Alliance,

Contact: Margaret Lochrie (Chief Exec),
69, Kings Cross Road,
London WC1X 9LL
Phone: 0171 833 0991
Fax: 0171 837 4942

The Pre-School Learning Alliance has 20,000 members and is the single largest provider of education and care for pre-school children in England. Member pre-school groups vary to meet the needs of local families and communities. Many adults attend Pre-school Learning Alliance training courses.

Royal Society for Mentally Handicapped Children and Adults,

Contact: Fred Heddell (Chief Executive)
MENCAP National Centre:
123, Golden Lane,
London EC1Y ORT
Phone: 0171 454 0454

MENCAP is the largest national organisation in England, Northern Ireland and Wales exclusively concerned with giving advice and support to people with learning disabilities and their families. It runs residential, training and employment and leisure services. It produces a variety of publications.

The Children's Society,
Contact: The Chief Executive,
Edward Rudolf House,
Margery Street,
London WC1X OJL
Phone: 0171 837 4299

The Children's Society is a voluntary organisation of the Church of England and the Church in Wales. It works with thousands of children, young people and their families in over 90 projects throughout England and Wales. Its work includes: street work and refuges for runaways, family centres in areas of high unemployment, independent living projects for young people leaving care, and family placement for children with special needs.

The Council for Disabled Children (CDC),
8, Wakley Street,
London EC1V 7QE

The Council provides information sheets on disability, special needs and general children's services.

The Disability Alliance: Educational and Research Association,
First Floor East,
Universal House,
88–94, Wentworth Street,
London E1 7SA
Phone: 0171 247 8763 (Rights and Advice Line)
0171 247 8776 (General Office)

Disability Alliance provides a telephone advice service to disabled people, their families, carers and professional advisers on social security benefits. It produces the Disability Rights Handbook annually which is a fully comprehensive guide to disability benefits. It also runs training courses for advisers.

The Family Fund Trust,
P.O. Box 50,
York YO1 2ZX
Phone: (01904) 621115

The Trust helps families with very severely disabled children under 16. It gives grants related to the special care of the child – such as laundry equipment, holidays, outings, driving lessons, bedding and clothing. Apply in writing, giving the name and date of birth of your child and brief details of their disability and the kind of help you need.

Values Into Action (VIA),
Oxford House,
Derbyshire Street,
London E2 6HG
Phone: 0171 729 5436

VIA (formerly the Campaign for People with a Mental Handicap) is a national campaign with people who have learning difficulties. It campaigns for people to have rights and the dignity of a responsible place in society. It provides an information service, publishes articles and provides training.

Young Minds (The National Association for Child and Family Mental Health),
Contact: Lorna Cunningham
22a, Boston Place,
London NW1 6ER
Phone: 0171 724 7262

Young minds is an umbrella organisation for professionals working in the field of child and family mental health. It campaigns for early intervention and the provision of effective multi-professional services. It encourages and disseminates information on good practice to help troubled young people and their families.

DISABILITY – SPECIFIC CONDITIONS

The Anthony Nolan Bone Marrow Trust,
Unit 2, Heathgate Buildings,
75–87, Agincourt Road,
London NW3 2NT
Phone: 0171 284 1234

The Trust has the world's largest independent register of over 256,000 volunteer donors who are willing to donate their bone marrow to patients suffering from leukaemia and other blood disorders and whose only chance of survival is a bone marrow transplant. They will do this regardless of race, colour or creed.

Action for Myalgic Encephalomyelitis (M.E.) and Chronic Fatigue,
P.O. Box 1302,
Wells BA5 2WE
Phone: (01749) 670799
Phone: (0891) 122976 (24-hour Helpline)
Fax: (01749) 672561

Action for M.E. exists primarily to help sufferers and does so by providing a wide range of services, information and a journal. It also offers specific support to young sufferers.

AFASIC,
347, Central Markets, Smithfield, London EC1A 9NH
Phone: 0171 236 3632/6487
Fax: 0171 236 8115

AFASIC aims to increase awareness and recognition of communication impairments, leading to better medical and educational provision as well as training and employment prospects. It also assists children and young people to develop increased confidence and self-esteem by enabling them to participate more fully in society.

Association for Spina Bifida and Hydrocephalus
Contact: Peter Walker,
Education Adviser,
ASBAH,
42, Park Road,
Peterborough,
Cambs PE1 2UQ
Phone: (01733) 555988

ASBAH provides advice and information to young people, their parents and professionals. The educational adviser will liaise with LEA or advocate at meetings or SEN Tribunals when negotiating a satisfactory Statement of SENs. The adviser also gives lectures and talks on the educational implications of the disabilities.

Association for Brain-Damaged Children,
Clifton House,
3, St. Paul's Road,
Foleshill Road,
Coventry,CV6 5DE
Phone: 01203 665450

Association of Parents of Vaccine Damaged Children,
Contact: Rosemary Fox,
Hon. Secretary,
2, Church Street,
Shipston on Stour,
Warwicks CV36 4AP
Phone: (01608) 661595

The Association was established to pressure the Government for compensation for the families of children injured by immunisation. It is not an anti-vaccine group but believes it is unfair that some should suffer severe injury without proper compensation through participation in a programme from which the majority benefit.

ATAXIA,
Contact: Sue Grice, Services Co-ordinator,
Copse Edge,
Thursley Road, Elstead,
Godalming,
Surrey GU8 6DJ
Phone: (01252) 702864
Fax: (01252) 703715

ATAXIA fights Frederick's and other Cerebella Ataxias and crippling diseases of the nervous system. It raises money for research into ataxia and provides information and support to sufferers and their families. It also produces a quarterly magazine and has a limited welfare fund.

Belt Up School Kids (BUSK),
Contact: Pat Harris, Secretary,
2, Trelawney Close,
Castle Oak,
Usk, Gwent NP5 1SP

BUSK is a national pressure group
which aims to maintain and improve
safety standards on all school transport
whether this be home-to-school
transport or school trips. It has local
groups throughout Britain and
maintains an accident statistics register.
It offers advice and support to parents
and provides a Code of Best Practice for
LEAs.

John Kenworthy and Joe Whittaker
Bolton Dale for Inclusion
Faculty of Arts, Science and
Education
Health and Social Studies
Chadwick Street
Bolton BL2 1JW
Phone: 01204 528851/900600
Fax: 01204 399074

The Bolton Institute of Higher
Education is a centre promoting
inclusion for all leavers. In January
1997, with funding from the Barrow
Cadbury Trust, it established an Action
Research Centre for Inclusion. The work
of the Centre is co-ordinated by John
Kenworthy and Joe Whittaker. An
integral component of the Centre is the
publication of research data, articles and
other material which promotes
inclusion and challenges segregated
services. Contributions will be
welcomed by the Centre in a variety of
media including: audia tapes, video
tapes, photographs etc.; written
contributions should be limited to no
more than 20 pages. For further
information on this please contact the
Centre.

Breakthrough Deaf/Hearing
Integration,
998, Bristol Road,
Selly Oak,
Birmingham B29 6LE
Phone: (0121) 472 6447 (Voice)
Phone: (0121) 471 1001 (Text)

Fax: (0121) 471 4368

Breakthrough's aim is the integration of
deaf and hearing people of all ages
through a variety of projects,
programmes and training.

British Deaf Association,
40, Victoria Place,
Carlisle,
CA1 1HU
Phone: (01228) 48844 (Voice and text)
Text/Ansaphone: (01228) 28719
(After hours)
Fax: (01288) 41420

The Association is the national
membership charity which represents
the interests of Britain's profoundly
deaf people, all of whom use British
Sign Language. It protects and advances
the interests of Deaf people and informs
the hearing public about deafness.

British Diabetic Association (BDA),
10, Queen Anne Street,
London W1M OBD
Phone: 0171 323 1531
Fax: 0171 637 3644

BDA helps those living with diabetes
and funds research into the treatment of
complications and the possible
prevention and cure of the condition.

British Dyslexia Association,
98, London Road,
Reading,
Berkshire RG1 5AU
Phone: (01734) 662677
Phone: (01734) 668271 (Helpline)
Fax: 01734 351927

The Association is a national umbrella
organisation for children and adults
with dyslexia. Working through 100
local associations and 60 corporate
member organisations, it provides
advice, information and support and
also campaigns for improved provision
to dyslexic people in education and
employment.

British Epilepsy Association,
Anstey House,
40, Hanover Square,
Leeds LS3 1BE
Phone: (0133) 243 9393
Phone: (0800) 30 90 30 (Helpline –
Free call between 9.30am–4.30pm
Mon-Thurs and 9.00am–4.00pm
Friday)
Fax: (0133) 242 8804

The Association provides advice and
information on all aspects of epilepsy.

**British Retinitis Pigmentosa
Society (BRPS),**
P.O.Box 350,
Buckingham MK18 5EL
Phone: (01280) 860363
Fax: (01280) 860515

BRPS raises funds for scientific research
in pursuit of a treatment or cure for R.P.
It promotes and extends the Welfare
Support Services to cater for the special
needs of R.P. sufferers and their families.

Brittle Bone Society,
Ward 8, Strathmartine Hospital,
Strathmartine,
Dundee DD3 OPG
Phone: (01382) 817771
Fax: (01382) 816348

The Society seeks to promote research
into the cause, inheritance and
treatment of osteogenesis imperfecta
and similar disorders, characterised by
excessive fragility of the bones. It also
provides, advice, encouragement and
practical help for patients and their
relatives facing the difficulties of living
with brittle bones.

**Changing Faces: A Better Future
For Facially Disfigured People.**
Contact: Kath Lacy,
1 and 2, Junction Mews,
Paddington,
London W2 1PN
Phone: 0171 706 4232
Fax: 0171 706 4234

Changing Faces was launched in May
1992 to raise awareness and increase

resources devoted to the care and
rehabilitation of facially disfigured
people. It offers advice and information
to adults and children (and their
parents) who have a facial
disfigurement. This service is available
in person, by letter or phone. Support is
offered by experienced team members.

Child Growth Foundation,
2, Mayfield Avenue,
Chiswick,
London W4 1PW
Phone: 0181 994 7625/995 0257
Fax: 0181 995 9075

The Foundation provides information
and advice to parents of children with a
growth disorder. It is a parent support
organisation for Turner Syndrome,
Growth Hormone Deficiency, SOTOS
Syndrome, PSM Syndrome,
IUGR/Russell Silver Syndrome and
Bone Dysplasia Groups.

Cystic Fibrosis Research Trust,
5, Blyth Road,
Bromley,
Kent BR1 3RS
Phone: 0181 464 7211

The Trust raises funds to finance
research in finding a cure for cystic
fibrosis and to improve the care and
treatment of people with CF. It
establishes branches and groups
throughout the UK to provide support
and advice for those affected by CF,
their families and carers.

**Deaf Education Through Listening
and Talking (DELTA),**
Contact: Wendy Barnes, National
Director
P.O.Box 20,
Haverhill,
Suffolk CB9 7BD
Phone/Fax: (01440) 783 689

DELTA provides free written
information for families of deaf children
and for lay people interested in the
natural aural approach to the education
of deaf children. It also offers discussion
meetings and conferences. It's

Chapman clinic offers free weekly sessions for pre-school deaf children.

Downs Syndrome Association,
155, Mitcham Road,
London SW17 9PG
Phone: 0181 682 4001
Fax: 0181 682 4012

The Association provides support, advice and information on all aspects of the condition to parents, carers and interested professionals.

ENABLE,
6th Floor,
7, Buchanan Street,
Glasgow G1 3HL
Phone: (0141) 2256 4541

ENABLE is the main voluntary organisation in Scotland for people with learning disabilities and their families. It has 75 local branches providing mutual support and recreational activities. It also provides information, legal advice, housing for people with profound needs, training, employment, day services and respite care.

Epilepsy Association of Scotland,
National Headquarters,
48, Govan Road,
Glasgow G51 1JL
Phone: (0141) 427 4911
Fax: (0141) 427 7414

The Association promotes the interest and welfare of people with epilepsy and their families. Direct services are provided in the form of day care, employment, information and counselling services. It also promotes the interests of people through vigorous publicity and professional education programmes. Additionally, it supports medical and social research.

Federation of MS Therapy Centres,
Unit 4, Murdock Road,
Bedford MK41 7PD
Phone: (01234) 325781
Fax: (01234) 365242

MS Therapy Centres provide information, support and therapy including physio, diet, counselling and Hyperbaric Oxygen Therapy.

Friends for the Young Deaf (FYD),
East Court Mansion,
College Lane,
East Grinstead,
West Sussex RH19 3LT
Phone: (01342) 323444 (General)
Phone: (01342) 300081
(Operations/Appeals)
Minicom: (01342) 312639
Fax: (01342) 410232

FYD is a national charity which aims to provide an active partnership between Deaf and Hearing people, so that young deaf people can develop themselves and become active members of society. This is achieved through a unique project and training programme.

Handicapped Adventure Playground (HAPA),
Adventure Play for children with disabilities and special needs,
Fulham Palace,
Bishop's Avenue,
London SW6 6EA
Phone: 0171 736 4443
Phone: 0171 731 1435 (Info. service-Voice/Minicom)
Fax: 0171 731 4426

HAPA runs five fully-staffed adventure playgrounds in London which are open all year round to special school groups during term times. It also offers playschemes and after-school clubs. It has a national information service offering advice on resources in connection with all aspects of play, disability, training and support for others opening their own similar facilities.

Heartline,
Contact: Susan Keeling,
12, Cremer Plane,
The Chestnuts, Wildish Road,
Faversham ME13 7SC
Phone: (01795) 539 864

Heartline provides information, support and friendship to parents and families of children with heart disorders an important element of which is a bereavement support group. It also provides leaflets and newspapers.

Huntington's Disease Association,
108, Battersea High Street,
London SW11 3HP
Phone: 0171 223 7000
Fax: 0171 223 9489

The HDA aims to provide information and support to families and individuals. It raises awareness of, and provides information about, the disease. It also does this for health professionals and other service providers. It works through a national network of Regional Advisers and provides fact sheets and a physicians guide. It funds research into the disease.

Hyperactive Children's Support Group,
71, Whyke Lane,
Chichester,
Sussex PO19 2LD
Phone: (01903) 725182

The Group supports and advises parents of Hyperactive/ADHD/Allergic children through dietary/nutritional therapies. It also advises professionals when requested. It is a membership organisation and produces a handbook plus three journals per annum.

Leukaemia CARE Society,
14, Kingfisher Court,
Venny Bridge,
Pinhoe,
Exeter, Devon EX4 8JN
Phone: (01392) 464848
Fax: (01392) 460331

The Society provides counselling and information to patients and their families. In appropriate cases it gives financial and practical support.

Motability,
Gate House, West Gate,
Harlow,
Essex CM20 1HR
Phone: (01279) 635999
Phone: (01279) 635666 (Customer/Helpline)
Fax: (01279) 635677

Motability assists disabled people in receipt of the higher rate component of the Disability Living Allowance or War Pension Mobility Supplement to obtain new cars on lease or hire purchase or used cars and wheelchairs on hire purchase.

Multiple Sclerosis Society of GB and Northern Ireland,
25, Effie Road,
London SW6 1EE
Phone: 0171 610 7171 (General enquiries)
Phone: 0171 371 8000 (Helpline)
Fax: 0171 736 9861

The MS Society promotes research into finding the cause and a cure for MS. It also brings people with MS together for mutual support. It works for better services and a better understanding of the condition by the general public.

Muscular Dystrophy Group (M.D.) of Gt. Britain and Northern Ireland,
7–11, Prescott Place,
London SW4 6BS
Phone: 0171 720 8055
Fax: 0171 498 0670

The M.D. group is a national charity funding research into treatments and cures for M.D. and allied neuromuscular disorders. It also supports adults and children affected by these conditions with expert clinical care, counselling and grants towards equipment.

Myalgic Encephalomyelitis (M.E.) Association,
Stanhope House, High Street,
Stanford le Hope,
Essex SS17 OHA
Phone: (01375) 642 466

The Association gives support to all those affected by M.E. This takes the form of: advocacy and representation for DSS, employment and insurance, advice and support and the funding of research. It publishes a quarterly membership magazine.

National Advisory Service for Parents of Children with a Stoma,
Contact: John Malcolm, National Organiser
51, Anderson Drive,
Valley View Park,
Darvel,
Ayrshire KA17 ODE
Phone: (01560) 22024

The Advisory Service covers a wide range of intestinal and bladder related problems. It offers practical and emotional support to parents and children.

National Association of Colitis and Crone's Disease,
P.O.Box 205,
St. Albans,
Hertfordshire AL1 1AB
Phone: (01727) 844296

The Association provides general information about inflammatory bowel disease for sufferers. It promotes research into the treatment, management and causes of such diseases and publishes worthwhile results.

National Association for the Education of Sick Children,
18, Victoria Park Square,
Bethnal Green,
London E2 9PF
Phone: 0181 980 8523
Fax: 0181 981 6719

The Association aims to ensure that sick children do not miss out on education. Its activities include: research, publication of reports (including first national Directory of sick children's education), holding conferences, newsletter and other publications, reference point for parents, negotiations with individual LEAs planning cuts,

improving opportunities for professional development.

National Asthma Campaign,
Providence House,
Providence Place,
London N1 ONT
Phone: 0171 226 2260
Phone: 0345 01 02 03 (Helpline)
Fax: 0171 704 0740

The Campaign funds research into Asthma. It also provides support and information to people with Asthma, their families and those who care for them.

National Eczema Society,
163, Eversholt Street,
London NW1 1BU
Phone: 0171 388 4097
Fax: 0171 388 5882

The Society provides practical advice and information about eczema and its management and has a wide range of publications including information sheets, guides for health professionals and membership packs. It raises funds for research and has a small Welfare Fund. It also runs a joint holiday project with the National Asthma Campaign for children and young adults.

National Federation of the Blind of the United Kingdom,
Unity House,
Smyth Street,
Wakefield WF1 1ER
Phone: (01924) 291313
Fax: (01924) 200244

The Federation is an organisation of people who are blind or partially-sighted which seeks to convey to the authorities, from its own experience of sight loss, what are the real needs of the blind and partially sighted. It is primarily a campaigning organisation.

National Meningitis Trust,
Fern House,
Bath Road,
Stroud,
Glos GL5 3TJ
Phone: (01453) 751738
Phone: (0345) 538118 (Support line)
Phone: (0891) 715577 (24-hour
Information)
Fax: (01453) 753588

The Trust is a charity which works
towards alleviating anxiety and trying
to save lives by making people aware of
the symptoms of meningitis. It provides
information and supports medical
research towards the eradication of
meningitis. It also offers support and
comfort to sufferers and their families.

**Prader Willi Syndrome Association
UK,**
Contact: Mrs Rosemary Johnson,
Secretary
2, Wheatsheaf Close,
Horsell,
Woking,
Surrey GU21 4BP
Phone: (01483) 724784

The Association offers support and help
to those who live with, or care for,
someone with the syndrome. It
provides a range of information of an
educational nature for parents and
professionals.

**RADAR (The Royal Association
for Disability and Rehabilitation),**
12, City Forum,
250, City Road,
London EC1V 8AF
Phone: 0171 250 3222
Phone: 0171 250 4119 (Minicom)
Fax: 0171 250 0212

RADAR is a national organisation
working with and for physically
disabled people to remove architectural,
economic and attitudinal barriers. It is
particularly involved in the areas of
education, employment, mobility, social
services, housing and social security.

**Rare Unspecified Chromosome
Disorder Support,**
Contact: Mrs E Knight,
160, Locket Road,
Harrow Weald,
Middlesex HA3 7NZ
Phone: 0181 863 3557

The group offers support and contact
with other families with a child with the
same or a similar condition.

Rathbone Community Industry
Head Office:
First Floor, The Excalibur Building,
77, Whitworth Street,
Manchester M1 6EZ
Phone: (0161) 236 5358
Phone: (0161) 236 1877 (National
Information Line. Mon-Fri 9–5)
Fax: (0161) 236 4539

Rathbone C.I. helps young people and
adults with special needs to achieve
greater independence through
vocational education, training,
employment programmes and
residential services.

**'Reach' (The Association for
Children with Hand or Arm
Deficiency),**
Contact: Mrs Sue Stokes, Nat.
Co-ordinator,
12, Wilson Way,
Earls Barton,
Northants NN6 ONZ
Phone/Fax: (01604) 811041

'Reach' is an Association which
provides contact and support for
families with children having any form
of hand or arm deficiency. Such
deficiencies may be present at birth or
through accident or necessary surgery.

**Royal National Institute for the
Blind (RNIB),**
Contact: Helen Oldfield
(Information Officer)
224, Great Portland Street,
London W1N 6AA
Phone: 0171 388 1266
Fax: 0171 388 2034

RNIB is one of the UK's biggest and most diverse charities providing 60 different services for almost a million blind and partially sighted people. It has a very wide range of services for blind and partially sighted children, young people and mature students, including special schools and colleges and support services for those in mainstream schools.

SCOPE

For people with cerebral palsy,
12, Park Crescent,
London W1N 4EQ
Phone: 0171 636 5020
Phone: 0800 626 216 (Helpline – call free)
Fax: 0171 436 2601/1425

SCOPE (formerly The Spastics Society) works to achieve scope for people to live the life they choose. It is the largest charity in the UK working with disabled people and it provides a range of services including schools for children with cp.

Scottish Council for Spastics,

External Therapy and Advisory Services
11, Ellersly Road,
Edinburgh EH12 6HY
Phone: (0131) 313 5510
Fax: (0131) 346 7864

The Scottish Council for Spastics exists to enable the needs of people with cerebral palsy – and those with a disability resulting in similar needs – to be met. Services provided include: accommodation, advice and information, education, employment, skills for living, social services and therapy.

SENSE

The National Deafblind and Rubella Association,
11–13, Clifton Terrace,
London N4 3SR
Phone: 0171 272 7774
Fax: 0171 272 6012

SENSE is a national voluntary organisation which works and campaigns for people with a sensory disability. It provides services, advice, support and information for deafblind children and young adults.

Sickle Cell (Anaemia) Society,

54, Station Road,
London NW10 4UA,
Phone: 0181 961 4006 (Office hours)
Phone: 0181 961 7795 (Out of office hours)

The Society is a leading national health charity providing advice, counselling and financial support for the benefit of sufferers and their families. It has an information service for carers, employers and organisations that work with people with Sickle Cell.

Skill,

National Bureau for Students with Disabilities,
336, Brixton Road,
London SW9 7AA
Phone: 0171 274 0565 (Tel/Minicom)
Phone: 0171 978 9890 (Information Service: Mon-Fri 1.30–4.30pm) (Tel/Minicom)

Skill is a national voluntary organisation that is working to develop opportunities for young people and adults with disabilities and learning difficulties. It is concerned with further, adult and higher education, vocational training and the transition to employment. It aims to improve access to education and training for those with physical or sensory disabilities, learning difficulties, specific learning difficulties, medical conditions or mental health problems.

STEPS (National Association for Children with Lower Limb Abnormalities),

15, Statham Close,
Lymm,
Cheshire WA13 9NN
Phone: (01925) 757525

STEPS provides support and information to families by putting them in touch with each other using the STEPS contact register. It develops a network of branches and groups providing help and advice, including the use of specialist equipment. It also gathers and exchanges information with parents and health professionals through publications as well as organising a national conference.

The Dyslexia Institute,
133, Gresham Road,
Staines,
Middlesex TW18 2AJ
Phone: (01784) 463851

The Institute provides tuition using teachers with specialist qualifications and assessments using consultant psychologists. It also provides training for teachers.

The Dyspraxia Trust,
8, West Alley,
Hitchin,
Herts SG5 1EG
Phone: (01462) 454986
Fax: (01462) 455052

Dyspraxia is an impairment or immaturity of the organisation of movement, perception and thought – sometimes known as 'Clumsy Child Syndrome'. The Trust offers advice, information, support, professional and parental conferences and much more.

The Fragile X Society,
Contact: Lesley Walker
53, Winchelsea Lane,
Hastings,
East Sussex TN35 4LG
Phone: (01424) 813147

The Society was formed in 1990 to provide support and information to families and to encourage research. It also welcomes as associate members those with a professional interest in Fragile X.

The Haemophilia Society,
123, Westminster Bridge Road,
London SE1 7HR
Phone: (0171) 928 2020

The Society serves people with haemophilia and similar blood disorders. It represents the interests of such people by providing help, securing high standards of treatment and making representations to Government. It also publishes information for health care professionals.

The National Autistic Society,
276, Willesden Lane,
London NW2 5RB
Phone: 0181 451 1114
Fax: 0181 451 5865

Formed in 1962, the Society offers information, advice and support to people with autism, their families and their carers. It provides training and promotes research into autism. It produces a range of literature on autism, including a journal *Communication* and a newsletter *Connection*. It also offers a diagnostic and assessment service and runs its own schools.

The National Deaf Children's Society,
15, Dufferin Street,
London EC1Y 8PD
Phone: 0171 250 0123 (Voice and Text)
Fax: 0171 251 5020

The Society is an organisation of families, parents and carers which enables deaf children to maximise their skills and abilities. Through its national and regional staff it provides a range of services for families throughout the UK.

The Stroke Association,
CHSA House,
Whitecross Street,
London EC1Y 8JJ
Phone: 0171 490 7999 (10 lines)
Fax: 0171 490 2686

The Association funds research and helps stroke people and their carers directly through information, publications and welfare grants. In some areas, its Community Service Dysphasic Support and Family Support provide visiting services respectively for those whose speech is affected by stroke and for new stroke families.

Tuberous Sclerosis Association,
Contact: Mrs Janet Medcalf,
Support Services Coordinator,
Little Barnsley Farm,
Catshill,
Bromsgrove,
Worcs B61 ONQ
Phone: 01527 871898

The Association supports sufferers and their carers by promoting awareness of the condition, whilst also seeking the causes and the best possible management of TS. Its services include: telephone advice, literature and information, a benevolent fund, a family care officer, a regional support network, meetings and small group holidays.

Twins with Special Needs,
TAMBA,
59, Sunnyside,
Worksop,
Notts S81 7LN
Phone: (01909) 479250
Phone: (01732) 868000 (Helpline)

The group provides clinics and advisory support and information in relation to the 8000 multiple births that occur in the UK every year. Genetic problems are doubled if twins are dizygotic (identical).

UK Rett Syndrome Association,
29, Carlton Road,
London N11 3EX
Phone/Fax: 0181 361 5161

The Association offers sufferers, families and carers support, friendship and practical help. It sees its role as helping to influence professionals and to further progress in the fields of education, treatment, care and understanding of R.S. It also assists, where possible, with research projects into the cause and treatment of the disorder.

SELF-HELP ORGANISATIONS RUN BY DISABLED PEOPLE

Association of Disabled Professionals (ADP),
170, Benton Hill,
Wakefield Road,
Horbury,
West Yorkshire WF4 5HW
Phone: (01924) 270335 (Voice/Text)
Please ask for ADP
Fax: (01924) 276498

The Association is an organisation *of*, not *for*, disabled people. Members are drawn from the traditional professions, from executive and managerial employment and from self-employment. Nearly all are disabled, but anyone working in these areas who supports ADP's aims can apply for membership. It provides telephone and written advice on employment and related issues, and advises disabled people wanting to enter, or newly-disabled in, similar areas of employment. ADP works to promote improved facilities in training, education and employment for all disabled people. Its voice is respected in Parliament where it has members in both Houses.

Association of Partially-Sighted Teachers and Students (ABAPSTAS),
BM Box 6727,
London WC1N 3X
Phone: (01737) 761610
ABAPSTAS offers mutual support and advice, as a self-help group, to members who include visually impaired people interested in employment, education and training, and to influence policies regarding disability.

British Council of Organisations of Disabled People (BCODP),
Litchurch Plaza,
Litchurch Lane,
Derby DE24 8AA
Phone: (01332) 295551
Fax: (01332) 295580
Minicom: (01332) 295581

BCODP is Britain's national assembly of disabled people and was set up by disabled people's groups who recognised that disabled people needed to represent their own issues at the national level. BCODP promotes the 'Social Model' of disability and advocates for disabled people's full equality and integration into society.

British Deaf Association (BDA),

Contact: David Moller, Education Officer,
3rd Floor, 6–12, Emerald Street,
Bloomsbury,
London WC1N 3QA
Phone: 0171 405 4966 (Minicom)
Phone: 0171 405 4735 (Voice)
Fax: 0171 405 4796

The BDA teaches leadership skills, increase access to Sign Language and extend Deaf people's educational choices. It achieves this through activities such as courses for school leavers. It also negotiates on behalf of young Deaf people whose LEA has restricted their choice for further education.

Derbyshire Centre for Integrated Living,

Contact: Margaret Kemp, Inf. Officer
Long Close,
Ripley,
Derbyshire DE5 3HY
Phone: (01773) 740246
Phone: (01773) 748452 (Minicom)
Fax: (01773) 570185

DCIL is a development resource guided by the experience of disabled people. It works with disabled people and service authorities to bring about supports and services which break down barriers to the full participation and equality of disabled people.

Disabled in Camden (DISC),

58, Phoenix Road,
London NW1 1EU
Phone: 0171 387 0700 (Voice and Minicom)

Phone: 0171 387 1466 (Information and Advice Service – Voice and Minicom)

DISC is an umbrella organisation working with members, individual disabled people and other organisations to help initiate new projects, improve current services and facilities and represent the interests of disabled people. It produces a newsletter and a variety of publications and has a wheelchair loan service and a cassette reading/recording and Braille service.

GEMMA,

BM Box 5700,
London WC1N 3XX
Phone: 0171 485 4024 (10am – 6pm)

GEMMA is a national friendship and information network for lesbian and bi-sexual women of all ages. Its aim is to lessen the isolation of women and to increase awareness of the social needs of disabled bi-sexual and lesbian women. It produces a quarterly newsletter in print, audiotape and braille.

Greenwich Association of Disabled People's Centre for Independent Living (GAD),

Contact: Geraldine O'Halloran,
Christchurch Forum,
Trafalgar Road,
Greenwich,
London SE10 9EQ,
Phone: 0181 305 2221
Phone: 0181 858 9307 (Minicom)
Fax: 0181 293 3455

GAD provides advice and information on independent living, enabling disabled people to have full control over their lives by employing their own personal assistants. It offers training in management of personal assistants and disability equality training, counselling, advocacy and welfare rights provision. Also consultancy on access issues and civic rights campaigning.

Hampshire Centre for Independent Living,
Contact: Philip Mason,
4, Plantation Way,
Whitehall,
Bordon,
Hants GU35 9HD
Phone: (0420) 474261

HCIL is concerned with the practical issues of independent living and in particular those experienced by disabled people in gaining and using personal assistance, advocacy, training, support and co-operation. It provides an individual response to requests for advice and information on independent living.

Jennifer Trust for Spinal Muscular Atrophy,
Contact: Anita Macaulay,
11, Ash Tree Close,
Wellesbourne,
Warwick, CV35 9SA
Phone: (01789) 842377

The Jennifer Trust for Spinal Muscular Atrophy Support Group is run by parents and adults who have Spinal Muscular Atrophy. The main aim of the group is to provide information, understanding and friendship to those in need. It produces a quarterly newsletter and holds on an annual conference. It has a network of area contacts for both childhood forms and for adults who provide local support and advice.

Kingston Association of Disabled People (KADP),
53, Canbury Park Road,
Kingston-On-Thames,
Surrey KT2 6LQ
Phone: 0181 549 8893 (Voice and Minicom)

KADP works to increase opportunities for disabled people to lead independent lives as part of the mainstream society.

London Dial-a-Ride and Taxicard Users Association (DaRT),
St. Margarets,
25, Leighton Road,
London NW5 2QD
Phone: 0171 482 2325

DaRT represents the views and concerns of Dial-a-Ride and Taxi-card users and lobbies for accessible transport services for disabled people in the Greater London area.

LOOK, National Federation of Families with Visually Impaired Children,
Queen Alexandra College,
49, Court Oak Road,
Harborne,
Birmingham B17 9TG
Phone: (0121) 428 5038
Fax: (0121) 428 5048

LOOK is the only national organisation that provides practical help and support to families of visually impaired children. It brings together local groups of families to share information and offer mutual support. Its national office can provide advice, assistance and expertise, keeping local groups and individual members up-to-date with all key issues effecting their children. It helps families gain the best for their children.

National Federation of the Blind of the UK,
Unity House,
Smyth Street,
Westgate,
Wakefield,
West Yorkshire WF1 1ER
Phone: (01924) 291313
Fax: (01924) 200244

The Federation is an organisation of blind and partially sighted people whose aim is to help people have a better standard of living and to be independent. It also campaigns on behalf of blind and partially sighted people for better living standards.

People First,
207–215, Kings Cross Road,
London WC1X 9DB
Phone: 0171 713 6400

People First is an organisation run for
and by people with learning difficulties
to gain self advocacy skills and it
provides information, training and
advice on issues relating to people with
learning difficulties.

Spinal Injuries Association,
Contact: Linda Clarke, Welfare
Officer,
Newport House,
76, St. James Lane,
Muswell Hill,
London N10 3DF
Phone: 0181 444 2121
Fax: 0181 444 3761

The Association is a national self-help
group controlled and run by spinal
cord-injured people themselves to assist
those with similar disabilities to get
back to an ordinary, everyday life. A
large number of services are available.

Strathclyde Forum on Disability,
2nd Floor, Cortney House,
100, Morrison Street,
Glasgow G5 8LN
Phone: 0141 420 5633

The Forum promotes the benefit of all
disabled people who live in its region. It
aims to bring about the full and equal
participation of disabled people in the
life of the community.

**The National League of the Blind
and Disabled,**
Contact: Michael Barrett, General
Secretary
2, Tenterden Road,
London N17 8BE
Phone: 0181 808 6030

The League, which has been registered
since 1899, attempts to secure
improvements in the social and
economic conditions of blind and
disabled people.

**Waltham Forest Association of
Disabled People (WFADP),**
Units 13–14,
Alpha Business Centre,
South Grove,
Walthamstow,
London E17 7NX
Phone: 0181 509 0812

WFADP works to ensure equal rights
for disabled people. It provides a range
of training and support on
self-advocacy and independent living as
well as producing regular bulletins and
newsletters.

ORGANISATIONS OFFERING ADVICE ON SPECIALIST EQUIPMENT

**ACE Centre (Aids to
Communication in Education),**
Ormerod School,
Waynflete Road,
Headington,
Oxford OX3 8DD
Phone: 01865 63508
Fax: 01865 750188

ACE provides a focus of information
and expertise in the use of
micro-electronics as aids to
communication. It also provides a wide
variety of services and facilities ranging
from in-depth assessments of the
communication needs of individual
children and young people in full-time
education, training and software
development work.

**CENMAC (Centre for
Micro-Assisted Communication),**
4th Floor, Eltham Green Complex,
1a, Middle Park Avenue,
Eltham,
London SE9 5HL

CENMAC supports the communication
needs of children with physical
disabilities who are receiving their
education in both special and
mainstream schools throughout the
Inner London area. Through the
provision of appropriate technological
aids, it aims to help each child gain full

and equal access to the National curriculum. Children may be referred at any age.

National ACCESS Centre,

Contact: John Goodacre, Centre Manager,
Hereward College,
Bramston Crescent,
Tile Hill Lane,
Coventry CV4 9SW
Phone: (01203) 461231
Fax: (01203) 694305

The Centre provides a service based on independent advice, training, assessment and support to clients with physical disabilities, sensory impairments or learning difficulties. Staff support clients to make informed choices about a range of micro-technologies, low tech aids and study strategies. A range of training courses are offered.

Disabled Living Foundation,

380–384, Harrow Road,
London W9 2HU
Phone: 0171 289 6111
Fax: 0171 266 2922

The DLF is a national charity providing practical, up-to-date advice and information on aspects of living with a disability for disabled and elderly people and their carers. Write for a copy of *With a Little Help: A guide to equipment and services for independent living.*

Glossary of Terms

LEGAL

1981 Education Act

Law which was seen as encouraging the integration of children with special needs. However, in most LEAs it has had very limited impact because it contained three 'get out' clauses which served to ensure that segregation continued.

1988 Education Reform Act

Law which imposed the National Curriculum in schools, gave schools greater control over their own finances and gave school governors greater powers in schools. All of this has served to fundamentally change the relationship between the school and the LEA.

1989 Children Act

Law which made the welfare of the child the main consideration when deciding how to help children in need.

1993 Education Act – Section 3

Replaced the 1981 Education Act. The 'Code of Practice' describes how this should work in respect of the identification and assessment of SENs. Most pupils with special needs are expected to be supported in mainstream schools without Statements. However, the requirement to integrate is still qualified by the three 'get out' clauses which were carried over from the 1981 Act. A new system of Tribunals was introduced so that LEA decisions can be more effectively challenged by parents.

1996 Education Act

GENERAL

Assessment

In the context of special needs education this usually means testing a child to compare her with other children. If she achieves a relatively low score, she can be labelled as having SENs and may actually be placed somewhere other than in an ordinary class in her own local school. Assessment should be a process to build up a picture of the child's strengths and needs.

Death Making

A term used by Wolf Wolfensberger in connection with his concern over 'threats to the sanctity of life of handicapped and afflicted people'. He takes the view that technological advances have made society much more 'eugenic' in the selection of those who are to live and those who are to die. He is concerned by the growth of euthanasia of foetuses and new-born infants and sees this as a growing trend in the management of the elderly.

Disability Awareness Training

A programme of training to sensitise professionals and others to the oppression experienced by disabled and learning impaired people.

IEP (Individual Educational Plan)

An individualised programme of study designed specifically for a child with a learning difficulty.

IQ (Intelligence Quotient)

A psychological term which is used to summarise a person's learning potential. A person's IQ (other things being equal) is in fact quite a good predictor of achievement, but it represents a summary of a number of different cognitive abilities and needs to be treated with some caution. Used positively, an IQ test can yield some useful diagnostic information about an individual's learning strengths and weaknesses – but such tests have historically been used as tools of oppression to segregate those not welcome in the mainstream of community life.

Local Education Authority (LEA)

A Local Education Authority is an organisation whose responsibility it is to manage the educational needs of those who live within its geographical boundaries. Its major task is to provide schooling for children and young people in the age range 5–19 years.

Named Person

A term introduced by the 1993 Education Act which refers to the person who will advise and support the parents of a child who is to receive the protection of a Statement of their special educational needs.

Parent Partnership

A term used to describe a possible state of affairs in which professionals work very closely with the parents of children with special educational needs.

Special Educational Needs (SENs)

Educational needs that some children have which most educationalists find puzzling and sometimes threatening. Such needs are called 'special' so that some of the children who experience them can be dealt with in atypical and socially devaluing ways, such as by being removed from the ordinary classroom so that the teacher will be able to feel more comfortable. Precisely the same thing happens in colleges of further education. The usual assumption is that the problem lies within the child rather than that the teacher and the school are having difficulties in teaching properly.

Special Needs Tribunal (SNT)

A system (set up under the 1993 Education Act) by which a parent can appeal against a decision made by the LEA.

Statement (of SEN)

Legal document drawn up by the LEA to describe the child's special educational needs and what they propose to do with the child. For many children this will automatically lead to compulsory segregation.

Statementing (process/procedure)

A long and bureaucratic process by which an LEA determines a child's special educational needs and the provisions that must be made to meet those needs.

PHILOSOPHY / LANGUAGE

Advocacy

Speaking up or pleading on behalf of another person or group with the aim of safeguarding the interests and rights of that person, or group.

Age-appropriateness

Treatment/management of another person in accordance with an acknowledgement of their actual chronological age rather than their level of understanding. Such treatment might include such issues as their appearance, dress, personal possessions, behaviour and the way they are approached, treated and addressed.

Community competence

The level of understanding a non-disabled person has of the needs of disabled or learning impaired people.

Conflict of Interest

The dilemma faced by a person (professional) when they are required to act honestly in the interest of one party which, if they did, would prejudice their position with another.

Deviancy

Appearance, speech or behaviour which is grossly atypical or otherwise in conflict with the accepted norms of the culture in which an individual lives.

Distantiated

Put at a distance, separated from others. This is the stock general, societal and service system response to individuals and groups seen as 'deviant'.

Full inclusion

Being a full member of an age-appropriate class in one's neighbourhood school or college, doing the same lessons as the others with the others and it mattering if you are not there. Plus you have friends who spend time with you outside school or college.

Functional integration

Being educated alongside other children in a mainstream school.

Hidden curriculum

The crucial informal learning that goes on in schools and colleges – the unplanned, un-measured curriculum.

Iatrogenic disease (illness)

Illness caused by medical intervention.

Ideology

A systematic set of ideas (a science) or habit of thinking on the basis of a theory of ideas about economics, politics, social welfare policy or whatever.

Inclusion 'With'

Local mainstream schools welcoming each child whatever their abilities and needs. They will be fully involved within the school on an age-appropriate basis and mix with all other children in their ordinary classroom, playground and neighbourhood. Mainstream schools will change for the better for all children when they become inclusive.

Ineducable

Incapable of learning anything worthwhile.

Integration 'In'

Children receiving help to attend ordinary mainstream schools. Sometimes their involvement with other pupils is less than desired and the commitment by staff to their presence is conditional. Integration tends to focus on fitting the child in to current school arrangements, but it is likely that inclusion can grow through providing integration.

Intentional relationship building

The activity of bringing people together in the hope that bonds will be formed and friendships formed.

Learning difficulties (moderate/severe)

Problems in learning those things which most other people find little difficulty with.

Locational integration

Being educated on the site of an ordinary school or college but not necessarily alongside or 'with' other typical students.

Marginalisation

The process of moving away (unwanted individuals or groups) or separating from the mainstream of community life and activity.

Means-led (services)

Services (usually statutory) which plan to make provision for individuals and groups on the basis of what they feel they can afford rather than on an honest assessment of the *needs* of those to be served.

Medical model (of disability)

Disability is seen as part of a person that needs to be 'cured' or 'fixed'. The person is understood in terms of what they *cannot* do rather than what they can and their abilities and rights are denied. This view leads to the attachment of negative labels which serve to further stereotype the individual as 'not one of us', which in turn legitimates their separation to the margins of society.

National Curriculum

A set of subjects which, by law, all children in England and Wales must pursue unless they attend a private fee-paying school – in which case they can choose not to.

Needs-led (services)

Services which try, as best they can, to make provision on the basis of the needs of those being served.

Normalisation /Social Role Valorisation (SRV)

Using valued means to support and enable people to live valued lives/ develop valued social roles.

Outreach work

Segregated settings trying to give children experience in valued mainstream settings.

Paradigm

A set of assumptions, beliefs, concepts and practices. An accepted way of interpreting the world.

Segregation

The enforced separation of individuals from other valued social groups. In the case of disabled children, their being separated from their peers and sent to separate schools, classes and units. For many children this is the start of a career of rejection and exclusion from ordinary life from which they will never fully recover.

Social devaluation (personal)

Having a low value placed by society on one's abilities, appearance or behaviour.

Social Imagery

The way in which an individual or group is construed by others. Such imaging is usually mediated by the association of symbols or images which, in the case of devalued people, involves the projection of social stereotypes.

Social Integration

Disabled children and young people being allowed to mix socially with their peers outside lesson time – at play and lunch times.

Social Model of Disability

Disability is seen as part of a person that can lead to social oppression. Recognition of the person's abilities and rights is central to their being. Society at the moment does not expect the disabled person to be a full participant and people need to work to remove the social, economic and architectural obstacles faced by disabled people.

Socially valued

That which is esteemed or prized within a particular culture.

'Special' (children)

A word used in condescension towards disabled children and young people. The use of the term sends mixed and confusing messages, but is exploited by professionals to separate out children who they feel would not be welcome in ordinary educational and social settings.

Special school

A segregated establishment mistakenly characterised as a 'school' which serves as a holding centre for children who have a learning difficulty or disability.

Taster (Teaser) Integration

The practice of taking children from special schools or classes for short periods to ordinary classrooms in mainstream schools without any intention that they should eventually be included.

Unconsciousness

Those thoughts, beliefs and assumptions upon which human beings act without knowing they are doing so.

Government Departments

Department of Education (DOE), Sanctuary Buildings, Great Smith Street, London SW1P 3BT (0171 925 5000)

Department of Health (DOH) Skipton House, 80 London Road, London SE1 6LW (0171 210 3000)

Special Educational Needs Tribunal, 71 Victoria Street, London SW1H OHW (0171 925 6925)

Welsh Office, Education Department, Phase 2, Government Buildings, Ty Glas Road, Llanishen, Cardiff CF4 5NE ((01222) 761 456)

Helpful Publications

SPECIAL EDUCATION LAW/STATEMENTING/PRACTICE

ACE (1992) *ACE Special Education Handbook: Education Act 1981* (5th Edition), Advisory Centre for Education. From ACE, 18, Aberdeen Studios, 22, Highbury Grove, London N5 2EA.

ACE (1993) *A Guide to the Education Act 1993* by Rick Rogers. Advisory Centre for Education.

Audit Commission/HMI (1992a) *Getting in on the Act – Provision for Pupils with Special Educational Needs: The National Picture* (HMSO).

DFE (1994) *Code of Practice: on the Identification and Assessment of Special Educational Needs*.

DFE: *Special Educational Needs – A Guide for Parents*. For copies of the guide in Bengali, Chinese, Greek, Gujerati, Hindi, Punjabi, Turkish, Urdu or Vietnamese, phone (01787) 880946. For copies in Welsh, contact the Welsh Office in Cardiff.

HMSO 1993 *Education Act*.

Friel, J. (1997) *Children with Special Needs: Assessment, Law and Practice – Caught in the Acts*. (4th Edition). Jessica Kingsley Publishers.

INTEGRATION

Crabtree, C. and Whittaker, J. (1997) *How Independent Are the Independent Special Needs Tribunals?* Bolton: Action Research Centre for Inclusion. Bolton Institute.

Crabtree, C. (1997) *Unspeakable Acts*. Bolton: Action Research Centre for Inclusion. Bolton Institute.

Jupp, K. (1992) *Everyone Belongs: Mainstream Education for Children with Severe Learning Difficulties*. Human Horizon Series, Souvenir Press.

Learning Together Magazine. Now no longer published, but back copies are available from J. Hall, 2 Devon Terrace, Ffynone Road, Swansea SA1 6DG.

O'Brien, J. and Forest, M. *et al. Action for Inclusion*. Inclusion Press. Available from J.Hall, 2 Devon Terrace, Ffynone Road, Swansea SA1 6DG.

O'Brien, J. and Tyne, A. (1981) *The Principle of Normalisation: A Foundation for Effective Services*. Published by ChM (Now VIA), Values Into Action (VIA), Oxford House, Derbyshire Street, London E2 6HG. Phone 0171 729 5436. VIA (formerly the Campaign for People with a Mental Handicap) is a national campaign with people who have learning difficulties. It campaigns for people with learning difficulties to have rights and the dignity of a responsible place in society. It provides an information service, publishes articles and provides training.

Rae, A. (1997) Survivors from the Special School System. Bolton: Action Research Centre for Inclusion. Bolton Institute.

Wolfensberger, W. (1972) *The Principle of Normalisation in Human Services.* Toronto National Institute on Mental Retardation.

Whittaker, J. and Kenworthy, J. (1997) *The Struggle for Inclusive Education – A Struggle Against Educational Apartheid.* Bolton: Action Research Centre for Inclusion. Bolton Institute.

CSIE's Integration Charter

1. We fully support an end to all segregated education on the grounds of disability or learning difficulty as a policy commitment and goal for this country.

2. We see the ending of segregation in education as a human rights issue which belongs within equal opportunities policies.

3. We believe that all children share equal value and status. We therefore believe that the exclusion of children from the mainstream because of disability or learning difficulty is a devaluation and is discriminating.

4. We envisage the gradual transfer of resources, expertise, staff and pupils from segregated schools to an appropriately supported and diverse mainstream.

5. We believe that segregated education is a major cause of society's widespread prejudice against adults with disabilities. De-segregating special education is therefore a crucial first step in helping to change discriminatory attitudes, in creating greater understanding and in developing a fairer society.

6. We believe that efforts to increase participation of people with disabilities or difficulties in community life will be seriously jeopardised unless segregated education is reduced and ultimately ended.

7. For these reasons we call on Central and Local Government to do all in their power to work as quickly as possible towards the goal of a de-segregated education system.

References

ACE (1994) *Special Education Handbook: The Law on Children with Special Needs* (6th Edition). London: ACE Publications

Adams, F.J. (1990) *Special Education in the 1990s*. Harlow: Longmans.

AEP (1989) *Integration: Problems and Possibilities for Change: Report of the Working Party on the Educational Integration of Children and Young People who have Special Needs*. Durham: Association of Educational Psychologists.

AEP 14/94 (1994) *The CSIE Integration Charter Circular of the Association of Educational Psychologists*. Durham: AEP.

Audit Commission/HMI (1992) *Caught in the Act*. London: HMSO.

Audit Commission/HMI (1992a) *Getting in on the Act – Provision for Pupils with Special Educational Needs: The National Picture*. London: HMSO.

Audit Commission/HMI (1992b) *Getting the Act Together – Provision for Pupils with Special Educational Needs: A Management Handbook for Schools and Local Education Authorities*. London: HMSO.

Audit Commission (1994) *The Act Moves On: Progress in Special Educational Needs*. London: HMSO.

Bank-Mikkelsen, N. (1980) 'Denmark.' In R.J. Flynn and K.E. Nitsch (eds) *Normalisation, Social Integration and Community Services*. Austin: Pro-Ed.

Barnes, C. (1991) *Disabled People in Britain and Discrimination: A Case for Anti-Discrimination Legislation*. London: Hurst and Company.

Berger, P. and Luckman, T. (1966) *The Social Construction of Reality: A Treatise in the Sociology of Knowledge*. London: Penguin Books.

Bledstein, B.J. (1976) *The Culture of Professionalism: The Middle Class and the Development of Higher Education in America*. New York: W.W. Norton.

Blumer, H. (1969) *Symbolic Interactionism*. Englewood Cliffs, N.J.: Prentice Hall.

Booth, T. and Potts, P. (19??) Integrating Special Education. Basil Blackwell.

Carson, S. (1992) 'Normalisation Needs and Schools'. *Educational Psychology in Practice Vol 7, 4, January 1992.*

Carson, S. (1995) *Pilot Evaluation of a Special Needs Provision in Schools within South Glamorgan using PASSING – Programme Analysis of Service Systems Implementation of Normalisation Goals*. Unpublished.

CSIE (1991) *Latest Segregation Statistics Give Cause For Concern* (press release). Centre for Studies on Integration in Education.

CSIE (1994) *Segregation and Inclusion: English LEA Statistics 1988–92*. Pub Centre for Studies on Inclusive Education. Research by Brahm Norwich.

DES (1944) *Education Act 1944, Part II*. London: HMSO.

DES (1965) *The Organisation of Secondary Education*. Circular 10/65. London: HMSO.

DES (1986) *Reporting Inspections: HMI Methods and Procedures*. London: HMSO.

DES (1989) Assessments and Statements of Special Educational Needs: Procedures within the Education, Health and Social Services. London: HMSO.

DFE (1992a) *Choice and Diversity: A New Framework for Schools*. London: HMSO CMD 2021.

DFE (1992b) *Special Educational Needs: Access to the System*. London: HMSO.

DFE (1992c) *HMI Framework For The Inspection of Schools*.

DFE (1994) *Code of Practice: On the Identification and Assessment of Special Educational Needs*. London: Central Office of Information.

Disabled People's International (DPI) (1981) *Proceedings of the First World Congress*. Singapore: DPI.

Emerson, E. (1992) 'What is normalisation?' In H. Brown and H. Smith (eds) *Normalisation: The Reader for the Nineties*. London: Routledge.

Fallers, L.A. (1961) 'Ideology and culture in Uganda nationalism.' *American Anthropologist 63*, 19.

Friel, J. (1995a) *Children with Special Needs – Assessment, Law and Practice: Caught in the Acts* (3rd Edition). London: Jessica Kingsley Publishers.

Friel, J. (1995b) *Young Adults with Special Needs – Assessment, Law and Practice: Caught in the Acts*. London: Jessica Kingsley Publishers.

Gibran, K. (1926) *The Prophet*. London: William Heinemann Ltd.

Hall, J.T. (1992a) '"Token" Integration: How else can we explain such odd practices.' *Learning Together Magazine*, Issue 3, October 1992.

Hall, J.T. (1992b) 'Segregation by another name?' *Special Children 56* , April 1992.

Hall, J.T. (1992c) 'Social role valorisation and special education.' *Learning Together Magazine 3*, October 1992.

Hall, J.T. (1993) 'Securing an Inclusive Placement'. *Leaving Together Magazine*, Issue 6, December 1993.

Hall, J.T. (1994) 'School-based advocacy for children with special needs'. *New Learning Together Magazine: From Special Needs & Inclusions*, Issue 2, September 1994.

Hansard (1993) 29th April. London: HMSO.

Haskell, T.L. (1984) *The Authority of Experts: Studies in History and Theory*. Bloomington, In: Indiana University Press.

Heraud, B.J. (1970) *Sociology and Social Work*. London: Pergamon International Library.

Hirst, P.H. and Peters, R.S. (1970) *The Logic of Education*. London: Routledge and Kegan Paul.

HMSO (1981) *Education Act*. London: HMSO.

HMSO (1988) *Education Act*. London: HMSO.

HMSO (1992) *Choice and Diversity: A New Framework for Schools* (Cmnd. 2021). London: HMSO.

HMSO (1993) *Education Act* (Including Schedules and Regulations 1994). London: HMSO.

HMSO (1994) The Special Educational Needs Tribunal Regualtions 1994.

HMSO (1978) *Warnock Report: Special Educational Needs* (Cmnd. 7212). London: HMSO.

Hurt, J.S. (1988) *Outside the Mainstream: A History of Special Education.* London: B.T. Batsford Ltd.

IPSEA (1994) article in Times Educational Supplement 25.3.1994.

Kellmer-Pringle, M. (1975) *The Needs of Children.* London: Hutchinson.

Kelly, G. (1955) *Psychology of Personal Constructs.* Vols. 1 and 2. New York: W.W. Norton.

Kuhn, T.S. (1962) *The Structure of Scientific Revolutions.* Chicago: Chicago Press

Lusthaus, E. (1985) '"Euthanasia" of persons with severe handicaps: refuting the rationalizations.' *The Association for Persons with Severe Handicaps (JASH)* 10, 2, 87–94.

McKnight, J.L. (1987) 'Regenerating Community'. In *Social Policy.*

Merton, R.K. (1968) *Social Theory and Social Structure.* New York: Free Press.

Lockhart, A. (1987) *Policy Statement on Special Education.* London: Newham LEA.

Nirje, B. (1980) 'The normalisation principle.' In R.J. Flynn and K.E. Nitsch (eds) *Normalisation, Social Integration and Community Services.* Baltimore: University Park Press.

O'Brien, J. and Forest, M. *et al.* (1989) *Action for Inclusion.* Inclusion Press. Available from J.Hall, 2, Devon Terrace, Ffynone Road, Swansea SA1 6DG.

O'Brien, J. and Lyle, C. (1986) *Framework for Accomplishment.* Responsive Systems Associates, 58, Willowick Drive, Decatur, Georgia 30038, USA.

OED (1989) Oxford: Oxford University Press.

Patton, M.Q. (1975) *Alternative Evaluation Research Paradigm.* Grand Forks, ND: University of North Dakota Press.

Poynter, R. and Wright, J. (1996) 'Taking Action – Your Child's Right to Special Education'. Birmingham: Questions Publishing Company Ltd.

Quicke, J. (1982) *The Cautious Expert: An Analysis of Developments in the Practice of Educational Psychology.* Buckingham: The Open University Press.

Sarason, S.B. and Doris, J. (1979) *Discussion of the Right to Education for All Handicapped Children Act.* (Public Law 94–102, 1975) USA. Educational Handicap. Public Policy and Social History. New York: Ever Press.

SEN Tribunal (1995) *President's digest to August 1995.*

SEN Tribunal (1995) *Annual Report 1994/95.*

Skrtic, T.M. (1991) *Behind Special Education: A Critical Analysis of Professional Culture and School Organisation.* Boulder, CO: Love Publishing Company.

Swann, W. (1991) Segregation statistics – English LEAs: Variation between LEAs in levels of segregation in special schools 1982–90. London: CSIE.

Tomlinson, S. (1981) *Education Subnormality: A Study in Decision-Making.* London: Routledge and Kegan Paul.

Tyne, A. (1995) 'Critique of Social Role Valorisation.' *CMHERA Newsletter* September.

Wittgenstein, L. (1953) *Philosophical Investigations.* Oxford: Blackwell.

Wolfensberger, W. (1972) *The Principle of Normalisation in Human Services.* Toronto: National Institute on Mental Retardation.

Wolfensberger, W. (1975) 'The Origin and Nature of our Institutional Models'. Syracuse, New York: Human Policy Press.

Wolfensberger, W. and Glenn, S. (1975) *PASS Programme Analysis of Service Systems: A Method for the Quantitative Analysis of Human Services.* Handbook (3rd Edition). Toronto: National Institute on Mental Retardation.

Wolfensberger, W. and Thomas, S. (1983) *Programme Analysis of Service Systems Implementation of Normalisation Goals.* NIMR Publications.

Wolfensberger, W. (1985) 'Social role valorisation: a new insight, and a new term for Normalisation'. *Australian Association for the Mentally Retarded Journal 9, 1,* 4–11.

Wolfensberger, W. (1987) *The New Genocide of Handicapped and Afflicted People.* Syracuse, NY: Syracuse University Training Institute.

Wolfensberger, W. (1992) *A Brief Introduction to Social Role Valorization as a High-Order Concept for Structuring Human Services.* (2nd rev. ed.) Syracuse, NY: Syracuse University Training Institute for Human Service Planning, Leadership and Change Agentry.

Wright, J. (1995) From Bill to Act: the passing of the 1993 Education Act. In Potts, P., Armstrong, F. and Masterton, M. (1995) 'Equality and Diversity in Education: National and International Contexts (Open University)

Yates, M. (1994) 'The Special School Survivor'. *New Learning Together Magazine, Issue 1,* April 1994.

Author index

Subject index